Rich Dad's
ADVISORS™

My poor dad often said, "What you know is important." My rich dad said, "If you want to be rich, *who* you know is more important than *what* you know." Rich dad explained further, saying, "Business and investing is a team sport. The average investor or small-business person loses financially because they do not have a team. Instead of a team, they act as individuals who are trampled by very smart teams." That is why the Rich Dad's Advisors book series was born. Rich Dad's Advisors will guide you to help you know who to look for and what questions to ask so you can go out and gather your own great team of advisors.

Robert T. Kiyosaki

Author of the *New York Times* Bestsellers
Rich Dad Poor Dad™
Rich Dad's CASHFLOW Quadrant™
Rich Dad's Guide to Investing™
and *Rich Dad's Rich Kid Smart Kid*™

Rich Dad's™ Classics

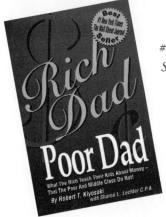

#1 *New York Times,* #1 *Wall Street Journal,* #1 *Business Week,* #1 *Publishers Weekly,* as well as a *San Francisco Chronicle* and *USA Today* bestseller. Also featured on the bestseller lists of Amazon.com, Amazon.com UK and Germany, E-trade.com, *Sydney Morning Herald* (Australia), *Sun Herald* (Australia), *Business Review Weekly* (Australia), Borders Books and Music (U.S. and Singapore), and Barnes & Noble.com.

Wall Street Journal, New York Times business and *Business Week* bestseller. Also featured on the bestseller lists of the *Sydney Morning Herald* (Australia), *Sun Herald* (Australia), *Business Review Weekly* (Australia), and Amazon.com, Barnes & Noble.com, Borders Books and Music (U.S. and Singapore).

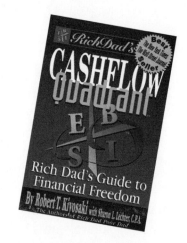

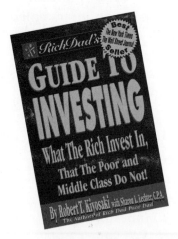

USA Today, Wall Street Journal, New York Times business, *Business Week,* and *Publishers Weekly* bestseller.

Wall Street Journal, New York Times, and *USA Today* bestseller.

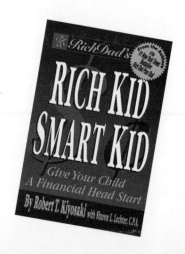

Rich Dad's Advisors™ Series

Rich Dad said,
"Business and Investing is a team sport."

Each of us has a million-dollar idea in our head. The first step in turning your idea into millions, maybe even billions, of dollars, is to protect that idea. Michael Lechter is an internationally known intellectual property attorney who is Robert Kiyosaki's legal advisor on all his intellectual property matters. His book is simply written and is an important addition to any businessperson's library.

Loopholes of the Rich is for the aspiring as well as the advanced business owner who is looking for better and smarter ways to legally pay less tax and protect his or her assets. It gives real solutions that will be easy to apply to your unique situation. Diane Kennedy offers over twenty years of experience in research, application, and creation of innovative tax solutions and is Robert Kiyosaki's personal and corporate tax strategist.

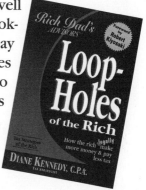

Your most important skill in business is your ability to communicate and sell! SalesDogs™ is a highly educational, inspirational, and somewhat "irreverent" look at the world of sales, communications, and the different characters that occupy that world. All of us sell in one way or another. It is important for you to find your own unique style. Blair Singer is respected internationally as an extraordinary trainer, speaker, and consultant in the fields of sales, communication, and management.

Rich Dad's
ADVISORS ™

Loop-Holes
of the Rich ™

How the rich legally make more money & pay less tax

DIANE KENNEDY, C.P.A.
TAX STRATEGIST

WARNER
BUSINESS
BOOKS ™

Published by Warner Books

An AOL Time Warner Company

Warner Books Edition

Copyright © 2001 by Diane Kennedy, C.P.A.
All rights reserved.

Published by Warner Books in association with CASHFLOW Technologies, Inc., and BI Capital, Inc.

CASHFLOW, RichDad, and RichDad's Advisors are trademarks of CASHFLOW Technologies, Inc.

 is a trademark of
CASHFLOW Technologies, Inc.

 Warner Business Books are published by Warner Books, Inc.,
1271 Avenue of the Americas, New York, NY 10020

Visit our Web site at www.twbookmark.com.

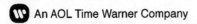 An AOL Time Warner Company

The Warner Business Book logo is a trademark of Warner Books, Inc.

Printed in the United States of America

First Printing: June 2001
10   9   8   7   6

LCCN: 2001088435
ISBN: 0-446-67832-5

Designed by imagesupport.com, LLC.

Illustrations by Sher Grotts.

Acknowledgments

There are many people that go into the creation of a book. I thank all of them! Special thanks go to:

Robert Kiyosaki, my friend, teacher, and mentor; Kim Kiyosaki, for her brilliant insights into marketing and business; and Sharon Lechter, who somehow can successfully combine style, grace, and power, and without whom none of this would be possible.

My friends and family who supported me through it all: Steve and Peggy Lee, Enid Vien and David Womack, Ginger Gibson, Dixie Norkoli, Jim Kelly, Esq., and Ben and Bryan Cooley. I am grateful every day that you all are in my life.

The people who are behind the scenes at the DKA CPA firm: Bev Adams, Sher Grotts, Kristi Harrison, Cheryl Otte, Neil Patel, Bernie Propst, and Jesus Sanchez. Your help and dedication beyond the call of duty gave me the opportunity to write the book.

My own very special advisors: Kim Butler, CFP, Renie Cavallari, George Krauja, Esq., Michael Lechter, Esq., Gabe Mendoza, Nancy Ogilvie, Kevin Stock, Dr. Van Tharp, and Dr. Allen Thomashefsky. It's been quite a ride.

The rest of the Rich Dad's Advisors, Dolf deRoos and Blair Singer. I am so honored to be in your company!

The Warner Books staff, and especially Rick Wolff. You all worked at an amazing speed to make this book possible.

To my clients. This book only exists because of your thoughtful and sincere questions.

Last, but only because it is the longest acknowledgment, my constant gratitude and love to Richard Cooley, who is my partner both in life and business. You possess the most amazing reservoir of patience and strength. For everything, thank you.

Contents

Foreword

My rich dad said,

"There is good income and bad income. If you want to become rich, you
need to know what kind of income to work for."

—Robert Kiyosaki

Starting with Nothing

Both my rich dad and my poor dad started with nothing. My real dad, the man
I call my poor dad, became a teacher. My rich dad, the father of my best friend,
had taken over the family business at age thirteen and never finished school.

In his midthirties, my poor dad went from teaching, to becoming a
school principal, back to the university for additional credits, and then on to
school administration. Our family moved from better neighborhood to better
neighborhood each time my dad was promoted.

In his midthirties, my rich dad continued to run the family business. He
began to invest in real estate and to start a number of small businesses. My
rich dad and his family continued to live in the same neighborhood and in
the same house.

In his forties, my real dad became the superintendent for the State of
Hawaii, reaching the peak of his profession. For his new position we moved
to the island of Oahu and into a very upscale neighborhood.

My rich dad, in his forties, also moved his family to the island of Oahu. But he moved to one of the richest neighborhoods, not just an upscale neighborhood. My rich dad was suddenly far richer than my poor dad—and earning much more money.

By the time both men were in their early fifties, the gap between their incomes and lifestyles was staggering. When I asked my rich dad why this was, he replied, "Because I work for a different type of income than your dad does, and I have better tax advisors than your dad."

One dad started with nothing and wound up with nothing. He worked hard, earned a lot of money, and paid a lot in taxes. The other dad started with nothing but wound up rich. He too worked hard and earned a lot of money—but he wound up very rich.

Fathering Advice About Money

As I was growing up, my poor dad often said, "Go to school, get good grades, so you can find a high-paying job." In contrast my rich dad would say, "How much money you make is *not* as important as how much money you keep. The trouble with a high-paying job is that the more you make, the less you keep."

Rich Dad's Lesson on Good Income and Bad Income

In my rich dad's mind, having a high-paying job was working for *bad* income. The reason he labeled income from a job *bad income* was taxes. He would say, "Taxes are our largest single expense in life. If you have a job, you have lost control of that expense. If you want to be rich, you need to work for good income. Good income is income that is taxed less and gives you more control over how much you pay in taxes and when you pay your taxes."

This book is about *legally* getting back more control over your money, including how much and when you pay your taxes.

Taking Control of Your Money

The words *tax loopholes* generate a secret and negative response for many people. As much as the word *loophole* has some mysteriousness attached to it, I have not yet met a person who has said "I am *not* going to take that deduction because I want to find *more* ways to pay *more* in taxes." Or "The government allows me this *write-off,* but I don't think I'll take it." Everyone I have met is interested in legally paying *less* in taxes, not more.

The Loophole of the Middle Class

"I bought a big house so I could write off my interest payment from my taxes" is a comment I often hear. In other words, millions of people are willing to give the bank a dollar in interest on their mortgage to get approximately thirty cents back in tax savings. If getting thirty cents back from a dollar makes sense to you, then I will offer you a better deal: Send me as many dollars as you want and I will send you back fifty cents for each dollar.

But for the middle class of America the interest deduction on a home mortgage is one of the last legal loopholes through which they can still exert some control over how much they pay in taxes. Their home is their largest investment and sometimes their only investment.

The Poor Do Not Have Loopholes

The poor people in America often rent because they cannot afford to buy a home. They have almost no tax loopholes available to them. In fact, the poor in America pay the highest percentage of their income in taxes, the middle class second, and the rich pay the smallest percentage.

Loopholes Are Incentives

My real dad—the man I call my poor dad—thought that tax loopholes were sinister and illegal. My rich dad saw them as *government incentives.* Rich dad would say to me, "The government offers me a different tax payment structure (loophole) because I create jobs. The more jobs I create, the better the economy and the more in taxes the government makes from my employees."

My rich dad also invested in real estate because real estate has so many tax incentives (loopholes). To this endeavor he would say, "The government needs people like me to provide low-cost, affordable rental housing to people who cannot afford to buy a home. If not for investors like me, there would be fewer rental properties, which would mean higher rental prices to the renter. That is why the government offers such tax breaks to people like me."

Rich dad saw himself as a business partner with the government. He would say, "The government offers me tax incentives (loopholes) to do many of the jobs the government needs done. I see myself as a business partner with the government, and your dad is an employee of the government. That is why I receive preferential treatment (loopholes on my taxes) and your dad doesn't."

More Than Just a Different Point of View

The second book in the Rich Dad series is *Rich Dad's CASHFLOW Quadrant.* The following diagram represents the CASHFLOW Quadrant:

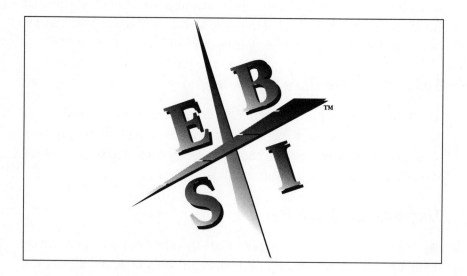

For those who may not have read the book, the letters represent the four different groups of people who make up the world of business:

E   stands for employee
S   stands for self-employed person or small business owner
B   stands for big business owner
I   stands for investor

Rich Dad's CASHFLOW Quadrant was written for anyone contemplating making a change in his or her financial or professional life, through changing quadrants. The challenge in making the change to a new quadrant is far more than just a change in a point of view. Such a change often requires a change in thinking, emotions, friends, and activities.

The Government Also Sees Things Differently

Rich dad pointed out that the government also sees thing differently, especially when it comes to taxes. When you look at the CASHFLOW Quadrant, you can clearly see the differences.

In 1943 the government passed the Current Tax Payment Act. What that act did was fundamentally take over all control of taxes from anyone in the E quadrant, by taking their taxes through withholding before they ever received their pay. The B, S, and I quadrants retained most of their tax advantages.

One of the reasons most employees have a difficult time getting ahead financially is that they work for what my rich dad called "50 percent money." He called it 50 percent money because regardless of how much a person made, the government historically took on average 50 percent of that money. Rich dad would say, "When an employee gets a raise, so does the government."

Rich dad always taught me to be aware of what kind of money I worked for. Today in the United States there are the following types of money:

- The first and most common is 50 percent money, which is the money you receive as an employee. That rate has been as high as 90 percent in the United States.
- The second is 20 percent money, which is money from investment capital gains. One of the advantages of investing in real estate is that this 20 percent money can easily be tax-deferred as well.
- The next is tax-advantaged money, which is income that you are allowed to deduct as expenses before paying taxes on that income. The S, B, and I quadrants still enjoy this type of income.
- The fourth type of money is tax-free money. The most common type of tax-free money comes from municipal bonds, yet for the sophisticated investor tax-free money is available in many other ways.

It is the differences in the percentage of taxes that caused rich dad to label income either good or bad. It all had to do with the percentage paid in taxes.

The S Quadrant Loses Control in 1986

In 1986 the government passed the '86 Tax Reform Act, which took away many of the tax advantages the S quadrant once enjoyed. After 1986 most highly paid professionals—such as doctors, lawyers, accountants, engineers, and architects—no longer had the same tax advantages the B and I quadrants could use.

Will the government take away the tax advantages of the B and I quadrants? My rich dad's reply was, "The people in the B and I quadrants perform many of the activities that the government wants and needs done. The people in these quadrants create new jobs, create the goods and services necessary to support a civilized society, as well as build the housing for people to live in."

Seeing himself as a partner with the government, rich dad invested heavily into affordable housing for low-income workers. By the time he was fifty he had built over 500 homes for low-income families, as well as nearly 700 apartment units for renters. The properties were clean and well managed, and tenants usually stayed there for years. Rich dad also owned hotels that catered to tourists who were on a budget.

My poor dad owned one piece of real estate, and that was his house. Although my rich dad was providing housing for many people, as well as jobs for hundreds of people, my poor dad still thought it unfair that my rich dad used the tax loopholes to get rich.

This Book Is About Partnership

Regardless of your point of view on taxes, this book is written for individuals who are ready to take more control over their taxes by seeing themselves as business partners with the government. This book is not about *tax avoidance* or, worse, *tax evasion,* which is illegal.

Do you need to gain more control over your taxes? Look at the value of the work you perform from the point of view of being a business partner helping the government do the job it has been mandated to do by its citizens. That is the point of view my rich dad took whenever he found out what the government wanted done and then did it if the job and tax incentives fit his plan. *Read this book from my rich dad's point of view, instead of the point of view of just paying less in taxes.*

A Final Word on Taxes

Rich dad believed in paying taxes, and that taxes were a necessary expense of living in a civilized society. He would say, "If not for taxes, we would probably not have the police to protect us and the firemen to put out our fires. Without taxes there would be fewer schools, fewer teachers, and an even wider gap between the rich and the poor. Without taxes we would not have courts, judges, and a legal system through which we can resolve our differences, and keep outlaws away from those who want to live within the law." But while he believed in paying taxes, he still wanted to have some control over how much he paid and when he paid it. In exchange for that control he was willing to be a partner with government.

All Quadrants Pay Taxes

So the final word on taxes is that all quadrants are required to pay taxes. One important distinction is that people who operate from the B quadrant have the most options when it comes to tax loopholes and may even find it appropriate to pay taxes from all four of the different quadrants. For example, rich dad sometimes found it more advantageous to pay taxes as an E, S, or I, even though he operated out of the B quadrant.

The point is that people solely in the E quadrant have the fewest options and have the least control over

- How much they pay in taxes;
- When they pay their taxes;
- Which quadrant they pay their taxes from; and
- The tax loopholes or tax incentives available to them.

The Price of Not Needing Advice

Because my poor dad worked from the E quadrant, *he did not need tax advice.* A mass-market tax-preparation firm was all he really needed. Because my poor dad did not need a CPA, he never had one on his team—and because he never had a CPA on his team he learned very little about how the rich earn more and pay less in taxes. His financial education remained stagnant. His need for job security cost him because he made more and more in the E quadrant but kept less and less due to increasing taxes.

A Most Important Loophole

One of the most important loopholes my rich dad had was the loophole known as *professional services.* Rich dad said repeatedly, "Business and investing are team sports." My rich dad was allowed to deduct the professional services of his accountant, attorney, bookkeepers, et cetera, through his businesses. My rich dad often said, "I became a financially smart businessman because the government helps me pay for the best financial and business education in the world. Hiring the best professional services is the best tax loophole and incentive in the world."

A Very Important Advisor

I feel honored to have Diane Kennedy write this book for the Rich Dad's Advisors Series. Not only is Diane a very important advisor, she is a friend and a mentor to me. Few people have taught me more about how the tax system works for the rich and how to play the game of the rich.

Diane lets me do what I do best, which is make money, and then provides me with the strategy and guidance to keep as much of my money as possible. I have learned so much from Diane . . . and Diane Kennedy is one of my most important advisors.

Diane is the tax strategist that wealthy entrepreneurs seek out. She does herself what she advises her clients to do. I am honored to have Diane's book join the Rich Dad Advisors Series. It answers a question I am often asked, "Tell me how you earn so much and pay so little in taxes." Instead of saying, "I don't know. My accountant tells me how," I can now say, "Get Diane Kennedy's book, *Loopholes of the Rich.*"

Read this book to find out why and how the rich get richer. As my rich dad said, "There is good income and bad income." Find out how you can earn more and more *good* income.

—Robert Kiyosaki

AUDIO DOWNLOAD

In each of our books we like to provide an audio interview as a bonus with additional insights. As a thank-you to you for reading this book, you may go to the Web site www.richdad.com/advisors and download "How to Build a Tax Savings Team."

Thank you for your interest in your financial education.

The Rules Have Changed

Are You Living Your Dream . . . Or Your Nightmare?

Are you one of the millions today who keep working harder and harder and receive less and less in return for their effort? Just where does that money seem to go? And, even more frightening, where does all your time go? Many today are waking up to the realization that they have somehow gotten old, and their life so far has only been about striving—with nothing to show for all the years of work.

Where Did It All Go Wrong?

The biggest expenses for the average American are interest and taxes. Both of these expenses put *your* money in *someone else's* pocket. The interest that you pay on your home mortgage, car loans, credit cards, and the like is income to someone else. The taxes you pay go to support the government without much input from you. In other words, the typical middle-class wage earner works to pay other people. And, worse yet, the average American seemingly has no say in how the money is spent. No wonder you feel out of control sometimes!

The middle-class dream has become a nightmare. You can't work harder at your job and expect to get ahead. And, even worse, you might not know it until it's too late. You might find out that you have no future just as you're ready to retire and enjoy your "golden" years. That's when you find out the pension you hoped for is gone. That's when you find out your house costs you more in property tax and insurance than you can afford. And, too late, you find out you now have outdated skills for the job market. This is one nightmare that doesn't end when you wake up. You don't even know you're in the nightmare until you wake up and find out you have no money and no future.

The good news is that there still is a dream possible for you. And, that future is possible no matter where you are today. It doesn't matter where you live. It doesn't matter how much money you have now. It doesn't matter how much debt you have. But the way to realize the dream, and end the nightmare, is not the way your parents taught you.

The plan of your parents—work hard, save your money, and collect your retirement—was effective for them, but it doesn't work now. *Loopholes of the Rich* was written to provide the information you need to operate in today's world. In this book you will learn the new rules that the wealthy play by. And you will learn how you can play by the same rules.

A Word of Caution

You will hear ideas and examples throughout the book that will excite you. You will likely find that the people in the examples have situations very much like yours. You will want to do something—be moved to take action. That's great! The caution is that you must follow all the steps closely. One of the fundamental, key steps is the need to have a good team. Find good advisors and then trust them to give you the best advice.

The Two Fatal Flaws on the Road to Wealth

There are two fatal flaws a business owner can make. The first is to do the *right thing* at the *wrong time.* The second is to do the *wrong thing* at the *right* time.

You might have heard this before, but it is more than a cute saying. It is only by doing the *right thing* at the *right time* that you will maximize your full potential.

RIGHT THING AT THE WRONG TIME

We all have a tendency to wait too long to act. That is the result of a physical law in the universe—inertia. We can't (or don't) believe that we need to take action until it's too late. Waiting too long is doing the *right thing* at the *wrong time.*

Have you ever missed out on a stock deal by waiting too long? You knew that the stock was a good buy but you wanted to talk to just a few more people or do just a little more research. By the time you felt you had enough information to act upon, it was too late—the price had climbed and it was no longer a bargain. I see the same thing every day in the real estate market, (something I follow closely). By the time the majority of investors are interested (and feel safe) in a neighborhood, the prices are sky-high—it is the visionaries that create and profit from the market. When you do the *right thing* at the *wrong time,* you are failing to act.

It's easy to identify someone who is doing the *right thing* at the *wrong time.* They will say things like, "I need to find out a little more information" or "Let me ask around a little first" or "I have *just one more* question." Now, all these actions are good. The problem comes when that is as far as they go. *One more* question leads to *one more* question, and on and on. The *little* more information is never enough. They get stuck in analysis paralysis.

I think of it as someone who is at a clay skeet shooting range. Picture someone shouting "pull," followed by the clay skeet flying across the sky. Here is where timing is so important. They lift their shotgun to their shoulder and pull the trigger with it aimed at the sky, long after the skeet has passed the mark. That is doing the right thing at the wrong time.

WRONG THING AT THE RIGHT TIME

When have you done the *wrong thing* at the *right time*? Perhaps you acted emotionally without thinking out the consequences or without the right kind of information. A good example of that plays out daily in the mutual fund portion of the stock market. As the value in the stock market rises, more and more people invest—at higher prices. Then, when the stock market value drops, these same people sell. The change in the market means that most likely some kind of action should be taken, but they act in exactly the opposite way. When you do the *wrong thing* at the *right time,* you demonstrate the need for more education.

You can identify the person doing the *wrong thing* at the *right time.* They will say things like, "Do *something,* even if it's wrong" or "Just *do* it." Again, the call to action is very important, but don't jump until you know where you want to land. Thoughtless action can be just as dangerous as inaction.

Picture yourself back at the shooting range from the previous example. This time as the shooter calls "pull," they aim the shotgun at the ground, completely opposite from the trail of the skeet, and, at the precise moment that the skeet is in the sky, they pull the trigger, shooting into the dirt. The shooter did the wrong thing at the right time.

How to Improve the Odds

Doing the *right thing* at the *right time* means that you need to have the best financial knowledge and the best timing. The best way to create the balance needed between financial *education* and the necessary calls to *action* is by creating a team. Your team should encourage and move you in the right direction. In Chapter 3, you will learn how to find, evaluate, and work with the right team. No one person can have all of the answers. A team makes you stronger. With their help and advice, you can pull the trigger at the right time to hit the mark of your financial success.

The "Do It Yourselfer"

Every so often, as I speak at seminars, a participant's questions make it clear that they intend to do it themselves in attempting to find the right business structure for their business. I am reminded of a true story a friend of mine told me, years after he had graduated from medical school. My friend's story, as he might tell it, follows:

It had become evident who the top student in his class was by the second year of medical school. In fact, this particular young man was so far advanced that he had trouble communicating with any of his fellow students and many of the professors. As his knowledge, and his conceit, grew, he began to believe that he was more competent than *anyone* else in the medical profession. This was in spite of the fact that he was only in his second year of medical school.

With that belief, he self-diagnosed a potential appendix problem for himself and determined that he should have surgery to have the troubled appendix removed. Of course, he felt that no one was as good as he was, so he also decided to remove the appendix himself.

He gave himself local anesthesia and rigged up mirrors on his narrow dormitory bed so that he could view the operating site—his own abdomen. His skill might have been top-notch, but he couldn't stanch the flow of blood quickly enough and soon passed out from the loss of blood. Luckily, he was discovered before he died from the failed surgery attempt.

He was trained, he was competent, *and* he almost died
trying to do it himself!

The Bottom Line: Use trained professionals; don't try this by yourself.

What You Will Learn in Loopholes of the Rich

Loopholes of the Rich came about as a result of my years of experience working with people who searched for ways to reduce their taxes and increase their wealth. After talking to literally thousands of people from all over the United States and Canada, from all walks of life, with different assets, education, and circumstances, I found that there were often similar questions and stumbling blocks that they all encountered. That is why this book was written—to create a common ground of understanding as a foundation upon which you can build with your own personal advisors.

The first statement that I generally hear from someone just starting is "I don't know where to start!" They ask, "What do I do first?" Usually they have a stated goal of what they want, such as pay less taxes and protect their assets. But they might not know what it is they really want. After a few minutes of conversation, we usually discover that what the person is really after is a sense of control and understanding about their own finances. They don't feel good about what they have done to date. They want to know that someday they will be able to have true financial freedom. And they want to know that they have that freedom protected. In other words, they want to be able to keep their financial freedom.

Perhaps you have longed for the same goal. As you read through this book, you will likely find some of your current ideas challenged. And, even more important, you might find that your friends and current advisors will challenge the ideas presented here. That doesn't mean that your friends are wrong and it doesn't mean that the ideas in the book are wrong. What it does mean is that we all understand things within our own framework and point of view. If something comes along that is not in that point of view, we can either reject it as incorrect or we can try to adjust our point of view to accept it. If you choose to accept different ideas, then you can experience growth and more depth of understanding. That is really what is book is about—to give you different ideas about things you might already think you know.

Above all, I have striven to present the ideas in a format that makes them easy to understand. We will be discussing complex tax strategies and tax law. You can't learn that from reading just one book. You actually can't ever say you have completely learned it, because tax law is constantly changing as new cases are decided, refinements added by additional Treasury regulations, and, of course, the inevitable changes to the tax code by Congress.

How the Book Is Set Up

The book is divided into six sections. Each section is important and builds upon the other. I suggest that you read the book through once, completely. Then go back to more closely read the chapters that are most applicable to your own circumstances. The six sections are:

I. THE FIVE STEPS TO FINANCIAL FREEDOM
Learn the Five STEPS to Financial Freedom so you can achieve the ultimate in tax savings and start building wealth today.

II. THE THREE STEP TAX FORMULA
This easy Three Step Tax Formula sums up the over 500,000 pages of tax code, regulations, rulings, and procedures. Learn how you can quickly and easily master this formula with practical how-to information.

III. PICKING THE RIGHT BUSINESS STRUCTURE
One of the most often asked questions by the new business owner is "What type of business structure should I use?" How can you know which is the right business structure for you? What are the most important issues for you?

IV. TAX PLANNING E-T-C

Learn how to take advantage of E-T-C to reduce your taxes even more. This is a new way of looking at *how* and *when* you pay taxes.

V. C CORPORATIONS

One of the most important tools to wealth building can be the proper use of your own C corporation. Just owning a C corporation isn't the path to wealth: You have to know what to do with it, too. Learn the potential pitfalls of C corporations and how you can avoid them, along with ways to take money out of your own C corporation. Also, learn to master the advanced techniques for use of Nevada corporations.

VI. KEEPING IT LEGAL AND SAFE

Set up your business and accounting to keep what you earn safe from frivolous lawsuits. Learn how to minimize the risk of IRS attack. Reduce the risk *of* an audit and reduce the risk *from* an audit.

BONUS

- IRS Business Types
- The 300+ Business Deduction Checklist
- Real-Life Tax Strategy Examples
- Sample Forms

Two Couples—Two Different Financial Strategies

Throughout the book, you will see the stories of two different clients unfold. You may find that you have similarities to one of these two clients. The clients are actually amalgams of real-life examples. Everything you will read about these clients and their personal experiences has happened to someone. The examples are real, but specific details have been changed. Plus, of course, the names have been changed.

Ted and Ellen are based on the characters of people I have known for a long time. In fact, I had gone to school with someone like Ellen. They got trapped in the middle-class nightmare—working hard, not home much with their two children, and tired most of the time. They were looking for a way out. They weren't afraid to try something new, and they were bright, hardworking people. But they didn't want to risk their family's security along the way.

Nick and Sue came to me after they already had a business developed and after meeting with various other advisors. They, unfortunately, had jumped, without knowing where they were jumping to, or where they were going to land. As a result, their tax strategy was not clear and was in direct conflict to their best interests. They didn't know what they were doing wasn't right, and were appalled to learn that they had inadvertently stumbled into an area that they didn't understand. Worse yet, they didn't have the tools to know that their advisors didn't understand the issues either. There was a lot of education and "un-education" required, as well as undoing the mistakes. For Nick and Sue, it was a more difficult path than normal, because of the fixing that had to be done. But in some ways it was also easier, because they already had the resources and knowledge of how to run a business and how to make business decisions.

These two couples are in very different situations, with issues unique to each one. You may find elements of either or both couples in your own situation. Every client of mine has had many learning experiences along the way to their business success. My hope is that you can learn from these experiences as you read about them. Every lesson you learn and *apply* from someone else is one fewer lesson you won't have to learn the hard way. I don't know about you, but that sounds a whole lot easier to me!

Interspersed throughout the narrative of these two couples, you will find other explanations and many forms. I encourage you to complete the forms and questionnaires that are applicable to your situation. These are tools that I use in my CPA practice with clients every day. My sincere wish is that you will have the same good results our clients have experienced. Above all, I wish you success and happiness in your business ventures, and, in fact, in all of life's adventures.

Meet Ted and Ellen: *What Went Wrong?*

"What went wrong?" was the first thing that Ellen, my old college pal, said to me when we met to catch up one day.

"We planned everything—good education, good career—and we're making more money than we ever thought we would," she continued. "Yet we live hand-to-mouth. They are talking about downsizing where Ted works, and I worry that we'd be out in the street if that happened to him." She was obviously upset.

"Ellen, the one thing I know is that you are not alone!" I replied, reflecting on my experience with clients in my tax practice.

When Did the Dream Die?

Years earlier, I had met Ted and Ellen soon after we all graduated from college. They were looking forward to building their life together—a nice house in the suburbs with the two children they planned. And back then, even though it was barely two decades ago, we all knew the surest route to success was the tried-and-true formula—get a good job, save to buy your first home, start your family, and live happily ever after.

Ted and Ellen were hardworking and achieved their success—new home and family—faster than most. And then one day I ran into them again. The first thing I noticed was how tired they both were. Ellen hadn't been able to be the stay-at-home mom that she wanted to be and was exhausted from juggling the demands of a typical eight-to-five job with the demands of caring for their eight-year-old son, Josh, and three-year-old daughter, Sarah.

Ted worked days at a job for the state, a safe, secure job with good benefits that were quickly being taken away. He was worried about how much longer he would have that job and had started a computer consulting business on the side. He spent his evening and weekends locked away from his family in a corner of the family room working on his computer.

Both Ted and Ellen felt guilty about the time they spent away from their children and they worried about money for their future (would there be money for the children's braces, education, and so forth), and about their own personal future (would there be anything left for them when they were ready to retire?).

We met as friends, but it soon became apparent that I could help them in a professional manner.

I had established my career as a tax advisor and strategist for the wealthy, and as a result had learned many of the techniques the wealthy used. The simple fact is that the wealthy approach their tax and financial planning in a radically different way than what we have been taught.

Ted and Ellen were happy to discuss their financial plans with me. Together, we created a strategy that reduced their income tax and used the money they previously paid to the government to build wealth, tax-free, for their future. That means that much of the money they used to spend on taxes is now being used to build their future.

In a series of conversations, they learned the basics of devising a tax plan, and then, together, we built a customized tax strategy, using the approach of the wealthy.

How You Will Learn

The easiest way to learn is from modeling other people's success, such as how the wealthy use corporations and other business structures to gain wealth. In *Loopholes of the Rich,* you will read of Ted and Ellen and later of Nick and Sue. Each milestone, challenge, and decision they faced has been faced by others. You can learn from their successes and how they dealt with their challenges.

After each bit of their story, there will be discussions and explanations that outline the issues and when and how these same issues could be applicable to you. Extensive checklists follow these stories along with forms you can use to set your own course toward wealth. These forms are used in the process we use every day in our business to evaluate our clients' plans and paths—where they are and where they are going.

No matter where you are on the path to wealth, there is something in this book that can work for you. You will be shown how to *practically* apply the things learned.

After each step or knowledge building block, consider what your first action should be. This is critical to making change in your life. Get the education and then take the action!

LOOPHOLES
OF THE RICH

Part I

The Five STEPS to Financial Freedom

Chapter 1

The Five STEPS

"First, I want to go through the first five steps of wealth creation," I said as I began my first meeting with Ted and Ellen. "And there is good news—you've already handled some of the steps. Plus, even better news—you have the opportunity to maximize what you already have going for you by identifying what you're doing right and learning from that when we go through the first five steps.

"We're going to go through some basic fact-finding questionnaires and review your past tax returns," I continued. "I must warn you, some of this may be uncomfortable. But it's important that you're honest with yourself because that is the only way to truly make a positive change."

The three of us then reviewed the STEPS program that we use in my CPA firm. The acronym STEPS stands for five different parts of the program. Following is the information we provide to new clients.

Five STEPS to Financial Freedom Program

Success leaves a trail. One of the easiest ways to have your own success is to follow where others have gone before. We all have different goals and come from different circumstances, but there are five basic steps that will ensure the best possible results for everyone, no matter where you are now. These five STEPS are:

S   Starting Point

T   Team

E   Evaluation/Strategy

P   Plan and Path

S   Starting Point (reevaluation)

S IS FOR STARTING POINT

First, you need to know where you are. It's like having to get on the scales before you start a new diet. You might not want to really know what the numbers say. But you do need to know your starting point.

That's just how it is for your financial plan. Your best results will come when you can take a realistic look at where you are financially—without excuses, blame, or justifications. Find out where you are, so you can plot an accurate course to where you want to be!

T IS FOR TEAM

After you have a good idea of where you are, you will need to start to think about the members you need for your financial team. Most likely, the main members of your team initially will be advisors, educators, and mentors. But your team can also include customers, clients, vendors, business alliances, and friends, among others. You can make conscious choices about the members of your team. You can learn how to evaluate what you need and how these people will fit into your plan. Finally, you can recognize the hidden influences they have on decisions you have made and will make in the future.

Remember: The members of your team will *help* you or *harm* you as you follow your own financial path.

E IS FOR EVALUATION/STRATEGY

After you know where you are and begin to assemble your team, it is time to call on your advisors to help you evaluate where you are and design a personalized strategy for you to achieve your goals. No one team member—your tax strategist, bookkeeper, legal counsel, or financial planner—will make all of the decisions. It is through the cooperative work of your whole team that you will receive the best advice and plan creation.

P IS FOR PLAN AND PATH

After S, T, and E, you now need to move forward on the path and implement the strategy designed. This can be the hardest part as you move into previously unknown financial waters. You will want to make sure that the team you have in place has experience in the necessary areas and can give you good advice based on their own personal education, experience, and special skills.

S IS FOR STARTING POINT (REEVALUATION)

You've taken the first four steps and now you need to again evaluate where you are. Just like a rocket going to the moon needs continual calculations to keep it on its path, you must constantly evaluate where you are and where you are going to ensure that you reach your goals.

By taking the time to thoughtfully consider where you are and where you've come from, you put yourself in a position to achieve the optimum results.

These five STEPS to financial freedom can start you and your family on the path to financial freedom *today.*

What Would Financial Freedom Mean to You?

After you go through the first five STEPS, you are ready to go on to the Three Step Tax Formula. This is actually a very easy formula used to calculate taxes, and you will learn how to control each aspect. You will learn how to pick the right business structure for you, the secrets of tax planning E-T-C, the traps of C corporations (and how to avoid them), advanced tax strategies, and, perhaps most importantly, how to protect what you have.

Upon hearing this brief outline, Ted and Ellen enthusiastically made a commitment to the program and we agreed to meet every month to examine their progress.

S Is for Starting Point

"The first letter *S* stands for Starting Point," I began our first program meeting. "In other words, realistically speaking, where are you financially right now? This can be the most difficult step you take in pursuing your financial dreams. You must have true courage to face the reality of what the numbers will say about where you are right now. In many ways, your financial statement is the report card for your financial life. Remember that this is a necessary first step and its only purpose is to determine the starting point. It doesn't have to be a portent for the rest of your life. To change, though, you must first know where you are.

"Through many years of working with clients, I have realized that it is easy to put off the work you need to do to pull together your first financial statement. There are always emergencies to deal with—and many of them are financial in nature. To avoid having to constantly deal with those financial emergencies, you must change how you view your finances. To do that, you need to be able to step back and truly see where you are. If you care about better results for you and your family, this is the most important step you can take."

T *Is for Team*

"Only after you have a good idea of where you are and where you are going, can you start putting together your plan for your team. Most likely, the main members of your team initially will be advisors, educators, and mentors. But team members can also include customers, clients, vendors, business alliances, and friends, among others. It also includes family members. Now, there are some limits to how much you decide to change your team. I don't know how practical it would be to try to find a new family," I said, as Ted and Ellen chuckled.

"But it is good to recognize the hidden influences they had into decisions you have made and will make in the future. The most important part of Team is the conscious choices you will be able to make about the type of advisors, educators, and mentors you need. You will learn how to evaluate what you need and how they will fit into your plan."

"I know that people around us have a lot of influence," interjected Ellen. "I never thought about consciously choosing who they would be."

"Ellen, the most important part to remember is that the members of your team will *help* you or *harm* you as you follow your own financial path. It is vital that you look at them and their prospective role with wide open eyes," I said.

E *Is for Evaluation/Strategy*

"The most accomplished navigators know that you need two crucial facts—where you are and where you want to be—to know how to set a course," I continued explaining to Ted and Ellen. "In financial matters, it can become more complicated, as it might not be clear what you need to do to get from point A to point B. You have to be able to evaluate the various tools, methods, and advisors to determine how they will work to help you achieve your personal goals. This program will teach the difference between merely buying a financial-planning product, and designing a strategy and then determining which financial-planning products to buy. With the knowledge of how you are going to move from where you are to where you want to be, you can make intelligent, thoughtful decisions about the best products to buy, the best advisors to add to your team—and, thus, reach your goals much more quickly."

"Wait a minute!" exclaimed Ted. "That's what I want you for—to tell me what to do and then I'll just go do it."

"I understand, Ted. In fact, all of this information and preparation can seem overwhelming. The best way I can explain it is by telling a story I first heard told by Stephen Covey.

"The story begins with a group of workers deep in the jungle given the task of forming a pathway. They organize and make good progress. At some point, one of the leaders dispatches a man up a tree to determine how much farther they need to go. The lookout climbs up a tall tree—higher and higher—until he can see over the jungle canopy. He looks from side to side clinging to his precarious perch. Meanwhile, the men below keep working assiduously at clearing the brush. The lookout's voice pierces down through the canopy to the men below. He yells, 'Stop! Wait a minute!' The men keep working under the urging of their leader. The lookout again calls out, 'Stop!'

"Finally, the leader shouts back, 'Be quiet! We're making great progress!'

"The lookout's voice then calls out, 'Wrong jungle!'"

As Ted and Ellen smiled, I explained, "The point is you need to know where you are and where you're going. Plus, you need to have the strategy mapped out. Otherwise, your hard work may be taking you in the wrong direction.

"When you know where you are and where you want to be, you can design the pathway that is right for you. You can get help along the way, but no one will ever know your own unique situation as well as you do and, frankly, no one will ever care as much as you do. Do you really want to turn over the planning of your life to someone else?" I asked.

"I guess I see your point," said Ted. "But we just have so little time now. How can we make enough time to do all this planning?"

"That's the one piece of good news that I can give you," I assured him. "Our firm has done this for a lot of years and has streamlined the process. The Five STEPS to Financial Freedom are admittedly harder the first time through, but then it becomes second nature to you. And, in fact, it will be exciting to you as you achieve good results."

P *Is for Plan and Path*

"None of this means a thing without taking action to implement the strategy," I went on. "This is probably the second biggest stumbling block, behind failing to first get a strategy, that I see clients run into. It's scary to try something new and, in addition, there is a point where you might have a lot of great ideas but not have a clue about where to start. That's a large distinction between our firm and others—we specialize in implementation (action). We'll go through the steps necessary to put your plan into place.

"But no matter who you choose to have on your team, this is the point where you need to rely on your advisors. They need to understand your goals and have the experience of achieving the same goals for other clients. You will be moving into uncharted waters for you. Make sure you have an experienced guide along for the ride!"

S *Is for Starting Point—Again (Reevaluation)*

"Finally, reevaluation is necessary to determine where you are now after you have designed and implemented your own Evaluation/Strategy and Plan and Path. I have a view of the world that I call the bumper car analogy. Remember when you used to go the fair and ride on the bumper cars?" I asked Ted and Ellen. They quickly nodded their heads.

"You never quite knew when someone was going to run into you or where they were going to come from. They might be specifically targeting you or they might just be trying to follow their own path and you happened to get in their way. Well, that's how I choose to view the world. There are six billion people in bumper cars and most of them are going somewhere. They may not have a specific goal in place. They may just be traveling in circles. And there are some that decide they are going to target you. But the fact is that you are going to collide with many of these six billion bumper cars as you are trying to follow your own path. You are going to get knocked off your path. That means that you can't continue on the same line you had drawn originally. You need to constantly be reevaluating where you are. Plus, you might find as you move toward your goal that it is no longer exactly what you want. So, point B (your destination) can change. As your goals change, your strategy and your team need to adapt. You may need to make changes in your team. Therefore, it is necessary to again look at the first four steps. The quicker you can reevaluate, and do it without regrets, blame, or justification, the faster and better your results will be.

"Well, that's the initial phase of the plan. What do you th—?" I hadn't even finished the question before both Ted and Ellen jumped in with enthusiastic responses.

SUMMARY

Success leaves a trail. Success leaves a trail that can be followed by everyone. When you make the decision to have different financial results, you will discover that you will change the things you do.

The Five STEPS to Financial Freedom. The first five STEPS on the road to financial freedom are S—Starting Point, T—Team, E—Evaluation/Strategy, P—Plan and Path, and S—Starting Point (Reevaluation).

S—Starting Point. Starting point determines where you are first. No matter what self-improvement plan you start—health, education, financial, or some other—you first need to measure where you are.

T — Team. The team you choose will be the ones who support you, or who hinder you, as you make changes in your financial life.

E—Evaluation/Strategy. You have the facts of where you are and an idea of where you want to go and you have assembled your team. Now, together, you will come up with an analysis and evaluation of what those numbers mean and what strategies you will employ to move forward.

P—Plan and Path. The fourth step is implementation. Design your plan, chart out your path—and do it!

S—Starting Point (Reevaluation). Take some time and assess where you have gone. You have made use of your team, who analyzed and designed a strategy, and you acted upon it. Where did you go? What is the next step?

Change can be uncomfortable. Whenever we move outside of the box that is familiar, we are in unknown territory. We are suddenly vulnerable in new ways. Things that happen at this point will unsettle us more than normal and we will naturally go rushing back to what we know—our own personal box. That is why the STEPS are designed to first include a team that supports you and helps you develop your own strategy and plan for implementation. You will be constantly reassessing to discover what works and what doesn't work. But you won't be alone!

Chapter 2

Starting Point

S *Is for Starting Point*

"As I've mentioned, the first letter *S* stands for Starting Point," I continued in my first formal meeting with Ted and Ellen. "This step may be the most painful as you examine where you are today. You won't have the crutches of what I call 'story' to help you along. No excuses, no blame, no justifications—just a realistic look at where you are financially. That is the first part. The second part of Starting Point is identifying where you want to be. You will learn how to clearly define where you want to be financially, so you can design the path to lead you to that goal."

Where Are You Now?

"Today we're going to talk about how to figure out where you are financially. And, because it is financial, we will have to do this using financial terms and constructions."

"Wait a second!" exclaimed Ellen. "I'm not good with numbers. That's what we want *you* for!"

"Ellen, I can't tell you how many times I have heard that. You're right that I have more education in working with accounting, but the fact is that no one will ever care about your financial well-being as much as you do." I paused as they chuckled. "I can tell you've run into the people who want to tell you that they really care about you, but—"

"But it seems like what they really care about is my money!" exclaimed Ted.

"Right—you got my point. But there is another reason why it makes sense for you to be involved in this information-gathering stage: because no one knows more about where you are now and what your plans are better than you do. The financial education you can gain by honestly completing the forms to determine your own financial situation can be worth far more than anything else you do," I added.

"I've seen many, many people reach this initial stage when they first call our office. They are told about the need for them to make the commitment to complete the first-step questionnaire and they hesitate. It seems that the person who never has time to devote to compiling their financial information is the same person who never has time to plan. Their life reflects that as they lurch from crisis to crisis. The person who doesn't think it is important for them to compile their financial information also tends to view their financial education as not important. Unfortunately, that is also reflected in their life. After hearing literally thousands of excuses, I've found that most of them tend to be merely variations of the same one. Sadly, none of the excuses help the person who makes them . . . or believes them. Life, and opportunity, continue to pass them by."

How to Find Out Where You Are

I have found that there are two reasons that people don't take stock of where they are. First, there is a lot of resistance because they don't want to know the answer. It's easy to spot those people, because they will be saying things like: "It's so bad, I can't ever get out" or "All I need is to make more money and then the problems will all go away" or "I know all that stuff already."

The second reason is because a lot of people are afraid of numbers because they never learned basic financial literacy. This is not their fault. Our school system does a very poor job of teaching basic financial skills. Many people not only don't know how to balance a checkbook, they don't even understand *why* you need to balance your checkbook. I can't tell you how many times I have heard business owners tell me that they know how much money they have in their bank account because they just called the bank and asked the balance. Of course, that doesn't take into account any checks that haven't cleared yet, or deposits that the bank hasn't posted. Still, many people continue to try to run their business with just that kind of inaccurate information. These people are also easy to spot; they say: "I just was never any good at numbers" or "The numbers don't matter anyway" or "My accountant does that all for me" or "I'd know but my wife/bookkeeper/banker/fill-in-the-blank can't keep track of the numbers."

Excuse No. 1: "I don't want to know the answer." Regarding this excuse, I can only say that just like I know I have to occasionally get on the scales and weigh myself—it is just as imperative that you occasionally get on the financial scales and weigh where you are. That is the only way you can measure progress and see where you are. There is no easy solution here—it is a case of just doing it.

Excuse No. 2: "I don't know how." There are some fine products available to help you build your skills. The best I have found for determining where you are today are the book *Rich Dad, Poor Dad,* and the CASHFLOW™ 101 game by Cashflow™ Technologies, Inc. These products promote financial literacy, which is a core requirement to anyone hoping to improve their financial situation and create personal wealth.

Following this chapter are worksheets excerpted from *1st Step to Financial Freedom,* an audiotape set with Diane Kennedy, CPA, and Robert Kiyosaki.

I encourage everyone to take the time to sit down and fill out these worksheets. If you are married, include your spouse in the process.

Have you ever been lost in a large shopping mall? I have. When I'm not sure where I am, I use the directory map to find out where I want to go. But knowing where you want to go isn't much help unless you first know where you are. Complete the worksheet (Fig. 2.1) at the end of this chapter to locate your personal "you are here" arrow on your financial map.

Jean's Great Deal

I received a call the other day from a client of mine. She was a highly educated medical doctor with a flourishing practice. But if she didn't work, she didn't get paid. She wanted to make her money work for her, instead of always having to work for her money.

That meant her goal was to build assets. I was happy to hear that she had bought her first piece of rental property. She was proud that she had found the ideal property and had diligently filled out the cash-on-cash analysis forms I had provided her. The cash-on-cash analysis form is an excellent way to evaluate a potential investment. (The cash-on-cash ratio tells you what the annual return is on the cash you have invested. It is one of the best tools for comparing real estate investments with other forms of investments.) You can see a copy of this form in Appendix D.

We set a time to meet the following day, and when I arrived Jean immediately showed me the sheet listing the projected rental income, with the vacancy factor, repairs, and maintenance allowance, property tax expense, insurance expense, and the property mortgage payment deducted. She had left the cash-on-cash calculation blank, though. She had trouble with that calculation and, after looking at her numbers, I knew why.

The problem was that the cash-on-cash ratio tells you the rate of return for your investment, and in her case, there was no return! The property expenses exceeded the income. I gently pointed that out to her and her response was "Isn't that great! I can write the expenses off on my taxes!"

I then spent the rest of our appointment explaining that tax-write-off schemes only give you back cents on the dollar. She was not getting return for her money. Plus, she was one of those higher income tax-payers who don't even get the minimal benefit of write-offs.

By the end of the appointment, Jean had decided to sell the property and take a capital loss that hit her once, instead of the continued drain of a tax write-off.

To paraphrase a popular saying:

> If you think getting a financial education is expensive . . .
> try ignorance.

Know Where Your Money Goes

As can be seen in the story about Jean, I do not advise my clients to create additional expenses just for the tax write-off. Instead, I advise them to first look at where they already spend money. They usually will look at the past three months' spending and take an average of their expenses to use as the monthly numbers. This can be a painful experience, as some of my clients have to come face-to-face for the first time with where their money really goes. Don't cheat yourself! Do this exercise accurately and with as much detail as you can. The more care you take, the better the results.

Your business must track income and expenses so your CPA can accurately prepare your tax return. But what do you do about your personal expenses? Our clients find more tax deductions and have better financial planning tools when they track their personal expenses as well as their business expenses. You can do this by using a bookkeeper or through a personal money-management software program.

I have discovered that clients who do not accurately track their personal expenses *always* and *without exception* shortchange themselves. They can't substantiate the deductions they can take and they simply don't remember many of them.

Take advantage of every deduction by knowing where *all* your money goes.

Where Are You Today?

Your financial statement tells your financial story. Figure 2.1 is the form "Where Am I Today?" This is the tool you'll use to record the details of your financial story. You'll be filling out this sheet gradually, as you go through the process of putting your information in order. The following sections will walk you through that process.

INCOME AND ASSETS

Income can be one of three types: earned, passive, or portfolio. You work for earned income. Assets that you own generate passive and portfolio income. We follow the Rich Dad theory of assets as explained in the Rich Dad series by Robert Kiyosaki and Sharon Lechter, CPA. Simply stated, the Rich Dad definition of an asset is something that puts money in your pocket. Otherwise, it is just considered a doodad. So, for example, a rental house would be an asset, but your personal residence would be a doodad. The rental house puts money in your pocket, your personal residence takes money out of your pocket.

Your banker, however, includes doodads as assets. But counting them as assets won't make you rich.

EARNED INCOME

Earned income is what you earn when you work for your money. It's income you're paid for doing a job as an employee, or income you pay yourself as a self-employed person.

Job Income

Job, or employee, income is reported by your employer at the end of each year on a W-2 form.

Self-Employment Income

Self-employment income is the income you make working for yourself, whether as a sole proprietor or in a partnership, corporation, or limited liability company. Remember, this is income you receive only when *you* work—it is not income you receive from your business working for you, which would belong under "Business (NET)" (see below).

PASSIVE INCOME AND ASSETS

Passive income is income you've earned from assets you own, such as a real estate investment or a business.

Real Estate

What you earn from a rental property is real estate income, and you'll see this listed on your financial statement in the Income section as "Real Estate (NET)." *Net* means the income you have left over once total expenses for the property are deducted. To determine your net income from a single rental property, subtract expenses from the rental income received. Enter the net income figure next to "Real Estate (NET)."

As mentioned above, real estate—that is, the property itself—can also be an asset. When determining the value of your real estate for the Assets section of your financial statement, you'll need to be honest with yourself and use a fair market value for the property—that is, the amount for which you could sell it today. Subtract the balance owed on the mortgage(s) for the property from the fair market value. Enter the value of the property next to "Real Estate" in the Assets section. If you have more than one property, total the separate values and enter that figure.

Business (NET)

Business income is the income you receive from businesses in which you own an interest, whether they are partnerships, limited partnerships, corporations, or LLCs. This is *not* the self-employment income you listed under "Earned Income"; this is income you receive from your business working for you. You'll see this as "Business (NET)" in the Income section of your financial statement. Again, *net* refers to the income you receive once all expenses have been deducted. Enter net business income next to "Business (NET)" in the Income section. If you have more than one business, add the net income figures and enter the total.

Your business can also be an asset. When determining the value of your business (or an investment you've made in a business) for the Assets section of your financial statement, you'll have to ask yourself, in all truthfulness, how much the business could be sold for today. Subtract debt that the business owes from the fair market value. It's possible that your net business value is a negative amount. Record the value, whether positive or negative, next to "Business Value (NET)" in the Assets section.

PORTFOLIO INCOME

Portfolio income consists of interests and dividends derived from investments such as paper securities, as well as royalties from products or services you create.

Now move to the Assets section of your financial statement. List the current (month's end) balance for each bank account you have: for example, checking, savings, and money market funds.

Add together all the bank account balances. Next to "Bank Accounts," record the total. For each stock or mutual fund you own, list the market value at month's end.

Add together all the stock and mutual fund values, then enter the total next to "Stock." For each type of bond you own, record the month's end market value.

Add together all bond values, then enter the total next to "Bonds."

Now move down to "Receivables" in the Assets section. A receivable is money owed to you, usually in the form of an IOU or a note receivable. There may be an amortization schedule that identifies the value of the note at any given time. For each receivable, record the most accurate balance of the amount owed to you. Total all your receivable balances, then enter the number next to "Receivables" in the Assets section.

Royalties

The IRS classifies royalties as portfolio income. Royalties are any income earned from intellectual property you've created. The income is usually generated from the sale or license of patents, copyrights, tapes, books, CDs, or oil and gas properties. Record the royalty amount, or the total of all royalties, in the Income section next to "Royalties."

Having filled out your entire Income section, you can enter your total income on the appropriate line there. You've also filled out the first half of your Assets section. Subtotal your assets and enter the number on the appropriate line.

DOODADS

This brings you to "Doodads," in the Assets section of your financial statement. As discussed earlier, doodads are things you once probably thought of as assets. Your banker calls them assets, but they are not assets in our definition unless they put money in your pocket. Examples of doodads would be your personal residence, your personal car, jewelry, furniture, sports equipment, and other personal belongings.

Now that you have your assets subtotal and your doodads total, you can figure out your total assets. Note that there are separate versions for total assets—a banker version and a Rich Dad version. This is a reflection of the different approach bankers and Rich Dad take toward doodads. To calculate the banker version of total assets, add your assets subtotal and your doodads total and enter the figure on the appropriate line. To calculate Rich Dad's version, enter only your assets subtotal next to "Total Assets (Rich Dad Version)."

EXPENSES AND LIABILITIES

You'll recall that expenses are not the same as liabilities. The typical monthly amount you pay on a liability is your expense related to that liability. Expenses include monthly payments you make for things such as utilities, food, and entertainment. You will be filling out separate Expenses and Liabilities sections.

Review several months' worth of all your bills, including bills for credit cards and for doodads like your car and home. If you're employed, review the deductions on your paycheck; if you're self-employed, estimate how much you pay for such things as taxes and insurance. Whatever your situation, select the month that represents your typical expenses. Basically what you'll be doing, as you read on, is recording each monthly expense in the Expenses section of your financial sheet, and recording the related balance due in the Liabilities section.

Taxes

If you receive a paycheck, your pay stub will give you the total amount of taxes you pay. These typically are federal income, state income, Social Security, disability, and Medicare. Total all your monthly taxes and deductions and enter the total next to "Taxes" in the Expenses section of your financial statement. If you are self-employed, you will need to estimate the amount of monthly taxes you pay.

Credit Cards

Enter the monthly payment, or the total of all monthly payments, next to "Credit Card Payments" in the Expenses section of your statement. Record the balance owed of all credit cards next to "Credit Cards" in the Liability section of your statement.

Home Mortgage

Total the monthly payment for each mortgage you hold on your home and for each equity line of credit or other home loan.

Cars

Total the monthly payments for all cars you own and record in the Expenses section. Total the balance due on all car loans and record in the Liabilities section.

School

Fill in the monthly payment for each school loan you're paying off in the Expenses section. The total amount due should be recorded in the Liabilities section.

Remaining monthly expenses might include, for example, utility payments, grocery bills, and travel and entertainment. Enter the total next to "Other Payments" in the Expenses section. Now you can add up all your expenses in the Expenses section and enter the figure next to "Total Expenses."

PERSONAL LOANS AND OTHER DEBT

Now that you've completed your Expenses section, turn your attention to the remainder of the Liabilities section. For any additional loans or debts you have over and above what you owe on credit cards, cars, school loans, and your home, record the total balance due as a liability. For instance, perhaps you owe money to your parents but are not currently making payments. The total balance you owe them should be listed as a liability, even though you aren't making payments and therefore have no related expense for that liability.

Enter the total of all personal loan balances next to "Personal Loans" in the Liabilities section of your statement. Enter the total of all other-debt balances, next to "Other Debt" in the Liabilities section. Now add up all the liabilities listed in this section, and enter the figure next to "Total Liabilities."

NET WORTH

Remember, Rich Dad wouldn't consider your home, car, furniture, clothes, collectibles, or other personal property financial assets unless and until they were sold for a profit. That's why you'll see two versions of net worth in the Liabilities section of your financial statement. One is the banker version, which includes doodads. The other is the Rich Dad version, which excludes them.

Follow either one of the two equations below, depending on which version you want. Remember, the Rich Dad total is the more truthful reflection of where you are financially; it is how a sophisticated investor would view your financial statement:

Total assets (banker's version, with doodads) − total liabilities = your net worth

Total assets (Rich Dad's version, without doodads) − total liabilities = your net worth

A quick glance at the totals in each section of your financial statement— total income, total expenses, total assets, and total liabilities—will give you a general idea of where you are financially. As you look at these totals, make sure you also review the cash flow patterns in the upper-righthand side of the statement. Generally speaking, if the money you have coming in as income goes right out as expenses, you've got the cash flow pattern of the poor. If your income is used to pay expenses and liabilities, then the cash flow pattern of the middle class best describes you. You're bringing in money through earned income, which pays expenses and buys more liabilities. In either case, poor or middle class, you can read on, get your financial house in order, and change your pattern to that of the rich.

Where Are You Going?

"The second thing you did," I said to Ted and Ellen, "that really helps is taking the time to prepare a financial statement that shows where you want to be. You've put some time into coming up with your goals and you've also put a deadline on accomplishing those goals. You'd be surprised how many people have a vague idea that they want to be 'rich,' but don't know what 'rich' means to them.

"One great advantage I have in my business is that I get to see clients over time and really observe what works and doesn't work. I'll never forget two clients I first saw about ten years ago. Both were in construction trades and both made the same amount of money ten years ago—$50,000. The first guy is still making about $50,000 a year. At least, last I heard he was, because he's not a client anymore. The second guy is now living in a house worth $5 million and his income is always around $1 million per year."

"I want to be like the second guy," Ted exclaimed. "What did he do—invest in something on the Internet?" he asked.

"It wasn't a get-rich-quick scheme," I replied. "Instead, it had everything to do with how he approached his business. There were a lot of differences in how both these men ran their businesses; the primary difference was that the second client had a goal. He then could compare exactly where he wanted to go with whatever decision had to be made in his business or whenever a new opportunity presented itself," I continued. "He could just ask himself, 'Does this support the goal?' If it did not, it didn't matter how much money he could make or how much in love with the idea he was, he didn't do it. For him, setting a goal created a touchstone to measure everything else against."

How to Know Where You Want to Be

Using the financial statement format shown in this chapter (Fig. 2.2), create the financial statement for where you *want* to be. You can use the second set of financial statements.

Talk the goals over with your family members. Think about the life you want. Where do you want to live? Do you still want to work? How much passive income (income you don't work for) do you need to support that lifestyle?

Then, complete the forms on pages 25 and 26.

1. Income and expenses statement. What will your expenses be in your ideal life? How much passive income do you want? How much portfolio income do you want? Will you have a business that provides income without working? Start by completing the Income and Expenses parts of the scorecard. For purposes of this exercise, complete the Income section and then calculate one third of that amount for taxes. (After the exercise is completed, you might want to review this percentage with your tax advisor.)

2. Assets and liabilities statement. Next, add some realism. Divide the target amount of passive income by the estimated return you would expect on your assets. For example, if you want $10,000 per month passive income ($120,000 per year) and you expect 10 percent return on your assets, you would divide $120,000 by 10 percent for $1.2 million. That's the amount of assets you would need working *for* you. If you determine that you want $10,000 per month passive income with 10 percent return, then enter $1.2 million into the Assets column of real estate. If you want portfolio income, perform the same calculation. For example, if you want $5,000 per month in portfolio income and expect a 5 percent return, you would need to have $1,200,000 invested (portfolio income percentages generally are less than passive income percentages). If you have a business, calculate the value of the business by multiplying the monthly cash flow by 96. How much and what kind of debt will you have? (Do not put business or real estate debt in this column.) It is your personal choice on whether you want to have a mortgage. Some people need the comfort of knowing their home is paid for, no matter what. Other people see the 7 percent or 8 percent mortgages that are available as cheap money that is available for investing.

Remember that the assets you listed need to work *for* you, they can't be the so-called assets that merely *cost* you. An asset that works *for* you would be a rental house where you collect positive cash flow. A doodad would be your personal residence.

Keep the two worksheets in a safe place. You will want to refer to them many times as you follow your personal path to wealth.

Back to Ted and Ellen—Keeping Track of Where You Are

"Wow! I know where I want to concentrate my time now," Ted exclaimed. "It looks like I get a whole lot more bang for the buck when I put my time into my business and pay attention to what I'm doing."

"I was hoping you'd say that, Ted. I agree. You're going to get the best results in the shortest time by concentrating on your business. You've already made a good start and that's the best way for you to reach the goals you've set for yourself and your family. We're going to go into the plan next, but first I want to talk about your current bookkeeping."

"Oh, I keep track of that myself with a software program. It's all in there," Ted replied matter-of-factly.

"I'm sure you have all of the information in the program, but what I see here is not in a usable fashion for an accountant. You see, there is a very strict format that an accountant uses to present data, one that is *legally* required whenever you prepare a filing for a business tax return. You might have kept track of income and expenses in the past using a program that tracks personal financial information. That would be sufficient for a sole proprietorship filing a Schedule C on a personal return. But as soon as you form any business structure such as a partnership or corporation, you are required to track under a double entry bookkeeping system."

"So now I have to learn bookkeeping, too? I am beginning to wonder why *anyone* even bothers with a corporation or partnership!" exclaimed Ellen.

"Remember when we talked about the need for a plan first?" I asked. "One of the things we will look at is the cost/benefit of incorporating your business. There are costs that you need to look at before you jump into any business, or for that matter, make personal decisions. The need to have accurate bookkeeping is one of the costs that you weigh against the benefits. And you don't need to do it yourself! We just factor in the cost of a bookkeeper. The good news is that it becomes a very easy decision to include this in your plan when we reduce the decision to dollars and cents."

"Okay, well, let's see what the plan needs to look like," answered both Ted and Ellen, with some trepidation.

I paused, wondering if I should add that they would get real familiar with bookkeeping terms before we were done. It's one thing to know how to debit and credit (it's better to hire that skill), and an entirely different thing to know how to read what the bookkeeper tells you. I thought that would be better said another day.

Worksheet

"WHERE AM I TODAY?" MY FINANCIAL STATEMENT

Name: _____ Date: _____

INCOME		
Earned Income		
Job and Self-Employment	$	
Passive Income		
Real Estate (Net)	$	
Business (Net)	$	
Passive Income Total	$	
Portfolio Income		
Interest	$	
Dividends	$	
Royalties	$	
Portfolio Income Total	$	
TOTAL INCOME	$	
(Earned + Passive + Portfolio)		

Cash Flow Patterns

Of the Poor

Of the Middle Class

Of the Rich

EXPENSES	
Taxes	$
Credit Card Payments	$
	$
Home Mortgage (Rent)	$
Car Payments	$
Food and Clothing	$
Other Payments	$
TOTAL EXPENSES	$
NET MONTHLY CASH FLOW	$
(Total Income less Total Expenses)	

What story do your numbers tell?

_____
_____
_____
_____
_____
_____

ASSETS		LIABILITIES	
Bank Accounts	$	Credit Cards	$
Stocks	$	Car Loans	$
Bonds	$	School and Personal Loans	$
Receivables	$	Home Mortgage Loan	$
Real Estate	$	Other Debt	$
(Fair Market Value less Mortgage)			
Business Value (Net)	$	**TOTAL LIABILITIES**	$
ASSETS SUBTOTAL	$		
Doodads			
Home	$		
Car(s)	$		
Other	$		
Doodads Total	$	**NET WORTH per Banker** $	
		(Total Asset per Banker less Total Liabilities)	
TOTAL ASSETS per Banker	$		
(Assets Subtotal + Doodads)		**NET WORTH per Rich Dad** $	
TOTAL ASSETS per Rich Dad	$	*(Total Asset per Rich Dad less Total Liabilities)*	
(Assets Subtotal only, do not add Doodads)			

FIG. 2.1

Worksheet

"WHERE AM I GOING?" MY FINANCIAL STATEMENT

Name: _____   Date: _____

INCOME

Earned Income

Job and Self-Employment	$ _____

Passive Income

Real Estate (Net)	$ _____
Business (Net)	$ _____
Passive Income Total	$ _____

Portfolio Income

Interest	$ _____
Dividends	$ _____
Royalties	$ _____
Portfolio Income Total	$ _____
TOTAL INCOME	$ _____

(Earned + Passive + Portfolio)

EXPENSES

Taxes	$ _____
Credit Card Payments	$ _____
	$ _____
Home Mortgage (Rent)	$ _____
Car Payments	$ _____
Food and Clothing	$ _____
Other Payments	$ _____
TOTAL EXPENSES	$ _____
NET MONTHLY CASH FLOW	$ _____

(Total Income less Total Expenses)

Cash Flow Patterns

Of the Poor

Of the Middle Class

Of the Rich

What story do your numbers tell?

_____
_____
_____
_____
_____
_____

ASSETS

Bank Accounts	$ _____
Stocks	$ _____
Bonds	$ _____
Receivables	$ _____
Real Estate	$ _____
(Fair Market Value less Mortgage)	
Business Value (Net)	$ _____
ASSETS SUBTOTAL	$ _____

Doodads

Home	$ _____
Car(s)	$ _____
Other	$ _____
Doodads Total	$ _____
TOTAL ASSETS per Banker	$ _____
(Assets Subtotal + Doodads)	
TOTAL ASSETS per Rich Dad	$ _____
(Assets Subtotal only, do not add Doodads)	

LIABILITIES

Credit Cards	$ _____
Car Loans	$ _____
School and Personal Loans	$ _____
Home Mortgage Loan	$ _____
Other Debt	$ _____
TOTAL LIABILITIES	$ _____

NET WORTH per Banker	$ _____
(Total Asset per Banker less Total Liabilities)	
NET WORTH per Rich Dad	$ _____
(Total Asset per Rich Dad less Total Liabilities)	

FIG. 2.2

SUMMARY

S **is for Starting Point.** First, know where you are. It doesn't matter where you are right now, just that you know *honestly* where that is. You don't even need to know why you got where you are. In fact, it would be better to suspend that part in you that wants to justify your situation. It doesn't matter *why,* just know *where.*

Why the starting point is important. All good programs that help you create change involve some way of measuring where you begin. That way you and your advisors can develop the best customized plan for whatever achievement you envision. In the case of financial change, it is a little easier because there is a way to do this through the use of easily measurable results (money!). You can tell where you are in terms of this measurement and be able to measure your progress. The fact that financial measurement is "easy" is what leads to the biggest problem, however. There is a lot of misinformation about finances. Plus, we are inundated with examples of tremendous financial success. You might be a victim of the media attention on the new wealth of the stock market, for example, and feel that you are somehow missing out. That may make it hard for you to face up to the story of your financial statement. If that is true for you, remember we don't care about the story. All we are looking for is the starting point. No matter what the numbers are, the important part is to step up and honestly face your true financial situation.

How to find out where you are. Use the forms at Fig. 2.1 and 2.2 shown in this chapter to determine your starting point. If calculating this is hard for you, consider buying (and playing!) the game CASHFLOW™ available through Cashflow Technologies, www.richdad.com, to expand your financial literacy. Finance is a language, just like English or Spanish. If you want to play in this game, you have to know the language! CASH-FLOW will help you learn that language.

Where do you want to be? Using the same form from above, now design your dream financial statement. Consider the dreams of you and your family. What do you need financially to make those dreams come true? What is really important to you? What wealth do you need to achieve those dreams? What income do you need on an ongoing basis? Complete the Income, Expenses, Assets, and Liabilities sections to reflect what your dream is.

Chapter 3

Team

Who Is on Your Team?

It was time for my second meeting with Ted and Ellen. In our first meeting, we had assessed their current financial status, their goals, and their personalized strategy to achieve their goals. And, right on cue, Ted had a concern.

"I was talking to my neighbor, who has a Harvard MBA, and I told him that we were going to probably do a corporation for my and Ellen's business. He said we shouldn't do that. I'm worried about what he said—after all he's a Harvard MBA," Ted said at the beginning of our meeting.

"And," added Ellen, "I talked to my friend who is a stockbroker and she said that my new business wasn't a good idea. She said that I'd never make any money at it."

I paused a minute before I replied. I had heard these and other concerns so many times before. The issue was always centered on whom my client chose to take advice from.

"I'm glad that you are excited enough about your plans to talk to others about them. And you've found out one of the frequent consequences of doing that. People will often try to dissuade you. Actually, you've had it pretty easy. I've heard a lot worse!"

Crabs in a Box

"There is a story I like to tell called the 'crabs in a box' story. This is actually based on my own experience growing up in Oregon. One of our weekend activities would be to go to the Oregon coastline and go crabbing for Dungeness crabs," I began my story.

"There are specially designed crab traps that you bait and throw into the ocean from the docks. The traps lure the crabs through a funnel-like opening that lets them in but doesn't let them out. Meanwhile, you just wait on the dock, usually drinking coffee to keep warm against the cold Oregon rain. After a while, you pull up the crab trap to see your catch. You carefully pick up the crabs while watching out for those big front claws and, after measuring and checking the sex of the crabs, keep the legal ones. And this is where it gets interesting. As long as you have more than one crab, you can put them in a very shallow box. I've seen them kept in a box that is barely five inches high. You see, even though the crabs could easily climb out and escape back to the icy cold sea, they don't. That is because as soon as one starts to explore the route of freedom, the other crabs in the box pull them back in.

"You will find many of your friends and advisors are like those crabs," I told them. "They know where they are and it's familiar, even if it is just a box, and they're all in it together. They pull others back into the box because they don't want them to leave. Part of the desire to pull the other back is because they are afraid for them. And part of the desire is that they don't want to see the other guy succeed, because it would mean that they would have to change themselves also—it would be a challenge to their own complacency.

"This is a common viewpoint in the human race. In fact, in Australia they have the saying about the 'tall poppy.' It is practically their moral responsibility to cut a friend down to size if they start rising above their present circumstances. In other words, they cut down the tall poppy."

I finished the story and glanced at Ted and Ellen. It looked like Ted understood the point of the story a little. Ellen still looked puzzled. I continued looking for an example to explain the phenomenon they were experiencing. I knew that if we found an easy way to explain it that it could help not only Ted and Ellen but a great many other people assess the members they need for their team as well as forewarn them about the reactions they will likely get from people around them.

Point of View

There are two main reasons why you might receive opposition as you bring about changes in your life. First, your friends or advisors can only see things from their own point of view. Second, change may be challenging to them and their own circumstances. You changing and growing may force them to confront things about their own situation that they do not want to look at.

You can view the concept of point of view as seen in Fig. 3.1.

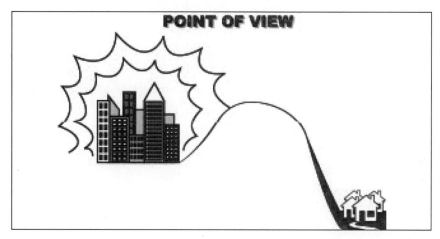

FIG. 3.1

Assume that you came from the little village shown on the far right and traveled to the top of the hill. From that vantage point, you can see the shining city that lies on the other side of the hill. The shining city can't be seen from the village and so when you travel back to the village, the people who live there tell you the shining city couldn't possibly exist.

That's what happens to many people when they decide to make big changes in their life. Perhaps they talked to advisors who had different outlooks or maybe they attended a seminar that opened up a range of possibilities to them. They then go back to their prior situation. They have seen what is possible and are excited about it. But people around them didn't have the opportunity to see the possibilities. They warn them that they can't achieve what they want, that it's impossible, that they won't succeed, or maybe that it's even illegal.

I am still amazed that when I make changes in my business life, I find myself going through the same cycle. Some people will tell me I shouldn't make the changes, or that I cannot. I understand what is happening, and, just like my clients, I will get feelings of self-doubt—am I doing the right thing?

If I step back for a moment, I recognize what is happening by the type of comments I hear from these people. They will say things such as "You didn't used to do it that way," "No one else does it like that," or "You will lose all your clients (friends)." You may have heard similar comments.

When You Hear Negative Comments

One way I respond to hearing negative comments regarding changes I am making is to go through the following mental review:

1. What has been the speaker's experience? People will speak from the point of view of their own experiences. If they have never had a successful business, or had a business that failed, they may feel that *you* can't have a successful business. They will be telling you that *you* can't succeed, but the truth is that they don't think that *they* could succeed.

2. What is their comment really saying? For example: "You didn't used to do it that way" could mean that they are afraid of change. Or "No one else does it like that" could mean that they are afraid to be different. Or "You will lose all your clients (friends)" could mean that they are afraid to change themselves because *they* might experience those losses. Or it could mean that they are afraid that your relationship with them will change.

If you hear critical comments from friends or advisors, keep them in perspective. In this case, it means *look at their perspective.* Do they know all the facts regarding your personal circumstances? Many times friends who *think* they know all about you in actuality do not. If they don't know all the facts, can they really advise you?

> The free advice you get from casual conversation is usually worth exactly what you pay for it—absolutely nothing.

Building a Team That Supports You

"I see now that even though my neighbor has a Harvard MBA, he has no experience in a business at all. He works for a university, which isn't even a for-profit venture," said Ted. "But who can I trust to listen to? I do need to talk to someone!"

I smiled. Ted did get it.

"Ted, that is where building a team is so vitally important," I answered. "You have a team around you already. The difference is that now you have the opportunity to make a conscious decision about who should be on your team. First, why don't you list all the people that influence you in your financial decisions."

Identifying Your Current Team

I had Ted do the following exercise: List the people you spend the most time with—your family, friends, co-workers, and so on. Try to list at least five people. Now, next to each person's name, write the experience this person has had in what you want to achieve. For example, if you want to achieve financial freedom by successfully investing in real estate that provides cash flow, you must determine what experience this person has in real estate. Do they personally have real estate that provides good cash flow? Have they achieved, or advised others who have achieved, financial freedom? Do they have the business and financial success that you want?

After you prepare the list, look at it with a critical eye. Are these people the advisors you need for the next step on your personal path to financial freedom? Do they have the needed experience to support your decisions and critically analyze them?

Who Do You Want on Your Team?

There is a whole range of types of people that you might like to have on your team, depending on your personal circumstances. At this point, Ted and Ellen had decided that they wanted to pursue their financial goals with three different businesses: 1) computer consulting; 2) multilevel marketing; and 3) real estate investing. Ted intended to work in computer consulting, so technically he would be a self-employed professional. However, their plan was that multilevel marketing and real estate investing would be how they would build their passive income—from real estate and from their own business. Ted and Ellen determined that their team would include the following members:

Ted's Business—Computer Consulting

Clients
Vendors
College instructor

Other computer consultants
Banker
Insurance agent
Bookkeeper

Ellen's Business—Multilevel Marketing (Direct Marketing) Business

Mentor in program
"Downline"
"Upline"
Potential prospects
Other multilevel marketing distributors
Motivational instructor
Bookkeeper

Future Real Estate Business

Successful real estate investor (mentor)
Real estate agent
Mortgage broker
House inspector
Insurance agent
Repairman
House cleaner
Real estate educator (through books, tapes, and workshops)
Real estate customers

Overall

Tax strategist
Attorney specializing in contracts
Attorney specializing in estate planning
Tax preparer
Financial planner
Stockbroker

You will likely find that you need different team members for your business and financial goals. Some typical financial advisors are:

Insurance Specialists

General insurance
Life insurance
Health insurance
Disability insurance
Errors and omissions insurance
Liability insurance

Accounting Specialists

Tax strategist
Bookkeeper
Accounts payable clerk
Accounts receivable clerk
Payroll clerk
Accountant
Auditor
Certified public accountant
Cost accountant

Corporation Specialists

Corporate administration
Corporation setup

Legal

Transactional attorney
Intellectual property attorney.
Real estate attorney

Financial

Banker
Financial consultant
Leasing company representative
Credit advisor
Investment advisor

How Do You Find the Right Advisors?

"That's some list!" exclaimed Ted. "How do I go about finding the right advisors?"

"Ted, there are actually two parts to that question: First, how do you find the pool of people to choose from? Second, how do you evaluate them once you find them? Does that sound right to you?" I asked them.

They agreed and we then discussed a number of ways to find advisors. They include:

- Check with local licensing boards (bar association for lawyers, state board for accountants, and so forth).
- Ask other business owners.
- Look for articles in the paper written by professionals and contact the author.
- Once you find one professional you like, such as a lawyer, ask him the name of a good insurance agent or any other professionals you're looking for.
- Seek out people who have achieved success and ask them for recommendations for advisors.

Evaluating Your Advisors

"Once you have your list of potential advisors pulled together, it is vital that you assess their ability and interest in working with you. We recommend that you complete an Advisor Checklist for each potential advisor for your team."

You can find a copy of the Advisor Checklist at the end of this chapter. Take the time to go through this checklist with each potential team member. The checklist will walk you through determining each person's experience in the area of the goals you seek. Most people use only one question—whether the person has the requisite credentials—to determine if the advisor is right for them. But your advisors are subject to the same issue of point of view discussed earlier in the chapter. The most effective team for you will be one that includes advisors that have the correct skills, credentials, and personal experience to help you achieve your goals.

"And, once you have your group of advisors, it doesn't stop there," I added. "The simple truth is that the only way to get different results is to do things differently. Your new advisors, if they themselves are financially successful, will be able to give you guidance in new ways of doing things. You will get the best results when you thoughtfully consider and act on the advice you receive from well-chosen advisors."

"We are really committed to making the changes needed to getting different results. Goodness knows, what we're doing hasn't been working so far!" exclaimed Ellen.

Ask the Right Person the Right Question

"I'm glad to hear that you have made a commitment," I said. "There are just a few more things I want to discuss regarding advisors before we close our meeting today. After you have surrounded yourself with good, qualified advisors, you will have one more skill to learn. That is to ask the right person the right question."

"But won't we have already established who our advisors should be?" asked Ted.

"We know that they will be the right advisors for your team. But speaking from personal experience, my clients have trouble deciding whom to ask when they have a question. For example, they will ask the banker an accounting question. Or they ask me, their tax strategist, a legal question," I said.

"Oh, I see," said Ellen. "Questions come up and it's easy to ask whoever is handy. I think the best way is to think about what questions you might have *before* appointments."

"Ellen, I'm so glad you said that. In fact, in my practice, I request that clients fax in their questions, or general topics, before appointments. That way I am sure to be prepared. My clients have thoughtfully considered what their questions are, and both of us make more efficient use of our time. I can also quickly redirect questions that I know should go to another advisor.

"I recommend my clients use that process with all of their advisors. I have advisors that I work with in my business, too. Even if the advisor does not request it, I always e-mail or fax questions or general topics to my own advisors before phone calls and appointments. That way they are always prepared and know in general what I want to talk about. It helps me get more focused on what outcome I want. I can tell my advisors appreciate it when I do that for them, and it certainly makes our time more efficient. And that means better advice for less cost."

Shhh . . . It's a Secret

"There is also the issue of confidentiality to consider when you discuss your financial, business, and tax strategies. You might have heard of attorney-client privilege," I began.

"Oh, yes," said Ellen. "You see that on the TV shows. If I tell my attorney something, it is privileged. They can't tell."

"Right, but you should probably have a lawyer explain exactly how that works if you ever find it a concern. For the past few years, CPAs have also been given the right of privilege on tax-related matters. There are some important distinctions though. In the case of CPAs, it is only for tax-related matters and, this is important, it varies from state to state. Talk to your CPA to find out what the state law is in your area. One solution that many people use is to have their attorney hire the CPA. In this way, the communication and work with their CPA falls within the attorney privilege. No one else has the right to call your strategy 'confidential' or 'privileged' because it can be subpoenaed. I have seen and heard many other people call their services 'confidential,' but the plain fact is that it won't stand up in a court of law *unless* they are CPAs (in some states), attorneys, or CPAs who have been hired by attorneys.

"Your banking and loan records with the bank can be subpoenaed. Your conversations with your insurance agent are subject to scrutiny. Also, be careful of what you tell your friends, because they can also be subpoenaed. The only way you can be sure to have the best asset protection is to keep the details of your business to yourself. Be careful with whom you share the details of your income and assets."

"But I've known my banker for years, he would never tell anyone anything about my business," protested Ted.

"Ted, if you are ever sued, he simply won't have a choice. The court can subpoena the bank's records and he will likely be called to explain all the documents—your loan requests, his notes from meetings, copies of your personal financial statements, and his recollections of your conversations. He might not want to do that, but unless he has the legal right to keep it confidential he will have to comply or face jail time. The strongest advice I can give you is to think twice before you talk to anyone about details of your tax plan," I concluded.

What Else?

What's missing from the lists of needed advisors? Obviously, the first thing you will notice is that there's nothing here on how you make money. That's your job! I have found clients will spend time trying to do their own tax planning, bookkeeping, legal work, or the like and ignore their business. They mistakenly do those tasks because they think they can save some money. But the fact is, though they may save some money on the cost of advisors, there is a much larger cost in the loss of income. They have become so focused on trying to save money by performing tasks they don't really understand that they don't concentrate enough on what they do know. You have to make it to save it! The other problem is that they have unknowingly put a ceiling on the amount of money that they can ever hope to make because they have slowed the growth of the business down to that of the slowest member— themselves! They have created a bottleneck in their own progress.

Some people take it to an even further extreme, trying to make their bookkeeper responsible for the business's profitability. The person who this profile fits will be the person who accusingly questions the financial statements: "I couldn't have spent that much money!" "Where did this money go?" The sad result is that the bookkeeper becomes afraid to bring bad news in and ends up quitting or not telling the boss the bad news. Either way, the owner has lost.

Bad news can be the best news you ever get when it comes to your business. It's the feedback that tells you quickly what's not working. Feedback about what does work can be slow and misleading. (How do you know that your product is selling so well because of the new ad campaign? Maybe it's only because the product is painted a different color.) On the other hand, if you get a financial statement that says your office supply expense amount has doubled, it is important to pay attention to that information.

Breaking the Need for Control—"I Can Do Everything!"

Learning to trust other people can be a big stumbling block to some people. It can be hard for these people to trust that someone else can do the job right.

I struggle with this problem myself, so I can empathize. I remember the story I once heard from another entrepreneur. His company could land two large projects if the presentations were good enough (which would really make a significant financial difference to the company). However, this person could not completely oversee preparation of the presentations while still maintaining his daily workload. For the first time, he had to rely on someone other than himself. He had left one person in charge of the final run-through so that he could attend a seminar. But his head wasn't in the seminar. Everyone knew that his thoughts were really still back at the office. The person he left in charge had been with the company for a while and was talented, reliable, and competent. But this was the biggest deal he'd ever seen. And it wasn't just one deal—it was two.

I'll never forget what our instructor told the other entrepreneur. As the other man continued to worry about his distant office and the unknown status of the projects, our instructor told my fellow participant, "You haven't really let go of the project unless you can allow it to fail."

For those of us who value perfection as the ideal, that might be the hardest statement you've ever had to read. Can you trust your team members enough to let a project go and allow it to fail?

How about trusting others? Can you trust your advisors to give you the best advice they can? Can you give them the freedom to work for you in their best capacity? And the biggest question of all: Can you trust yourself to pick the right advisors—then have enough trust to let them do their best?

If that doesn't seem possible, you might want to examine what it is that draws you to the need for control. What stops you from trusting the advisors you have? What would need to happen for you to believe they have your best interests in mind? Can you learn to trust yourself to make the best choice in advisors?

Work on Your Strengths . . . But . . .

The opposite of the person who wants to maintain control (the "I can do *everything!*" guy) is the "I could *never* do that!" guy.

You may have heard the saying: "Work on your strengths, not your weaknesses." This wisdom goes on to suggest that if you work on your weaknesses, at the end of your life all you will have will be some things you are just so-so at. But the fact is that there are simply some things that you cannot abdicate. You *must* do some things for yourself. For example, you can't pay someone to go to the gym for you. You can't pay someone to parent your children. (That's been tried before and the proof it doesn't work is the children who end up very close to their nannies and not really sure who their parents are.)

Just like maintaining close personal relationships and taking care of yourself, you alone are responsible for your own financial well-being. You *must* have the basics of financial literacy so that you can communicate with your advisors. The more you understand the big picture of your finances, the more success you will have.

In fact, after you understand how your personal financial statement works, you will begin to see that you can read the story of others' personal financial statements as well. You can see in a moment what their future will be—riches or bankruptcy. You will also be able to tell the financial story behind a business or investment you are thinking of making. You will be able to tell where the problems are and assess whether it is realistic for you to think that you can correct those problems to create wealth. Plus, you can see how that financial statement will blend with your own and if it will impact it positively or negatively.

No, you don't need to know whether you should debit or credit an account or how to post to a journal. But you do need to understand the financial statements that your accountant or bookkeeper gives to you. The bottom line is that no one (no matter what they say) will *ever* care as much as you do about your own financial statement.

We see the sad results of people who abdicate their financial responsibility—they are the movie stars, singers, athletes, and the like who have been rich and suddenly are bankrupt. Don't be one of those!

Building a Team

You've now found the right advisors, are clear on what they will advise you on, and know what your responsibility is, but how do you now mold this group into a team?

Speaking as an accountant, and understanding the phenomenon of most professional advisors, a large part of what we do is because of the benefit we can bring to our clients. We really do want our clients to win. So when we see behaviors and patterns of clients that work against their best interest, it's frustrating. Your advisors are in business, too. Professional advisors (whether CPAs, attorneys, financial planners, or others) not only have a desire for you to win, but they also must win. There is a universal principal of exchange. For long-term relationships to grow and last, there must be equal exchange, so that both parties win.

Spinning Dreams

"I just have one quick question . . ." I have heard many long conversations start with those six simple words and have learned to dread them. The question is usually short, but the details can take a half hour or more to explain, and then, at the end, inevitably, it is a what-if situation. Running what-if scenarios can be useful when taken with a grain of salt. It can also be the most debilitating indulgence you ever allow yourself. The human imagination has no bounds, and if you allow yourself you can always find one more what-if to run.

A good advisor has had personal success and so knows intimately what works and doesn't work. Spending your time, and your advisor's time, on what-if situations that are unlikely to come to fruition is a *waste of time.* Make the best use of your time and resources by being focused on what you want and the *likely* challenges you face. Once you have addressed these and have a plan on how to move forward, let the what-if scenarios go.

When Things Don't Work

"After you have your team assembled and you have discovered the best way to work together, there will be times when things don't work," I told Ted and Ellen. "Before we end this session on building a team, I want to touch a little on some techniques for ways to deal with the things that don't work. You have likely run into people who typify the three different behaviors people demonstrate when things don't work like they wanted. I hope the following examples help identify them more quickly."

We all make mistakes—or as we like to say, receive unintended results. We planned for one outcome and something else happened. Sometimes that is because we made mistakes and sometimes it is just life happening that gets in the way. The way you live your life, the extent to which you enjoy it, and the success you have will be all about how you handle those unintended results that come up. There are three basic ways all of us can handle them: 1) blame, 2) justify, or 3) take responsibility.

BLAME

You can always spot the person who handles responsibility by assigning blame. They have a lot of "story" around why something didn't happen as they wanted, and it's always someone else's fault. I bet you, like me, have heard the same story many times: "I'd be rich, if it weren't for my wife. She won't let me invest in anything." Or "My husband just doesn't have any insight into these things. He'd never understand." The person who deals with unintended results by laying blame can't ever get beyond what stopped them from getting the result they wanted. In fact, they can't ever get the lesson and see what they could do differently.

In every case, the person who makes these kinds of statements will ultimately blame team members for their personal financial future. You actually see the same thing with people who suddenly become rich and then have nothing. Very few of them ever say they didn't plan well or that they selected poor advisors; instead they are the first to blame their advisors for their loss of fortune. I can guarantee that those same people, if they ever get their wealth back, will lose it again because they haven't examined themselves.

My experience has taught me to be careful around people who deal in blame. If they deal from this mode, they are simply not going to grow beyond it. Another reason, and a more practical one, is that I know that no matter what we do or how well we do it, there will always be unintended results. That's how life works. I personally don't like being near someone who practices blame when there are unintended results—I might get caught in the crossfire! This is not a productive behavior to practice or to receive! Most good advisors will simply refuse to take this kind of person on as a client.

By the way, there will be times when you have a situation that clearly is a result of someone else's obvious actions against you. In that case, there clearly is blame if you want to assess it. But instead, is there a way to look at the lesson in this so that you can be sure you don't repeat it? Maybe you didn't select the best advisor. How can you make sure you do next time? Maybe there were some circumstances that occurred that you hadn't planned for. How can you plan for that next time? It is from the things that don't work that we learn the most.

JUSTIFY

I recently heard someone justify why he wasn't rich. I was at a seminar and the person next to me muttered his own justification under his breath, when the room was challenged to explore why they didn't have the financial freedom they wanted. My neighbor's response to the challenge was that "I could be rich, except I decided to take a more spiritual path." In other words, he used a spiritual viewpoint as an excuse as to why his business had failed. His comment also contained an unspoken criticism of anyone who was rich—he believed they couldn't be spiritual at the same time. The next time you hear someone say something as a justification for why they can't have something you think is possible, listen to what they are really saying. Chances are there is a statement within it—a kernel—that isn't true, and that is the part that is so grating. In fact, I know very spiritual people who are wealthy. I have a friend who has made a good living out of being what he calls a "social entrepreneur." He's touched a lot of lives positively with his for-profit business in a way that no nonprofit business had been able to.

Everyone has different goals and priorities, and that's one of the things that make life so interesting. It's okay to choose different goals than someone else, but don't lie to yourself in the process.

Another example of justification I heard one time was "I would be rich except that I don't have the education that is needed." In some cases, people might use justifying as a way to stop themselves without even knowing they do so. The person who justifies will, like the person who blames, not be able to learn from their unintended results. But in the case of the justifiers, they don't even get in the game, and they use justifying as their excuse for not doing so.

I don't see people who justify in my practice, because they haven't yet reached the point where they want to move forward.

TAKE RESPONSIBILITY

The final behavioral type comes from the kind of person we all like to emulate. In my opinion, they are the true heroes of humankind. These are the people who step up and take responsibility. This doesn't mean that they blame themselves (that would just be blame directed at themselves instead of others). No, it means they recognize that something didn't work and they keep going. They are like Edison, who said, when asked if he was discouraged by his failures, that he was not. In fact, he said he had not failed, he had just discovered a lot of ways that something didn't work. If he had indulged in blame or justification, he would never have gone on to make the inventions he did.

The client who regularly takes responsibility for his or her own actions is a joy and an inspiration to be around. I look forward to those appointments and they get my full attention because I am inspired, energized, and enthused by being around them. I know that they get the same results from everyone else around them, because they have the tangible results of their improvement in all aspects of their life. This is the best way to build a team to support you!

SUMMARY

Who is on your team now? The people around you—family, friends, advisors, and mentors—will greatly influence your future path. Everyone has a team already formed in their life. Sometimes, in fact, those people are the echoes of people you knew in the past and whose advice you still follow. Perhaps the biggest guide to your financial decisions are the words you remember a teacher telling you as a child. If that is true, and even though the person might no longer be active in your life, include them in the list. You want to consciously examine every single person who is influencing the financial decisions you make today. List these people and then write down what each person was able to accomplish in their own financial life. You might want to specifically ask yourself what experiences they may have had in the result you want. If your dream is to have a business that creates passive income with little or no work, do they (or did they) have that themselves?

Who do you need on your team? List all the types of advisors, mentors, and educators you will need to reach your goal. This list constantly evolves as your strategies, plans, and goals grow. One of the keys to success that the wealthy follow is to surround themselves with people who know more than they do. List every type of specialty you want to include as part of your ideal team.

Create a prospective list of team members. Compile a list of prospective additions to your team. Try to come up with at least three people for every category. At this stage, add every person you think might have the necessary skills and experience. Whenever you find one advisor that you like and want to work with, ask them for referrals for the others.

Assess your prospective team members. Complete the Advisor Checklist for each potential advisor. Do these people have the experience and credentials to support you? This is a very important step. You will be moving into an area where you will need to rely on the experience of your advisors. Make sure they have the ability to help you.

Examine how you will work with your new advisors. Your advisors will likely have ways of working that are new to you. Identify how they work best with their clients to produce the best results.

Build a team. The best advisors have a lot of people seeking them out. What can you do to make sure you have built the best relationships and to make sure that you don't get lost in the crowd? What can you do to build a team around you that cares about your results and feels involved in your progress?

Plan to handle unintended results. What plan do you and your team have in place in case you receive different results than you hope for? How quickly can you react with intelligent and planned action to these unintended results? Do you have a Plan B in the event Plan A doesn't work? And, on the flip side, what will you do if you receive much more than you had planned? Do you have a plan for checking your financial and tax needs on an ongoing basis?

The team you build consciously and thoughtfully can be the most important asset you have. Make the most of this asset you build to grow your financial future!

Advisor Checklist

For each advisor you are thinking of adding to your team, ask the following questions. You might want to complete a form for each potential member. Completing the checklist helps you make a more conscious decision about each person. The more you are conscious and focused on what you want, the more easily and quickly you will get what you want.

1. What role will this advisor perform as part of your team?

EXPERIENCE

2. How much experience do they have in delivering the specific results you are seeking?
3. What experience do they have with specific issues you will have?
4. What is the average income and business experience of their clientele? (Is this where you want to be?)

PERSONAL VIEWPOINT

5. Do they personally have experience in your proposed outcome?
6. Are they at an income/wealth level that is similar to where you want to be?

EDUCATION

7. Do they have the educational requirements for the role?
8. Do they have the necessary professional credentials for this role?

COMPENSATION

9. How are they compensated (flat fee, product sale, hourly)?
10. Do they have a vested interest in helping you achieve your desired outcome?

RESPONSIBILITY

11. Do they assume any responsibility? (The highest degree of responsibility will come from the person who signs the income tax return or gives you an opinion letter regarding a plan. These people put their credentials on the line.)

CLIENT CONTACT

12. How do they keep in contact with their clients (proactive, reactive)?
13. Is their response time comfortable for you?
14. Is this someone you could be honest with?

YOUR NEEDS

15. What can this advisor do to help you meet your goals?
16. Are you looking for someone you can model?
17. Do you expect to be educated by this advisor?
18. If you answered yes to No. 16 or No. 17, how would this advisor do this?

ADVISOR ORGANIZATION

19. Does the advisor have an organization that supports achieving your goals (not working by himself)?

Chapter 4

Evaluation/Strategy

Analysis

"It's nice to see you again. I know that the last few meetings—assessing where you are and evaluating your team—were a little rough on you both," I began, starting off the following meeting with Ted and Ellen.

"You're right. In fact, we wondered if we wanted to even continue going through with this. It seems so hopeless. I don't know how we are ever going to get to our goal of $5,000 per month in passive income," Ellen said dejectedly.

"You've already done the hardest part—assessing where you are and clearly defining where you want to be. Now let's write up your plan and start on your strategy. By the end of today's meeting, you will be able to see more clearly what you can do and that your goal is very achievable," I said with a smile. "You've shown a lot of courage to keep going. That tells me that you *will* succeed with the rest of this.

"But before we start your personal strategy and analysis, I also want to remind you about a conversation we had last month regarding the multilevel marketing opportunity. What have you decided about that?" I asked them.

In Business to Make Money

Previously, I had received a call from Ellen, obviously excited.

"Last night, we met with a new neighbor to talk about being a distributor for his network marketing company. Can we meet to talk about that?" began Ellen during an early morning phone call.

Later that week, Ted and Ellen came into my office to discuss the business opportunity that had captured their attention.

"I've had a number of clients do very, very well with network marketing," I told them. "Network marketing, which is also known as direct marketing or multilevel marketing, is really just a way of distributing products or services through a group (network) of independent distributors. Some companies also have distributor commission structures that pay different percentages on different levels of a distributor group. The great thing about network marketing is that you can work diligently in the beginning to form an income stream that keeps coming in, whether you continue to work or not. In many ways, a network marketing distributorship is one of the best kinds of businesses to be involved in. But you must set up the business correctly to be able to take advantage of all the deductions. Unfortunately, the IRS has established some precedents in designating businesses like this as hobby businesses."

"We want to make sure we do this right!" Ted and Ellen unanimously proclaimed.

"Well, first let's review the type of business you currently have. Right now, Ted's computer consulting business provides a monthly income in excess of all the deductions I believe we'll be able to take. There's no question that Ted's computer business is truly a business in the IRS's eyes. There wouldn't be a problem with deducting a loss, which is unlikely in any case.

"To ensure that the new business opportunity is really a business, I want you to review the Nine Steps to Business as you begin the new venture." I further explained to Ted and Ellen the importance of really running a business as a business.

"That makes sense to me," said Ellen. "I plan to make a lot of money with this! I am willing to do what it takes to make it work."

Ted and Ellen's Businesses

After reviewing the Nine Steps to Business (found at the end of this chapter), Ted and Ellen resolved to pursue the network marketing opportunity as a business. In Chapter 9, "Expenses," we will see how Ted and Ellen use the tax code to deduct many normal expenses they already have.

Ted was determined to make his computer consulting business a success as soon as possible, so he could leave his full-time job with the state. Ellen was resolved to seeing an income stream from the network marketing as soon as possible, so that she could spend more time with her children.

Hobby vs. Business

You undoubtedly have heard that you should "do what you love and the money will follow." That is true *as long as* that love is run like a business. Otherwise, you run the risk of being considered a sham business under the IRS's hobby loss rules.

If the IRS considers your business a hobby, you can only deduct expenses up to the amount of income. That means that you *cannot* take advantage of many of the special deductions for business. This ruling is especially detrimental in the beginning stages of a business, when most have expenses that exceed their income. In this case, the business loss is *not* deductible.

When Is a Business Not a Hobby?

There is a general rule of thumb that you might have heard that states that a business is not a hobby if there is income in three out of five years (three out of seven in the case of certain agricultural activities). Clearly, if you have net income (after expenses are deducted) that is taxable, the question on whether the business is a hobby is not valid. The three years out of five rule (or three years out of seven) is not hard and fast, though. In some cases, businesses have been disallowed during the loss years even when there was profit in other years. Additionally, other businesses have been allowed as losses even when there is a loss year after year.

The key deciding factors actually have to do with whether the business is run *like* a business. No one factor alone is decisive; all factors are taken into account.

Following are the nine steps to determining if you have a business, as stated directly by the Internal Revenue Code. If you follow these nine steps as the IRS dictates, you not only fulfill the requirements under the code, you actually are more likely to prosper. (This is an example of how the IRS actually *wants* you to succeed in your business.)

The nine IRS guidelines to having a business are:

1. You carry on the activity in a businesslike manner;
2. The time and effort you put into the activity indicate you intend to make it profitable;
3. You depend on income from the activity for your livelihood;
4. Your losses are due to circumstances beyond your control (or are normal in the start-up phase of your type of business);
5. You change your methods of operation in an attempt to improve profitability;
6. You, or your advisors, have the knowledge needed to carry on the activity as a successful business;
7. You were successful in making a profit in similar activities in the past;
8. The activity makes a profit in some years (how much profit it makes is also considered); and
9. You can expect to make a future profit from the appreciation of the assets used in the activity.

Following, at the end of this chapter, you will find the Nine Steps to Business form that you can use to make sure your business meets the necessary criteria.

When Is a Business Not a Business?

Why does the IRS go to so much trouble to make sure you have a business? The reason is because some people have taken advantage of the system that allows you to take business losses against other earned income. And so, in an effort to correct this situation, the pendulum has swung the other way. Instead of only having to prove you have expenses, you also have to prove that you really have a business when you have losses.

There are some industries that are particularly vulnerable to question by the IRS. These businesses fall into two general categories: 1) businesses that could have a hobby interest, such as animal breeding or training, or craft type industries; and 2) businesses that have the potential for personal use write-offs, such as some types of sales. The second business category, personal use, is particularly vulnerable subsequent to unfavorable court rulings against some multilevel distributorships abused by unscrupulous distributors. The companies were never at fault; it was the abuse by the distributors. *This does not mean* that multilevel marketers cannot be called businesses. It only means that multilevel or network marketers need to be especially careful to make sure they are being run as true businesses. If you fit this category, make sure you review the Nine Steps to Business with your tax advisor.

Ted and Ellen's Analysis

The stated goal for Ted and Ellen was $5,000 per month in passive income. Passive income means income that they don't need to work for—it just shows up every month. Prior to completing their analysis, Ted had been working a side business as a computer consultant and Ellen had begun working through a multilevel marketing opportunity. An MLM is also known as a network distribution opportunity, or direct marketing business.

Following is the process that they used for determining their personal strategy. They had spent a great deal of time analyzing how they wanted to achieve their goal. They would use two investment vehicles to get to their goal of $5,000 per month in passive income: Ellen's MLM business and real estate. They investigated both of these opportunities first. One primary consideration for Ellen was whether the MLM was even a business. They followed the guidelines of the Nine Steps to Business to ensure that it would be treated as a business.

Ellen felt that she had a realistic goal of $3,000 per month in passive income after three years in her MLM business. She had contacted her mentor in the program and knew that in order to have $3,000 per month she would need to have ninety people in her downline. To achieve that number, she would need to talk to 540 people. Her first goal, then, would be to talk to fifteen people per month. She wrote that goal down:

1. Discuss ABC Corporation with fifteen people per month.

She also knew that the people she brought into the program would need training and encouragement. She calculated that a new person would need eight hours of training and a more experienced person would need two hours of training. She averaged the time needed and wrote down her second goal:

2. Spend five hours each with new and current distributors.

The second part of their strategy to reach $5,000 per month in passive income was to invest in real estate. They knew that, historically, investors who bought smart could make an average of 20 percent return for cash on cash. Ted and Ellen wanted $2,000 per month, or $24,000 per year, for their investment, and so calculated that they needed to have $120,000 invested. (They calculated this by dividing the annual amount they wanted to receive [$24,000] by the expected return [20 percent].)

FORMULA: To determine amount needed to be invested.

Passive income goal per year _____ ÷ expected return _____ =

amount needed to be invested _____

After much investigation, they determined that the best program for them was to buy undervalued properties that required minor repairs and fix-up. They estimated that they would need an average of $10,000 per property, with a loan covering the balance of the purchase price. They would sell them using a lease purchase program that would remove them from the need of ongoing fix-up costs and headaches.

FORMULA: To determine investment necessary per house.

Down payment _____ + estimated closing costs _____ + estimated

repairs _____ + estimated carrying costs _____ = amount necessary

per house _____

At $10,000 per property, Ted and Ellen knew they would need to eventually purchase 12 properties ($120,000/$10,000 = 12). In order to meet their three-year goal, that would mean that they would have to purchase an average of one house every three months. Their next goal became:

FORMULA: To calculate the required number of houses.

Amount necessary to invest _____ ÷ amount necessary per

house _____ = number of houses needed _____

3. Purchase one new property every three months to lease option with estimated 20 percent cash-on-cash return.

They then took the three overall goals and further refined them.

1. Discuss ABC Corporation with fifteen people per month.
   a. Ask for referrals from thirty people per week.
   b. Discuss the program casually with three people each day.
   c. Set up meetings twice per month—first and third Saturday at home.
   d. Arrange for someone to watch Josh and Sarah on first and third Saturday.

2. Spend five hours each with new and current distributors.
   a. Set up call schedule to call new distributors each week.
   b. Meet with each new distributor at least once a month.
   c. Call each existing distributor each week.

3. Purchase one new property every three months to lease option with estimated 20 percent cash-on-cash return.
   a. Identify general location for property to purchase.
   b. Find real estate agent to work with for purchase.
   c. Attend real estate seminar to learn how to market lease purchase properties.
   d. Find $10,000 to invest every three months.

"Wait a second! All of this seemed doable, until we got to No. 3d. We are living practically paycheck to paycheck. There is *no way* we can find $10,000 to invest every three months! This whole thing just isn't going to work!" exclaimed Ted, exasperated.

"Wait a second," I said, trying to calm Ted down. "The first thing to remember is that you don't need to find it all at once. Actually, as Ellen's business begins to bring in more money, you will have more to invest. Plus, as you begin to have property paying you income, you will also have more to invest. Right now, concentrate on getting that first property. That way you can start the ball rolling."

Ted looked a little mollified, but still skeptical.

"It's easier to think about getting $10,000 instead of $120,000. But that seems just as unrealistic. I have no idea where we're going to get $10,000 to invest," said Ted.

"That's where the second part of the strategy comes in. We need to find some more available cash for you and Ellen," I said.

The Problem Is Your Paycheck!

"Where do I find more money? I know the answer to that. The problem is with my paycheck!" said Ted.

"If I just got paid more, these problems would disappear. In fact, that's why I started the consulting business at night. It's because I just don't get paid enough!" Ted stated again with certainty.

Ted and Ellen had done some real thinking about the steps necessary to be wealthy. Ted had listed the family's average monthly expenses. And, like many other Americans, their expenses equaled the amount of net income they had.

I looked at the information that Ted and Ellen had given me, and said, "Yes, the problem is with your paycheck. But the answer isn't to change the amount of money you *make*. Instead, change the amount of money you *keep*."

"But how do we do that?" asked Ellen. "We've tried to deduct everything we can, but every year we're lucky to break even on our taxes and not have to pay extra."

Earn-Tax-Spend Syndrome

"First, let me explain a little bit about the changes that have occurred in how taxes are paid in the U.S. Most people don't realize how new the concept of taxation by the federal government actually is. In fact, it wasn't until 1943 that the government began withholding taxes from employees. In less than sixty years, the middle class has become conditioned to having the government get their cut first," I started explaining to Ted and Ellen. I then showed them a diagram of how this works (Fig. 4.1).

"Ted, when you told me how much your income was, you automatically used the amount of net you had," I said. "The net income is the amount that is left after the government takes out their share. That is the amount of the paycheck that you bring home. We're going to talk about types of income later, as well as the importance of changing the earn-tax-spend syndrome of middle-class Americans.

"From 'your share,' you then have to pay all your expenses. So, even though you make a good salary, the real answer is how much you keep after the government is finished. If you're like most Americans, there isn't much

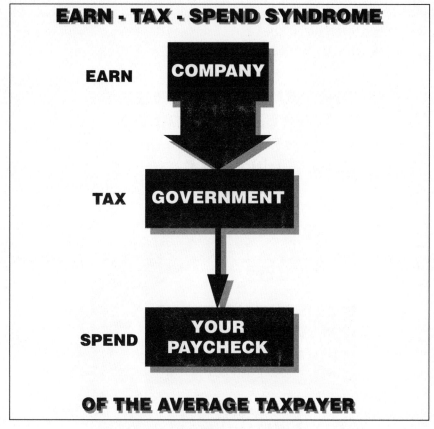

FIG. 4.1

left over to invest after you pay your expenses. So you really end up keeping little, if anything," I went on to explain.

"But a business, when set up the correct way, can reverse this process. We will discuss this in greater detail later. For now, just know that you can *control* the amount of money you spend on taxes. And taxes are the largest expense the average American has."

"The problem is my *paycheck!*" exclaimed Ted. "But it's not the amount that I get paid, it's the amount that I keep. I just pay too much in taxes. So how do we pay less?"

The Business Owner's Solution

"Here's the exciting news!" I said. "A business, when set up the correct way, can reverse this process. By identifying and documenting your hidden business deductions you can *control* the amount of money you spend on taxes. Remember, that is one of the largest expenses the average American has." I quickly sketched the business owner's system to wealth:

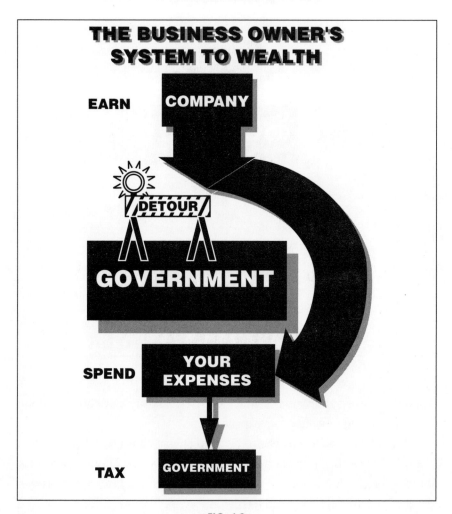

FIG. 4.2

Build a Business

"The question most asked of every CPA is 'How can I pay less taxes?' But the sad truth is that there is very little available in tax planning for the W-2 wage earner," I further explained to Ted and Ellen. "You've seen why that is with the diagram of the earn-tax-spend syndrome. Each year many high-income wage earners make the unfortunate discovery at tax time that deductions they thought everyone had, such as mortgage interest, go away as your income increases. It is extremely hard to build riches by increasing your salary."

"Wait a minute! An old buddy from college, who is a real estate broker, has been telling me the best way to save taxes would be to buy a bigger house. Do you mean I might not get the deduction? When did that change?" asked Ted, getting agitated again.

"I hear that comment a lot, Ted. The truth is that we have had a 'phase-out' of itemized deductions for quite a while now. That means as your income increases, you will lose deductions that you used to have. And if you are an employee, you have no control.

"Now the good news: You can still find a way to pay less in taxes. First, though, you need to have a business so you can take advantage of the special deductions available for business owners, and especially for those who operate their business as a corporation.

"And, even better news for both of you, you already have a good start toward taking advantage of those special deductions!"

What Is a Business?

There are many opportunities in today's world for starting a business part-time while you keep the day job. In fact, it's best that you continue with the day job until your business can support you.

In Ted's case, he clearly had created a position for himself as a self-employed person. This was a good starting point for him to begin tax planning as a business owner. You might want to consider what skills you have that can be turned into a business. As more and more businesses downsize, there are a great many start-up businesses based on consulting to the very companies that have laid off employees.

Another possibility is network marketing or purchasing a franchise. The benefit of starting this way is that the systems are already in place for your business. The key ingredient that you add in either case is that you follow the program, which generally means you start selling. Everything else that goes into a business (administration, fulfillment, customer service, accounting, and the like) is outlined in the program provided by the network marketing company or the franchiser. You just follow their system.

Still others become involved in real estate investing or stock trading. There are many winners and, unfortunately, losers in these areas. Invariably, it's not the system that contributed to the failure in these cases, but the lack of diligence of the person in following the prescribed program.

Regardless of what type of business you decide to start, the fundamental fact remains that you must run it *like* a business.

"It's good to know we've done something right," started Ellen. "But I've got to be honest—I'm not really sure what it is. Ted's job provides more money than his business. And the business takes whatever free time he has available. So why do you say that the business is something we've done right?"

"Your business does make money. But you aren't currently taking full advantage of what is available to you in tax planning," I explained. "And that is where the real benefit is in owning a business. You get the opportunity to control when and where you work, and the amount of money you make, *plus* you are able to take advantage of deductions for things you already are buying.

"You have a good sense now of where you want to go with your goals. The next step is to break down those goals into action items. You will find that for many of the steps—such as finding money for investing from tax savings—you will need advisors. Next time, we will talk about the very next step—building a team."

"For the first time, I'm feeling like I'm in control of our own financial destiny," said Ellen. "I know we don't have all the answers yet, but it doesn't feel as hopeless as it did!"

How Do You Design Your Own Strategy?

The strategy that Ted and Ellen designed actually had a number of parts. First, they knew where they were and where they wanted to go. One of the most important items to them was growing their passive income, something that would be accomplished through existing assets (the real estate and network marketing businesses). They identified the amount of passive income that they wanted, they set up the business strategy to help them accomplish their goal. This involved making assumptions. For instance, in Ellen's business, she estimated how many people she would need to talk to before a sale would be made. (No matter what business you choose, in some way you will have to market and/or sell. A great way to improve this skill is by reading *Sales Dogs*™, by Blair Singer, also part of the Rich Dad's Advisors series. You will need to control the amount of spending your business has so that you can keep some of what you make.)

Ted and Ellen then created a plan for what to do with the money they were able to keep from the money they made.

Ted and Ellen had their business strategies in place. Now it was time for them to design their tax strategies. The sequence is important—first design your business strategy and then design your tax strategy. You have to *make* the money before you can *save* it!

Ted and Ellen's Tax Strategy

"The biggest changes that I want you to make will be in the way you set up your businesses. Currently, all of your income flows into your personal income tax return. And by the time you add together your salaries and the income from the Schedule C computer consulting business, you end up in the highest tax bracket," I said.

"I want to first show you the changes that I propose, and then explain what these various structures are," I said, showing Ted and Ellen the diagram on page 62 (Fig. 4.3).

"You can see that I suggest that we set up an S corporation for Ted's computer consulting business and a C corporation for Ellen's new MLM business. The first year for these businesses is projected to show a slight gain, after the additional expenses, in the S corporation. The C corporation will likely have a first-year loss. The S corporation's income will flow through to you via a Schedule K-1. The C corporation will have a loss that will stay within the corporation." I paused, noting the glazed expression on Ted's and Ellen's faces.

"Wait a minute," I continued, "here's a diagram (Fig. 4.4) that I think will help you understand what I am talking about. You can see by this business structure diagram that income, or loss, that is generated by the business held within a partnership or within an S corporation flows through to the individual owner. It is then reported on the individual's tax return. A C corpo-

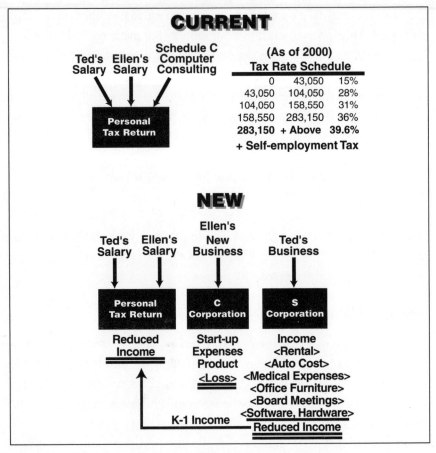

FIG. 4.3

ration, which is a different type of corporation, pays tax at its own level." (These types of corporations are explained below.)

When I realized that Ted and Ellen had understood the difference between the S corporation and the C corporation, I moved on to the various deductions they would be taking from the companies. Deductions will be covered in greater detail in Chapter 9, "Expenses," and Chapter 20, "Special Rules for C Corporations."

"There were a number of reasons that we chose to utilize these specific entities," I told them. "Ted's business is never going to be very large and, as a rule of thumb, I do not consider forming a C corporation for a consulting business unless earnings will be in excess of $30,000 to $50,000 per year. Also, an S corporation can work very well for the first year of business if it looks like you will have a loss, because the loss can flow through to your per-

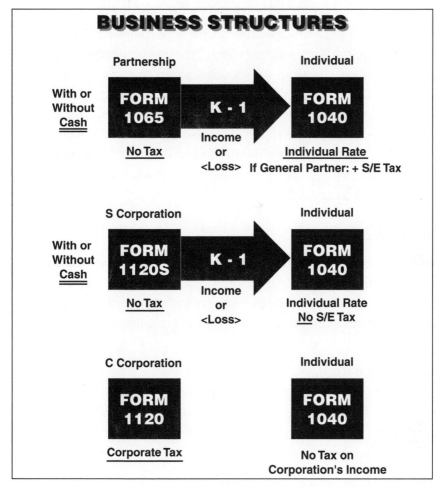

FIG. 4.4

sonal tax return. Of course, in your case, we are projecting close to a break-even year after we deduct all the expenses." I paused a moment, making sure that Ted and Ellen were following the discussion. They were.

"It may seem a little counterintuitive to set Ellen's business up as a C corporation," I continued, "because we fully anticipate losses in the first year. And I know that I just told you that losses in an S corporation can flow through to your personal return."

"I am very dedicated to making money soon in the MLM," interjected Ellen, "and more and more as time goes on."

"I know that, Ellen," I responded. "I also know, from our days in college, that if you make up your mind to do something you follow through and exceed everyone's expectations. That's why I have no problem with setting your business up as a C corporation *now.* If we weren't sure that the business was going to succeed, or you were a little less certain about your commitment, I would suggest an S corporation, which could then be converted to a C corporation at a later date when the business became profitable. The secret to MLM companies is that, with a dedicated effort, the income continues to increase. We know that Ted is going to continue with computer consulting as a way to get out of the full-time job, and then as a bridge into creating more passive income. But it won't grow much, and so it will be best to keep it as an S corporation."

Business Structures

When we began our strategy meetings, Ted and Ellen already had a fundamental understanding of the different types of business structures. For those of you who may not be as familiar with these structures, the following descriptions show the different types of structures and the pros and cons of each.

SOLE PROPRIETORSHIP

This type of business is taxed at your personal income tax rate, with self-employment tax (15.3 percent) in addition to your federal and state income tax. There is maximum liability. It does not require full-charge bookkeeping and is easy and low-cost to set up.

When Would You Use a Sole Proprietorship?

I would only recommend a sole proprietorship when it is clear that the owner will not keep good records, which are mandatory for the other types of businesses. Also, the business would have to be one in which there is *no* possibility of liability. For example, if you have a business that employs people, you should never operate as a sole proprietorship, as acts they commit could create liability for you. Thus, under a sole proprietorship business structure, *everything* you own is at risk.

PARTNERSHIP

There are two types of partnerships—general and limited. A general partnership has a minimum of two general partners. A limited partnership has at least one general partner and at least one limited partner.

The general partner for both a general partnership and for a limited partnership has full liability, including liability for acts of another general partner. A limited partner, present only in a limited partnership, has liability only to the extent of their investment. In other words, if they invested $10,000 in a limited partnership, they can only lose $10,000.

Income is taxed at the partner's level, *even if* there are no distributions. This is called "phantom income," which means that you as a limited partner, with no control, may be required to pay tax on income that flows through to you from the partnership, even if there is no cash to accompany it. *Caution*: Carefully read any partnership agreement to make sure that distributions are required to cover a portion of any attributed phantom income. A further word of caution: Contractual requirements to always pay phantom income could damage possible asset protection aspects of a limited partnership.

The general partner is required to pay self-employment tax on their income, in addition to the regular federal or state income tax. Note: A corporation *never* pays self-employment tax, so if a corporation is a general partner, there would not be any self-employment tax assessed.

When Would You Use a Partnership?

At this writing, I can't think of a single instance when I would recommend a general partnership. There is full liability for the partner from the business, *plus* for acts and contracts of your fellow general partner. I occasionally see general partnerships that have been in place for a number of years that merely hold property. I generally recommend changing the structure to protect the owner against liability that might occur from the property (hazardous waste dumped without your permission, someone who is injured while trespassing, and so on).

A limited partnership, on the other hand, is highly recommended for holding real estate. The best structure is to have a corporation, either an S corporation or a C corporation, as the general partner.

A limited partnership also protects the assets of the company against liability that might arise from the owner. In other words, if you own a limited partnership interest in an apartment building and you are sued because of liability that comes from you personally, then the ownership in the apartment house is protected against that danger.

LIMITED LIABILITY COMPANY

The latest entity of choice of many attorneys is the limited liability company (LLC), which is formed under state law. Laws for LLCs vary from state to state. As with all tax planning, but especially if you're considering an LLC, make sure you consult with a tax strategist *before* forming an LLC.

In many states, you are now able to use the LLC for *any* type of taxing entity. In other words, you can elect for your LLC to be taxed as, and treated in every other way similar to, a partnership, an S corporation, or a C corporation. There is a lot of misinformation out in the marketplace currently about LLCs. The truth is that they are neither the absolute answer to everything you would want nor the latest manifestation of evil incarnate. The biggest problem with LLCs today is that they have not been uniformly accepted by the states and you must be careful to discover exactly what the laws in your area will allow.

Throughout this book, you will see that I refer only to sole proprietorships, partnerships, S corporations, and C corporations because these are the four types of basic business structures for taxing purposes. The LLC emulates one or all of them.

S CORPORATION

An S corporation is a regular corporation in which you make a special election to be taxed as an S corporation. There are some further restrictions as to the number of shareholders and types of shareholders that are allowed. Plus, you have a restricted time period in which you can adopt the S corporation status.

The S corporation provides liability protection to the shareholders against acts of the business. In other words, if something happens within the business, the shareholders' other assets are safe. It does *not* protect the business against liability from the business.

Income from the S corporation flows through to the shareholders and is taxed at the individual's rate. Income from an S corporation is never subject to self-employment tax.

When Would You Use an S Corporation?

An S corporation is an excellent structure to use for a small business that is not expected to have taxable income that exceeds $30,000 to $50,000. It is also a good business structure to use for companies that fall into the category of personal service corporations (see Chapter 26), or for companies that anticipate an initial loss and wish to have it flow through to their shareholder owners.

The disadvantage of an S corporation is that it is taxed at the shareholders' income tax levels, and many of the employee benefits are less than within a C corporation.

C CORPORATION

The C corporation is different from all the other business structures. It is the only one that is taxed at its own tax rate schedule. In other words, you can take advantage of the graduated tax tables that are available to individuals *and* to corporations. Plus, a C corporation allows you to provide the greatest number of deductible employee benefits tax-free. The best of all worlds!

There is a great deal more about the significant benefits available for a C corporation in Chapter 20, "Special Rules for C Corporations."

When Would You Use a C Corporation?

More than any other, this is one business structure where you definitely need to have a well-thought-out plan *first*. Don't rely on free advice from your friends and other nonprofessional advisors. There are many benefits available, *as long as* the proper elections are made *initially*. This will be discussed further in Part V.

In general, I recommend a C corporation to a properly sophisticated business owner who: anticipates income in excess of $50,000 (after salary and benefits to him); has other significant personal income; and/or plans to make a public offering of the company.

Your Tax Strategy

Like Ted and Ellen, first determine what your business and investment strategies will be. If you don't have a business now, you probably are thinking of starting one. The simple fact is that the old way of working for someone else until you retire and collect your pension doesn't work anymore. Plus, the best tax breaks available are for those who own their own business. So, start with building your business.

You will need to make many assumptions in the beginning when you are building your business strategies: a reasonable, expected return; development timetable; number of customers you will need; who your clients will be; how to have marketing success; among many other important considerations. This is where your *team* comes into play. Use the experts you have assembled to see how reasonable your assumptions are. I also recommend going through the exercise of writing a business plan. There is some excellent software available at low cost that forces you to examine each element of your business plan. Take the time to put some thought into your business. You might have to live with your decisions a long time—make sure your business will go in a direction that makes you happy and works toward achieving your goals.

Then, examine your tax strategy for your businesses. Here is a systematic approach that we employ:

1. Identify key elements:
    a. Current marginal tax rate—Chapter 10
    b. Current hidden business deductions—Chapter 9
    c. Projected hidden business deductions—Chapter 9
    d. Current or projected passive losses from current investments—Chapter 19
    e. Current or projected investment expenses from current investments—Chapter 19
    f. Amount of lost itemized deductions—Chapter 9, Chapter 20
    g. Other taxing entities (dependents)—Chapter 17
    h. Projected income and type of business for new business—Chapter 7

2. From the data above, design your tax strategy. In some ways, this is more art than science. However, the critical part is that the information above needs to first be gathered. Your tax strategist will need this information for customizing the best possible plan for you. You simply cannot find a tax strategy in a box or copy it from someone else. The fact is that everyone has different and unique circumstances. What will work for one person and will best serve their needs might actually be illegal for another person.

SUMMARY

First, have a business. The tax code is written for business owners and, to a lesser degree, self-employed persons. There are simply no tax breaks available for employees. Yes, there are some deductions—such as the mortgage interest deduction on your home, charitable contributions, property tax deductions—but they are minor, available to all taxpayers, and actually phase out as your income increases. No, the only true tax breaks remain for those who have a business.

What is a business? In order to take business deductions you have to first prove that you have a business. The IRS will often challenge a business that appears to never make a profit and is something that might be fun for the owner, as a hobby, not a business. Typical challenges have been for horse breeding, training, and showing and craft-type activities. In this case, you can take deductions against income, but cannot pass any loss through to other income.

IRS Nine Steps to Business. The IRS has nine guidelines for determining whether you have a business. The checklist for the Nine Steps to Business follows this summary. The IRS is mainly looking for a businesslike manner; your time, effort, and intention to make this profitable; reliance on the income; losses that are either normal or beyond your control; change in attempt to achieve profit; you or your advisors have knowledge in this area; and you either have experience making a profit or you have reasonable expectation of a profit from future appreciation of assets.

Create a business strategy and set milestones. Determine the goals for your business and develop the strategy to achieve them. In the example in the text, Ellen had determined her end goal in gross income. She found experienced advisors who then worked with her to set the milestone goals on a monthly and weekly basis. She wrote down the milestones into an action plan and referred to that list daily. No matter what your business is, or what business goals you envision, you can also follow the same formula—use your advisors to help determine the milestones. List those into a handy reference and put that reference where you will see it regularly—such as your bathroom mirror or the refrigerator door. Then check your progress on an ongoing basis.

Earn-tax-spend. The average American is an employee. That means that for most of us, the government takes its cut of our pie before we can even miss it. You *earn* a paycheck, the government *taxes* that money, and you get what's left to *spend.*

Business owner's solution—earn-spend-tax. The only tax breaks left are for those people who have their own business. The business owner can look for legitimate ways to write off, or deduct, expenses that reduce the taxable income. The amount that is left is then taxed. In other words, a business can throw up a huge *detour* sign in the way of the government. They have to wait for what is left after the business owner's system to wealth.

After business strategy, comes tax strategy. A customized tax strategy takes into account the business structure, taxing structure, form and amount of income, hidden business deductions, and other taxing entities. You should identify key elements to your unique situation and also look at your personal short-term and long-term goals. Your tax strategy will likely have steps, or phases. Chart these out to determine how you will follow your own personal path to financial freedom.

THE NINE STEPS TO BUSINESS

INSTRUCTIONS: *Line One*: Fill in the name of your company.
Line Two: Fill in the type of business. You can use the IRS business type listing in Appendix A as a reference. Your accountant will use this listing to determine the business type when filing your tax return.
Questions: Answer the questions with yes or no. For no answers, see additional text. Every no answer weakens your position as a business.

Review this form with your tax advisor.

Name of Company _____

Type of Business _____

Businesslike Manner

1. Do you have a separate bank account for your business? YES / NO
2. Do you (or does your CPA) keep accounting records for your business? YES / NO
3. Do you keep copies of receipts in a filing system? YES / NO
4. Do you make an effort to collect accounts receivable? YES / NO
5. Do you review profit and loss statements regularly? YES / NO

Time and Effort

6. Do you keep track of time spent in your business activity? YES / NO
7. Do you keep track of business appointments in a schedule or diary? YES / NO
8. Do you have notes of conversations you have had with consultants or experts to enhance your business? YES / NO
9. Do you keep evidence from business seminars you have attended? YES / NO

Depend on Income

10. Will you need the income from your business for your lifestyle? YES / NO
11. Do you intend to replace your current job with this business? YES / NO

Reasonable Losses

If you have losses, do you have documentation that:

12. They are normal for the type of business you are in at the beginning? YES / NO
13. Or: Others have experienced the same kind of downturn? YES / NO

Effort to Make Money

If you have losses, do you have evidence that:
14. You have made changes to try to improve the business? YES / NO
15. You have investigated ways to make your business profitable? YES / NO
16. You have consulted with experienced business owners or other advisors regarding your business? YES / NO

Experienced Advisors

17. Have you identified the advisors you need for your business? YES / NO
18. Do your advisors have the business experience needed to give you good advice? YES / NO

Your Experience

19. Have you been successful in this kind of business before? YES / NO
20. Have you been successful in a similar business? YES / NO

Past Profit

21. Has the business been profitable in previous years? YES / NO
22. If so, has the profit been enough to make it sensible to continue? YES / NO

Asset Appreciation

23. Is the business building assets that will have future appreciation? YES / NO

Scoring the Test

For each of the nine sectors, rate how strong your case is as to business purpose on a scale of 1 to 5, with 5 being strongest. For the weakest elements, what can you do to strengthen your point?

Businesslike manner	1	2	3	4	5
Time and effort	1	2	3	4	5
Depend on income	1	2	3	4	5
Reasonable losses	1	2	3	4	5
Effort to make money	1	2	3	4	5
Experienced advisors	1	2	3	4	5
Your experience	1	2	3	4	5
Past profit	1	2	3	4	5
Asset appreciation	1	2	3	4	5

Example: You may have shown a slight profit in your business and thus answered "yes" to both questions 21 and 22. But you don't feel totally confident in this area, so you rate "Past profit" only a 3 or 4.

What can you do to improve your position? _____

_____

_____

_____

_____

_____

_____

Chapter 5

Plan and Path

Let's Get Moving!

"We sure have spent a lot of time getting ready; when are we going to start putting this all in place?" asked Ted.

"Wait a second, Ted!" exclaimed Ellen. "I don't know how this works. I don't know what to do first. Don't rush this!"

"You both have just summarized the two ways people approach tax planning," I said. "It can seem like a long process and you might be anxious to just move ahead—to do something! Or you can be concerned that you don't know what to do next and aren't really comfortable moving forward. Both are completely natural reactions.

"We know what your goals are," I continued, "and you have put your team together. Now let's start working with that team. My role will be designing and implementing your tax strategy to make sure you are taking full advantage of tax laws and protecting your assets."

Action

This next step might seem the most uncertain for you, as you start putting your plan into action. For Ted and Ellen, they already had begun their business and investment plans. They needed to get the correct business structures in place to take advantage of what they had. Your personal action steps might be entirely different. You might need to take action to investigate and start a business. You might need to get more education about the types of investments you need to make. Your advisors will be the ones to help you decide what your own personal action steps should be. Do not assume that because the next step for Ted and Ellen was to form various business structures that you should do the same.

Next Step

"We've sure come a long way from when we first met. I'm still not sure what the next step is, though. Where do we go from here?" asked Ellen.

"We've decided on the right structure for both of your businesses," I replied. "Additionally, when you begin buying real estate, we will determine the best business structures for that also. For now, we need to: 1) set up the proper structures; and 2) establish the best benefit plans and deductions. Then you must continue working with all of your other alliances (insurance agent, banker, bookkeeper, and so on) to get their help with the rest of the implementation process. You have begun this process with a significant difference from the businesses that fail every day. You followed the first three steps of STEPS—Starting Point, Team, and Evaluation/Strategy—and now you're about to embark on Plan and Path," I said.

"Now let's get busy!" Ted exclaimed.

Ellen nodded her agreement.

Implementing Your Tax Plan

As you work through the exercises in *Loopholes of the Rich,* you will begin to put together ideas for your own tax strategies. Your own plan will be different from Ted and Ellen's, so the details you've seen above won't be exactly the same for your business structures.

Ted and Ellen had already gone through Chapter 9, "Expenses," to look for hidden business deductions in their business. In some cases, special resolutions were required, which they prepared with the help of their other advisors. They also relied on their advisors to set up the business structures.

Ted and Ellen's Action Items

1. Incorporate Ted's business:
    a. File appropriate paperwork with state agency.
    b. After receipt of approval, apply for employer identification number (EIN) from the IRS (Form SS-4).
    c. Apply for local licensing—business permit, sales tax permit, whatever else is required.
    d. Apply for S corporation status from the IRS (Form 2553). (Note: Ted and Ellen live in a community property state and so, although Ted solely owned this company, Ellen also needed to sign off on the S corporation form.)
    e. Hold first stockholders meeting to elect board of directors.
    f. Hold first board of directors meeting.
    g. Prepare organizational minutes.
    h. Issue stock certificates.
    i. Open checking account with stockholder loan.
    j. Apply for credit card.
    k. Set up accounting information.
    l. Start filing system.
    m. Purchase assets at fair market value from old sole proprietorship.
    n. Notify customers of business structure change.
2. Incorporate Ellen's business:
    a. File appropriate paperwork with state agency.
    b. After receipt of approval, apply for employer identification number (EIN) from the IRS (Form SS-4).
    c. Apply for local licensing—business permit, sales tax permit, whatever else is required.
    d. Hold first stockholders meeting to elect board of directors.
    e. Hold first board of directors meeting.
    f. Prepare organizational minutes.
    g. Issue stock certificates.
    h. Open checking account with stockholder loan.
    i. Set up accounting information.
    j. Start filing system.
    k. Notify customers of business structure change.

Ted and Ellen are not beginning the real estate company immediately, and so are not spending the money to set up the business at this time.

Implementing Your Plan

The list above is just a general guideline. Every type of business, set of circumstances, and business locale requires different steps. This is where you will need to rely on the experience of your advisors to follow the appropriate steps.

SUMMARY

More education vs. action. I have seen clients frequently reach this phase of their personal program and freeze. They are conflicted between the need for more information and education versus the desire to get moving and do something. There is always fear when we move outside of our box. That is the uncertainty that keeps us safe in many cases. But it also keeps us static and unable to change. Rely on your team to motivate and support you through this phase. Make sure you have set up your program—then follow the guidelines the team has developed for you. You can make it happen!

Design your action items. From the third step of the program, Evaluation/Strategy, you set up milestone goals. Now take those goals and define what the action items are for each step. Break each down into manageable sizes. Don't let the overall goal overwhelm you—if you identified your dream correctly, it will overwhelm you. So don't look at the horizon too much, keep your eye on what is at hand. The time for assessment is coming. For now, trust your plan so you can plan your work.

Work your plan. After the action items are identified, it is time to move. You have planned your work—now work your plan, confident that you have a viable plan that has the endorsement of a solid base of advisors who have proven track records.

Chapter 6

Starting Point (Reevaluation)

How Did You Do?

"This last month sure was interesting. Some of the things we thought would work did and some didn't . . . I guess that's life, isn't it?" Ellen said at the beginning of our next monthly meeting.

"That's exactly why we have a plan to meet on a monthly basis," I replied. "I'm glad to see that you brought along your financial statements for your businesses. How is it working out with your bookkeeper?" I asked, looking at the paperwork their bookkeeper had sent along earlier.

"Well, to be honest, I still am not really sure that we're keeping track of all we're supposed to, plus I don't know if we're taking full advantage of the businesses," said Ellen hesitatingly.

"What Ellen isn't telling you is that I don't feel real comfortable with all of the deductions. More than anything, I'm scared of an IRS audit. I'd rather pay too much money than have them show up and put me in jail!" Ted exclaimed.

"Ted, I've heard that from clients before. The fear of the IRS is something that is pretty widespread in the U.S. today. In fact, the IRS tries to foster that fear as a means of self-regulating. I'm really glad you brought it up right away. Many times I will see clients that have something obviously stopping them, but they don't acknowledge it, or even realize it. We're going to go through a little exercise later that will help you identify what is stopping you. But, first, I want to walk you through the first part of the process."

Reevaluate

After you have gone through the first four steps of STEPS (Starting Point, Team, Evaluation/Strategy, Plan and Path), it is necessary to give the process a little time and then look at what has happened.

Do another assessment. Where are you now? What does your personal financial statement look like after a period of time (generally a month) has gone by? What does your business financial statement look like? Where do you need to improve? How does this financial statement compare with the previous one? Are you moving toward your goal? Ask yourself all these questions and give yourself honest answers.

After you have looked at where you are, decide what changes you need to make to your business strategy. You will likely have found things that worked and a lot of things that didn't work. Is your plan still on track to help you meet your goals? What new action steps do you need to take?

Then, look at your team. For each member, look again at how they help or hurt you as you move toward your goal. Have your needs changed? Are your advisors fulfilling what you needed? Do you need additional or different advisors?

The reevaluation can be the most enlightening exercise or the most demoralizing—it depends completely on how you view the process. As you evaluate each step, look at what got in your way. You might want to start keeping track of the things that go wrong. You especially want to note when something seems to bother you a lot.

Awareness

The first step toward change is awareness. I can listen to a person's conversation and in a matter of minutes assess whether they are on the path of wealth or not. You will hear patterns emerge as a person talks. These patterns generally represent the blocks that they have throughout their entire financial life. The tendency is to blame others for these problems. But the fact is that the one constant in all of this is ourselves. If we keep getting employees that we can't work with, why do we keep hiring them? If we can't seem to find a market that wants to buy our product, why are we not hearing what the market really wants?

The problem is never really about money. It's really about us.

What Stops You

After working with literally thousands of clients, I have discovered that there are some similar blocks that many possess. Review the list and see if any of them ring true for you.

Lack of education. Signs: "I never seem to find the good deals." "There aren't any good deals." "I don't know where to start." "I just need more money and everything will be okay." "I don't care what the numbers say, this is a good deal."

Lack of control. Signs: "I don't need to do a financial statement, let me just explain it all to you." "I don't have time for all of this." "I don't know how much money I've spent. That's up to the bookkeeper."

Too much control (lack of trust). Signs: "No one else can do this as well as I can." "I don't want to spend the money on advisors." "I can just read a book and understand this all." "Bookkeeping (legal, accounting, tax preparation, etc.) isn't rocket science."

Fear of loss. Signs: "I don't want the IRS showing up and arresting me." "My friends think I'm crazy for doing this." "Someone is going to sue me, I just know it."

Any of these blocks can stop you. And, at one time or another, one of these, or something like that, has probably been true for all of us.

How to Find Your Blocks

The easiest way to identify your blocks is to go through the reevaluation process periodically (I recommend monthly), looking at all aspects of STEPS (Starting Point, Team, Evaluation/Strategy, and Plan and Path). Write down everything that didn't work and then look back at the previous month. What patterns do you see emerging? What do those blocks mean? Can you get more education to help you make better decisions? Is fear immobilizing you? How real is that fear, and what can you do to change it?

One of the most common fears is the fear of the IRS. Chapters 30 and 31 specifically address how to reduce the risk both *of* IRS audit and *from* IRS audit.

Not Much Progress

"I feel like we didn't make much progress at all," said Ted at the end of the process. "Our business didn't make much money and our personal financial statements are actually worse because we spent so much money getting our businesses set up."

"It seems to me that the decrease is all due to money you invested in yourself and in your businesses," I replied. "At this point, I think we all agree that the plan is just beginning to work and there aren't many changes that need to be made. I do want to finish by talking about your concern about the money you have invested in your education and in your businesses to make sure you have the right structure and advisors in place. I believe that kind of investment actually brings you the highest possible kind of reward. We call it the Small Change Principle."

Little Changes Make Big Differences

For many people who are just starting out in their businesses, personal spending is typically less than usual. As a result, there will be less importance to finding the hidden business deductions. They might find that they only save $1,000 per year or less. (The average tax saved for clients of our firm is $80,000 per year and the average taxable income for our clients is $350,000 per year.)

Some people are disappointed to see only small savings, but the fact is that small changes you make now can give big results in the future. That is because of the magic of compounding—the Small Change Principle.

For example, $1,000 saved each year for twenty years at a very conservative rate of return of 10 percent will give you $63,000! As you weigh the pros and cons of taking advantage of the ideas in this book, don't think of the benefit you get now of $1,000—think of that pot at the end of the rainbow—$63,000.

You can also see the Small Change Principle in nonmonetary ways. Little changes you make in your knowledge and habits can make large changes over time. The overwhelming factor in both cases is the element of time. I have found that people overestimate what they can do in a year and underestimate what they can accomplish in twenty years. When you take the long-range plan on goals, you have time on your side. I don't know about you, but I'm looking for anything that makes it easier. And this is one plan that works.

There is a two-edged sword, though. If you are doing things wrong, it will also multiply over time and with volume. Even if you're starting small, it is very important that you get on the right path. Time will make it easier.

Positive Steps

My husband and I do the following exercise on a daily basis. Well, not exactly faithfully, but certainly whenever we find ourselves overwhelmed or feel that we aren't making forward progress.

For each day, either at the end of the day, or at the beginning of the next, write down five things that you did that worked ("wins"). List five things (on Fig. 6.1); don't go on to the next step until you have written down five things. Now next to each one of those items, say why that was important. After that is complete, write down what you want to do next to continue the progress for each of the five things.

If possible, find someone to share these wins with on a daily basis. This can be anyone—your spouse, your friend, your child. In fact, if you have a child that is discouraged in school, this exercise has a proven track record of changing that discouragement into confidence. Give it a try!

Why This Works

I believe that the best decisions are made from a feeling of strength and confidence. The worst of mankind's behavior comes out when someone feels beaten down and fearful. When there is hope, the best of mankind's behavior shines through.

You are making significant changes in the way you approach your finances and your business. You are changing the way you do things and the people you choose to advise you. And, subtly, surely, you are changing the way you think. That can be unsettling! Give yourself a break, and a pat on the back, by committing to perform this exercise for a month.

Date: _____

POSITIVE STEPS

What worked today? (wins)	Why was that important?	What next?
(1)		
(2)		
(3)		
(4)		
(5)		

FIG. 6.1

SUMMARY

Assess. On a scheduled basis (we recommend monthly), prepare new financial statements both for you and for your business. Your business should be kept separately, on its own set of books, and the financial statements should be prepared so that they accurately reflect the business. I don't recommend that you become an accountant. In fact, we encourage our clients to focus on what they do best and hire bookkeepers to prepare the financial statements.

Reevaluate. Now look at those new financial statements compared to your old ones. Make note of the changes you see. Did your personal assets go up or down? Did your personal spending change? How? Do not judge or justify the trends. At this point, just list all the items that look significant. If you have not done this exercise before, make sure your advisors are involved in this process. The ability to analyze financial statements is an important skill to learn and you want to make sure you learn it correctly.

Awareness. Study the trends. If this continues, would you be headed to wealth . . . or financial disaster? Now is the time to consider why the trends occurred. You don't need to justify the results, just identify the causes. By the way, many times start-up businesses experience losses in the beginning. Unless you have an investor or are working the business yourself, you will always have more cash outflow than cash inflow in the beginning. The test of a new business is how much money will be needed and how long before the tide turns. So don't judge your results—just look for realistic indications of trends and identify the strategies that need to be adapted. Also, look at your team again. Are they the correct team to help you achieve your results?

Look for blocks. What is stopping you from achieving what you want? List the reasons you aren't achieving the best possible results. Write down the things that didn't work. As you do this exercise regularly, you will likely see trends emerging. Do you need more education? Do you need to expand your team? Do you need to face some fears? We all have these needs and concerns as we change our personal paths. Make it easy on yourself and identify quickly where you want to concentrate additional growth and then do that.

Small Change Principle. Little changes make huge differences over time. When you are making little changes, you might lose sight of the bigger goal and the progress you are making. Acknowledge the positive steps. We recommend doing the exercise contained in this chapter as a way to reinforce what went right.

Celebrate! Above all, take time to congratulate yourself and celebrate. By the way, this isn't an excuse to go back to old bad money habits. Find ways to celebrate that don't cost money.

Part II

The Three Step Tax Formula

Chapter 7

The Three Step Tax Formula

It was a quiet afternoon, after a very busy morning, when Ted and Ellen next came into my office. They looked like I felt, tired, but happy with the work we had accomplished. I was excited that we were moving on to the next phase in the tax strategy.

We had clearly established where they were, where they wanted to go, had an evaluation and strategy developed, and then jointly designed the plan and path for them to take. A major part of that plan was to create some cash flow into their system and the most obvious way to do that was to reduce their largest expense—the amount of taxes they paid.

Ted and Ellen had two legitimate businesses set up and running—the computer consulting business and the multilevel marketing. They were beginning to look at real estate investing, but needed to free up some cash to start that flow going.

"It's been two months since we started working together," said Ted at the beginning of our meeting. "It's kind of funny, because before we met I thought all we would do was look for things to write off. We've done a lot of planning, and now we're just starting to look at the tax write-offs!"

"I think that a good CPA ends up having a lot of hats that they wear when they work with their clients," I said. "Looking for tax write-offs is a big part of tax strategy, but it is only part of the overall tax plan. *Plus,* the tax-reduction strategy is only just one piece of an overall path to financial freedom. Actually, we first determined what your goal was—financial freedom—and then quantified that. We set the path, and now we're going to review your tax situation and look at a way for you to pay less taxes immediately."

"Great! I'm always telling Ted we need to write off our meals. That's what you mean, right?" asked Ellen.

"That's part of it. When you read articles on saving taxes they always talk about write-offs, so it makes sense that is what you would think of. But there's more to a good tax plan. Let's review it all first."

Tax in the U.S.

The United States of America was based on a tax revolution. It seems that somehow Americans have lost sight of that fact when we look at all the obvious and hidden taxes we have in our life.

Income taxes are actually a recent part of our history. And as we've seen, even more amazing, payroll withholding of employees' taxes has been around less than sixty years. With payroll withholding, the government has been able to take its money first, and that has made all the difference.

Types of Tax

There are actually many different types of taxes. The most common are: 1) Social Security and Medicare tax, 2) ad valorem taxes (means "at value"—sales tax, excise tax, and other similar levies, 3) estate and gift tax, and 4) income tax.

SOCIAL SECURITY AND MEDICARE TAXES
Social Security and Medicare tax is based only on earned income. The Social Security portion is limited by a ceiling amount that is set every year. A few years ago, the IRS split off the Medicare portion—2.9 percent for both employer and employee portion—from the Social Security portion. When they did that, they removed the ceiling on Medicare taxes. Remember the next time you hear that the IRS has not raised Social Security taxes in a number of years, they are right. But they do raise the ceiling amount on which the tax is applied *and* the Medicare portion is now based on all earned income with no ceiling amount. That had the effect of raising the taxes a great deal.

The key to reducing Social Security and Medicare tax is to reduce the *character* of income. Remember that the tax is only applicable on earned income. In Chapter 8, "Income," we will discuss the different types of income and how you can change its character.

AD VALOREM TAXES

These taxes generally follow purchases or ownership of certain assets— such as luxury items, cigarettes, real property, and so forth. Remember that the taxes paid on asset purchases for business purposes will be an income tax deduction.

ESTATE AND GIFT TAXES

There is currently a federal estate tax for every estate whose net worth exceeds $675,000. There may also be an inheritance tax on the estate. The estate tax is a federal tax, while the inheritance tax is assessed by the state and varies from state to state. The tax is assessed on the estate, not the beneficiaries, but obviously the impact of that tax does significantly affect the beneficiaries. There is a gift tax, also taxable to the giver, for gifts of greater than $10,000 per year. If a gift exceeds $10,000, then the giver can elect to either charge the excess against the lifetime credit ($675,000 and increasing each year) or pay gift tax on the excess.

Estate and gift tax planning is a huge area of tax planning that is outside the scope of this book. Seek qualified estate planners to address your personal issues.

INCOME TAX

The main thrust of *Loopholes of the Rich* is to develop a tax strategy plan that reduces the amount of income tax that you pay. If that is your goal, too, you will enjoy this book, and particularly the next three chapters!

The Three Step Tax Formula

There are over 500,000 pages of written tax law. However, it is constantly changing and being modified. Congress begins the process of tax law by writing the IRS tax code. The IRS then interprets how to follow the code, by writing Treasury regulations. They modify and explain the regulations and code further through revenue rulings and revenue procedures. Also, taxpayers can ask for specific interpretations from the IRS through private letter rulings. Finally, the court system serves as an appeal function for IRS rulings. So, in order to have a good grasp of tax law, you would have to know all the current IRS tax code, Treasury regulations, revenue rulings, revenue procedures, private letter rulings, and court cases. The fact is that only a tax specialist could hope to have a grasp on all the tax law in effect. In addition, much of what is written is subject to interpretation, with often conflicting opinions between the various sources. I never recommend that my clients try to become tax experts. Rather, it is important that they understand fundamentally how tax is calculated. That is where the Three Step Tax Formula comes in.

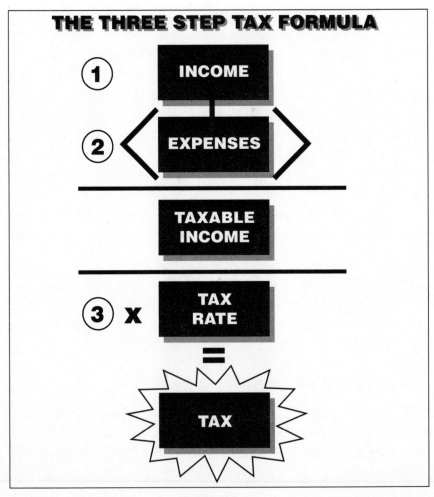

THE THREE STEP TAX FORMULA

1. INCOME
2. EXPENSES
   TAXABLE INCOME
3. X TAX RATE
   = TAX

FIG. 7.1

As you can see in the diagram, there are three different stages to the calculation of income tax. First you report income. From income you subtract deductible expenses to come to the amount of taxable income. The taxable income is then multiplied by the tax rate to determine the amount of tax. It sounds quite simple. The key, though, is in learning how you can manipulate, to your advantage, each of these stages.

1. Income. First, what is income? What are the different types of income? How can you change from one type of income to another and why does it matter? How can you turn taxable income into tax-deferred income or tax-free income?

2. Expenses. What expenses are deductible? How can you make use of multiple business structures to create expenses on one side that are not income on the other? What personal expenses do you have now that are really hidden business deductions?

3. Tax rate. One of the best provisions that we in the U.S. have, that other countries do not, is the ability to make use of a graduated tax rate. This means that there is not a flat rate applied to your taxable income. Instead, a portion of your income is taxed at one rate and then the next layer of income is taxed at a higher rate. If, for example, you have a tax rate of 28 percent for your personal return, this means that you have filled the portion allowed at 15 percent and for every additional dollar you make, you will pay 28 percent. You do not pay 28 percent on all of the income, just that final portion. We call 28 percent your marginal tax rate.

Chapters 8–10 will discuss each of these stages in more detail.

SUMMARY

Types of tax. The four main types of tax are 1) Social Security and Medicare tax, 2) ad valorem taxes, 3) estate and gift taxes, and 4) income tax. Social Security and Medicare tax is based on earned income. There is a limit on the Social Security portion, but the Medicare portion of the tax continues on all earned income. Ad valorem taxes are based on the value of the object being taxed—such as real property, luxury items, and so forth. Estate and gift tax is assessed based on transfers from your wealth to another through gifting or inheritance.

Three Step Tax Formula. There are three steps to the calculation of income tax. First, income is calculated. Then, deductions are subtracted. Finally, the tax rate is applied to the balance. Understanding this basic formula will help you understand tax advice and strategies. Think about how those strategies would affect your own personal tax formula.

Chapter 8

Income

Three Buckets of Income

I was sitting with Ted and Ellen in my office as we went through the Three Step Tax Formula. I knew they were anxious to see if I could really explain how tax planning worked in less than an hour, when it took the government over 500,000 pages to attempt to do so!

"Since the 1986 Tax Reform Act, the IRS has defined three different 'buckets' of income. It's important to know these types and understand where your income falls. The reason is that these different types of income are taxed differently. There are many restrictions on losses and expenses that are incurred within these three categories. For example, you are limited in the amount of passive loss that you can take against earned income. But I'm getting ahead of myself," I said. "Let's start with the three baskets of income.

"The three types of income are: 1) earned, 2) passive, and 3) portfolio.

"Examples of earned income are your wages from a job (even if the employer is your own company), net income from your sole proprietorship business (not incorporated), and income from your active involvement in a partnership."

"I just want to make sure I understand," said Ted. "A sole proprietorship is the type of business I had before I was incorporated—right?"

"Yes, a sole proprietorship is the default structure of most businesses," I said. "The biggest shock to sole proprietors comes the first year they have income from their business that is more than their expenses. That means that they have net income. It doesn't matter how much more they have in write-offs from other businesses or in itemized deductions, they will be subject to self-employment tax on the net income of the business. The self-employment tax in this case is the share of the Social Security and Medicare tax that both the employer and the employee pay. At today's rates, that is 15.3 percent in tax that most of these business owners didn't expect. Plus, of course, there is income tax, too. Sadly, the sole proprietorship is subject to self-employment tax and most of these owners have no idea that they need to prepare for it!

"The second type of income is called passive," I further explained. "Passive income comes from limited partnerships or limited liability companies where you do not have active involvement. Real estate rental income is also considered passive, even when you might have active involvement. Rental income (and loss) has some special rules of its own.

"The third type of income is called portfolio. Portfolio income occurs when paper assets such as stocks, bonds, and notes give off income in the form of interest and dividends," I concluded.

"The easiest way to think of this is: 1) earned income comes from something *you* do; 2) passive income comes from investment in businesses or real estate that works *for* you; and 3) portfolio income comes from paper assets."

Losses

Since 1986, U.S. tax laws have stated that losses can only be claimed against income in the same category. For example, passive losses can only be used against other passive income. You cannot take passive losses against earned income. Investment expenses, such as for margin interest or investment education, can only go against portfolio income. Of course, this is a simplified version of a more complicated piece of tax law. For example, you are allowed up to $25,000 in real estate losses against other forms of income in certain cases, provided your income is not too high.

Earned Income

The IRS defines taxable income as "gross income" and says that "Except as otherwise provided . . . gross income means all income from whatever source derived." That's a pretty sweeping statement.

Note that income includes the fair market value of an item or other service that you barter, or exchange, for.

Except as Otherwise Provided . . .

The IRS code states that unless otherwise provided, income is taxable. What are some of the obvious exclusions? "Income" excludes loan proceeds, gifts, and inheritances. When a company pays you back for loans that you have put in, it will be done tax-free also. The tax code also excludes many types of benefits that your business can pay you and deduct. In other words, your business can often pay you benefits that are a deduction for the business and are not taxable to you. More on that in Chapter 9, "Expenses." Depending on the form of business you have, you can also have tax-free withdrawals from the business.

> Key: Keep good records of all income, regardless of whether it is taxable or tax-free (loan proceeds or paybacks, tax-free benefits, gifts, or inheritance—which are not required to be reported), in case it is ever questioned by the IRS.

Tax-Free or Tax-Deferred Income

The IRS has provided ways to take what would otherwise be taxable income and turn it into tax-deferred or tax-free income. Tax-deferred income means that you put off having to pay tax until a later date. The benefit is that your money grows at a faster pace. For example, assume you pay tax at a 28 percent marginal tax rate and you invest $1,000 per year. After taking out for taxes, you actually have only $720 available for future investment. On the other hand, if all the amount can continue to grow, there is more available to grow. For example, if you invest $1,000 per year at 12 percent for twenty years, the difference between paying tax each year and being able to defer the tax to a future date would mean an additional $6,456 in wealth. If you invest for ten years, the difference is only $1,179. The unknown factors, of course, include the amount of interest you will earn and the future tax rate.

Tax-free income, on the other hand, means that not only does the investment grow without tax, but you can also liquidate that investment and take the value without paying tax on it.

Tax-Deferred

There are two primary ways to turn income into tax-deferred income. One is through a business structure or business entity that allows you to have tax-deferred income. This will be discussed in greater detail in Chapter 17, "Entity Selection." In this case, the form of the business that owns the investment will determine how taxing occurs.

The second way is through specific code provisions allowed for certain types of investments. Currently, under U.S. tax law you can exchange, in certain circumstances, to defer the gain. This is done, under specific laws, between corporations when you see mergers and reverse mergers, for example. The most common way an exchange is done is through a like-kind, Starker, or Section 1031 exchange. These are all different ways of saying the same thing.

The like-kind exchange is described in IRS Section 1031 and further defined in a court ruling, *Starker v. Commissioner*—hence the other names. For ease, we will refer to the exchange as a like-kind exchange. This is a specific exchange of real estate that has been held for business or investment. You cannot do a like-kind exchange on your personal residence or on non–real estate items. The like-kind exchange allows you to sell a piece of property that is highly appreciated and roll over the gain into another piece of property. The second piece of property merely has to be another piece of business or investment real estate. It does not need to be the same type of property. You can exchange from many properties into one property or vice versa. For example, you could exchange a single-family residence into an apartment building.

There are some rules for a like-kind exchange that must be closely followed. If you are considering a like-kind exchange, make sure you notify the real estate agent who is selling your property, as well as the title company. They will put you in touch with an exchange agent who will facilitate the sale.

A possible scenario could be that you have a rental that you have owned for a number of years. You originally purchased it for $100,000 and you have accumulated depreciation of $40,000. That means your basis in the property is now $60,000 ($100,000 − $40,000). Let's say you now get an offer of $200,000 for the house and decide to sell it. After the mortgage on the property of $55,000 and the commission and cost of sale of $15,000, you would net cash of $130,000. However, you would also have tax due on the $125,000 gain from the property. And, $40,000, representing the depreciation, is taxable at a higher rate.

Cash Received

Sale price	$200,000
Cost of sale	(15,000)
Mortgage	(55,000)
Cash received	$130,000

Gain on Property

Sale price	$200,000
Cost of sale	(15,000)
Basis in property	(60,000)
	$125,000

You could pay the tax from the gain on the sale of the property, or you could do a like-kind exchange. We'll complete the example with your decision to invest the cash you received into an apartment building. You know you want to buy an apartment building, but you don't know yet which one you want. That's okay. You first let the title company and your agent know that you want to do an exchange. They will help you find an exchange facilitator who will serve to hold the proceeds from the sale of the residential rental property while you look for your replacement property. You have to file a notice with the IRS within forty-five days that you intend to exchange your property and list possible replacements. You are not obligated to buy any of those properties.

You must find and close on another property within 180 days of the sale of the first property and you must invest all of the cash proceeds and all of the sales proceeds into another property. If you do not, the portion that you keep is considered "boot" and will be taxable. You still have the opportunity to roll over the rest of the gain.

Remember, though, that this is a tax-deferred transfer. You have taken the basis of the previous property and transferred it into the new property, so the gain of $130,000 has been rolled into the new property. If you sell that property, you will then have to recognize that gain, as well as any other gain from appreciation in the property that has occurred since you purchased it.

Tax-Free

Much like with tax-deferred income, there are two ways that you can have tax-free income. The first way is through the type of business or investment structure such as a Roth IRA or life insurance plan. These items will be discussed in more detail in Chapter 17, "Entity Selection."

The second way is through specific law. The best example of that currently is with the tax-free gain that is allowed through the sale of your principal residence. You can now deduct $250,000 (if you are single) of gain on the sale of your home you have lived in for two of the past five years. If you are married, the exclusion amount jumps to $500,000. If you have a passion for fixing up houses or have a knack for finding deals in real estate, this can be a tremendous benefit to your wealth. Look for properties that you can live in for two years and then sell to pocket the gain, tax-free. If you make $100,000 on a house in two years, which we recently did, consider how much that would mean in before-tax money. At a 40 percent tax rate, you would have to make $166,667 to equal that amount.

Why Type of Income Matters

Once you understand what is income (versus tax-free cash receipt, tax-deferred, or tax-free growth) and what *type* of income you have, you might find that you want to change the character of the income. Why?

Earned income means just that—you have to earn that. If your goal is true financial freedom, which means that money you don't have to work for (passive and portfolio) exceeds your monthly expenses, then you want to turn earned income into the other forms. You can do that with your business, particularly if it is in the form of a C corporation.

Also, since the 1986 Tax Reform Act, and the three-bucket approach to income, losses, and expenses from one bucket can only go against income from that same bucket. (See Fig. 8-1.)

One of the great benefits of owning real estate is that you can often have positive cash flow (cash inflows minus cash outflows) and yet still have taxable losses, which can offset other income. The losses come about from depreciation, which is a noncash expense.

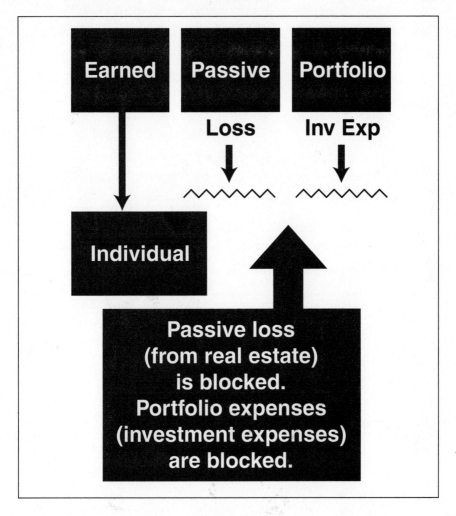

FIG. 8.1

The IRS caught on to that trick in 1986, and changed the law so that losses from real estate were largely blocked when they flow through to the highly compensated individual.

There are two ways around the block. A few years ago, responding to the powerful real estate lobby, the law was changed to allow people who are real estate professionals to claim *all* losses. In this way, the passive loss from real estate becomes a quasi-earned income. It is only considered quasi-earned, because it is allowed to offset earned income, but is not subject to the other taxes of earned income. It is the best of both worlds.

You must pass two tests to determine if you are a real estate professional. The two tests are:

1) More than half of the time you spend performing personal services in all trades or businesses must be spent doing "qualified real estate activities."

   And

2) More than 750 hours of the year must be spent in "qualified real estate activities."

   A qualified real estate activity is any activity in which you "develop, redevelop, construct, reconstruct, acquire, convert, rent, operate, manage, lease, or sell real estate."

Secondly, you can learn how to change the character of the income you make through your business from earned to passive. This is primarily done through the use of a C corporation, and will be discussed in greater detail in Chapters 20–28.

Why Doesn't Everyone Have a Corporation?

There are some cases where having a corporation doesn't make sense. The primary reasons are probably the most difficult for the business owner to see, unfortunately.

LACK OF A BOOKKEEPING SYSTEM

A corporation *must* have a financial statement as part of the tax return. That means that the business owner must have a true double entry bookkeeping system and, in all likelihood, hire a bookkeeper to get good, accurate numbers. It is often a surprise to new, naive corporate owners who show up with their typical shoebox of accounting records and discover that they can't do the accounting that way anymore. These are the same people that fail to give any real value to the function of a bookkeeper and either continue to limp along doing it themselves or go through bookkeeper after bookkeeper, complaining that they wanted too much detail and/or cost too much. The fact is that the biggest cost is in *not* running their business like a business. But if they don't want to do that, they can continue in a form less sophisticated than a corporation.

Solution: Follow the Five STEPS to Financial Freedom and get your team in place. An integral part of the team should be a bookkeeper that you can work with and who welcomes your questions. Learn from them—they can teach you much about your business.

NO PLAN

Forming, and especially dissolving, a corporation is costly and time-consuming. It isn't something to enter into lightly. If you aren't sure that you really need a corporation, and aren't sure what you will do with one, don't form one! I see people daily in my practice who have been sold on corporations and somehow have ended up with multiple corporations. But they don't know what to do with them. They are appalled to learn about the complex process that is required to liquidate a corporation.

Solution: First, have a plan of what you will do with your business, and get the best advisors to assist you in meeting your goals.

WRONG STRUCTURE

There are some business transactions that do not work well within a corporate structure. For example, real estate is much better held within either a limited partnership or a limited liability company. This is because distributions from a corporation must be made at fair market value. So if you planned to buy an apartment house and then when the value went up exchange it under like-kind exchange rules for deferred tax, you could not do so easily through a corporate structure. However, it could be done through a limited partnership.

Solution: Again, have a good idea of what you want to accomplish and then get the best advisors. Follow the Five STEPS system.

INITIAL LOSSES

In some cases, you may want initial losses to stay within the corporation and roll forward against future years' income. But if you are uncertain as to the success of a particular venture or have an immediate need for losses, you may want to have a flow-through entity in order to take the losses on your personal return. An example of a good business structure in a case such as this is an S corporation.

Solution: The answer to all the potential troubles that might occur with the wrong business structure is to follow the Five STEPS system. Find the best advisors for what you want to accomplish.

Just as with the Five STEPS to Financial Freedom, the critical first step for determining how to change the character of your income is determining your starting point.

SUMMARY

Three buckets of income. The three types of income are earned, passive, and portfolio. Earned income comes from work you perform. Passive income comes from investments or businesses that work for you. Portfolio income comes from paper assets—such as notes and stocks. Losses, in general, from portfolio investments or passive investments cannot offset earned income.

Earned income. Most Americans primarily have earned income. This is the income you earn from a job or from your self-employed profession—where you work for the money. You may have others that support you in your function, but make no mistake—if you don't show up, there's no money. The IRS will assume that any money you have or deposit will come from earned income unless you can prove otherwise. For example, if you have a business make sure you clearly distinguish loans and other nonincome deposits. Also, make a note in your personal records of any gifts of cash or inheritances.

Passive income. Passive income and losses come from businesses that produce distributions such as S corporations or partnerships. Passive income also includes income and losses from real estate.

Portfolio income. Portfolio income comes from paper assets such as notes, stocks, and bonds. It includes interest and dividends. There are often also expenses associated with paper assets such as margin interest expense, investment education, portfolio management fees, and so on. These are investment expenses that can only be used against portfolio income.

Tax-free income. Some structures and investment vehicles allow for tax-free growth. Examples of these are the Roth IRA and whole life insurance. There are also some cases under specific tax law that allow tax-free income—such as from the sale of a principal residence.

Tax-deferred income. Income can also be deferred to a future time. Two examples of this are pension plans, which are a deduction currently, grow tax-deferred, and are taxable when withdrawn, and like-kind exchanges for real property. There are also similar exchanges available for life insurance policies under a different code section.

Chapter 9

Expenses

Hidden Business Deductions

"We've reviewed the first part of the Three Step Tax Formula—income," I said to Ted and Ellen, continuing our meeting. "Now let's go through the expenses portion. First, let's look for the hidden business deductions."

"Finally!" exclaimed Ellen. "Now I can get the list of what I can deduct from my company."

I sat for a moment before responding. I had heard this from almost every single beginning business owner I had ever met—and some not so beginning. It seemed that everyone was looking for the "magic list," but the fact was there was no magic answer.

"Well, I guess, Ellen, you could say that you can deduct anything that helps your business," I started slowly, still thinking furiously.

"In fact, the Internal Revenue Code says pretty clearly what is deductible. Let's see if I can find that code section," I added, reaching for my pocket guide of the tax code.

Twenty-Seven Words

That day I showed Tom and Ellen Internal Revenue Code Section 162(a). This code section says, in just twenty-seven words, what you can deduct for your business:

There shall be allowed as a deduction, all the ordinary and necessary expenses paid or incurred during the taxable year in carrying on any trade or business.

"But who decides what is 'ordinary and necessary'?" asked Ted.

"That's the problem, Ted," I replied. "It's all subject to interpretation, like a lot of the tax code. In this case, there have been a lot of federal court decisions trying to interpret what those words mean," I continued, this time turning to my online tax research program.

"Okay, here's the definition that is the consensus of those decisions," I said after reviewing the material.

I showed Ted and Ellen the following definitions of "ordinary" and "necessary."

Ordinary expenses: Expenses that are normal, common, and accepted under the circumstances by the business community.

Necessary expenses: Expenses that are appropriate and helpful.

"That's pretty broad," noted Ted. "There certainly is a lot of latitude in what is normal, common, and accepted in any area by a group of people."

"Exactly, Ted!" I exclaimed. "And that is why having a tax professional advising you on your strategy is so necessary. For one thing, although you clearly will know your business better than an outside advisor, they will know what has been allowed in previous court cases. They also can add some perspective to what you plan. The key is that it must start with you.

Overview of the Deduction Discovery System

Most taxpayers understand the importance of deductions. This is an area that everyone, even employees, are constantly striving to derive more benefit from. If you look at many ads—such as from real estate agents touting home ownership, they use "tax-deductible" as a reason to purchase. Everyone is looking for ways to reduce their taxes by finding deductions.

In the case of a business owner, there are many more deductions available than for an employee. The simple fact is that for a highly compensated employee, they have *no* deductions available to them. But the business owner will always find something they can deduct, no matter how much their income is.

Why look for deductions? It's simple—the more tax deductions your business can take, the lower your taxable income is.

The deduction discovery system was developed to identify what deductions you might already have and to find ways to legitimately write off future expenses that are planned.

First, though, let's go over the most commonly overlooked business deductions. Chances are you have these deductions available already for your business.

The Commonly Overlooked Business Deductions

Following are the business deductions common to almost all businesses. Take the time to review the list and make a note of ones that might be applicable to your business. (Refer also to Appendix B, "300 + Business Deductions.")

AUTO EXPENSE

There are many ways to deduct the cost of an auto. And that can be confusing. Using the values for the year 2000, here are the simple facts about autos:

• You can buy the car in your business. The business can deduct the cost of maintaining the car (gas, oil, repairs, tires, car washes, and so forth). Plus, the business can deduct the interest portion of any payments and then depreciate the car, using the limits established by the government. For vehicles purchased in 1999, the depreciation amounts are: Year 1—$3,060, Year 2—$5,000, Year 3—$2,950, Year 4 and on—$1,775.

• Your business can lease the car. For "luxury automobiles," defined in 1999 as anything worth more than $15,500, a small amount will not be able to be deducted. For example, a vehicle worth $31,500 will have to have $260 of the lease added back in the first year.

• You can buy or lease the car yourself, and be reimbursed for mileage at the current rate. In 2000, the amount was $0.325 per mile. The payment is deducted from the business income, but is not considered income for you.

• If you buy a vehicle that is over 6,000 GVW (gross vehicle weight), the luxury automobile limitation does not apply. In this case, your business can depreciate the vehicle just like it was any other piece of income. That includes being able to make a Section 179 deduction of $20,000 (in 2000) right up front.

BAD DEBT

Bad debt is a commonly misunderstood deduction. It is most often overlooked at the personal level, though, and not at the business level. An individual can write off as bad debt loans made to anyone that have been "written off" with no hope of collection. An individual can also take a deduction for debt or expenses paid on behalf of others that will not be repaid. The burden of proof will be on whether the item is actually a gift. To prove a bad debt, you must attempt to collect just as you would with any other debt. I recommend that my clients first have a note drawn up for all loans and then show proof of collection attempt by sending a letter with a return receipt requested demanding payment.

Where most people will overlook the bad debt expense at an individual level, they will mistakenly try to take a bad debt expense deduction for a business when it is not allowed. The only way that a business can take a bad debt expense is if the income was first reported and tax was paid on it. In other words, if your business is accrual-based, which means that accounts receivable are counted as income even if they have not been collected, then when that receivable is not collected, there is a bad debt expense. Most small businesses, however, are cash-based, which means that income is only counted when it is received. There cannot be a bad debt expense offsetting income, because the accounts receivable income was never recognized.

"Wait a second!" interjected Ted. "This is something I know about. I know that in my business I don't have to pay tax on income until I receive payment. But I have a client right now that I don't think is going to pay me. I sold him some software and spent time installing it on his computer. So I have true costs in that software and the time I spent. There is expense and lost income!"

"Ted, I know it doesn't seem fair," I answered. "But in this case, you will only be able to deduct the money you spent on the software. You won't be able to take it as a bad debt expense, though; you only get a deduction for the cost of the software. So, for the product, you don't have a loss that you can deduct."

"Okay, I understand that, but what about my time? Doesn't that count for anything?" asked Ted.

"You could take a deduction for the amount you weren't paid *if* you first recognized it as income. For example, if you were to book the sale to that customer and your time, there would be an offset to income. That is how large companies do their accounting system. Then, when these companies can't collect, they have a bad debt expense." I paused, checking with Ted to see if he was following the logic. He was. "Now, in your case, you do not book the income in the first place, so there is nothing to deduct against. The net effect for the large company is to have zero income. You would also have zero income, because it was never booked in the first place. Don't feel alone in struggling with this concept; it is one of the most difficult areas for most new small business owners to understand."

BUSINESS START-UP

There are many expenses *before* you begin your business. And, unfortunately, since one of the steps is setting up your accounting system, and the expenses occur first, you might forget them. Here is a checklist of common start-up expenses that you can deduct (or capitalize and deduct over sixty months). It is not complete. Use it as a memory jog for items you can deduct in your business.

- Legal expenses (will need to be amortized over sixty months). These are costs that you pay to an attorney or document preparation service to prepare the initial paperwork for your business. These need to be amortized over sixty months. In other words, you can subtract 1/60 of the cost each month. After the business is going, most legal fees are deductible immediately.
- Business structure setup (amortized over sixty months). This includes the costs you pay to have special business structures set up—such as the cost of forming a corporation.
- Filing fees. These are the costs paid to the state and local agencies for the privilege of doing business and include business licenses, state filing fees, fees for lists of directors, and others. The exact fees will depend on the type and location of your business.
- Accounting fees. Hopefully, you will consult with an accountant and bookkeeper to get your books set up as soon as possible. Those costs are deductible.
- Office equipment. There is a lot of office equipment needed for a basic office in this electronic age. Computer, printer, fax machine, phone— these are just a few of the items needed. Many people already have some of these items before starting a business. Your business can pay you the fair market value for these items from its proceeds, but you need to track the expenses first.

- Office furniture. Office furniture can include your desk, tables, chairs, and filing cabinets, as well as art you hang on the walls.
- Cost of investigating business (seminars, books, travel, advisors' fees). A prudent business owner takes time to investigate and learn all they can about their business first. This can include going to seminars, buying books, subscribing to magazines, dues to professional organizations, travel to look at other businesses, and talking with advisors.
- Office setup costs (stationery, business cards, logo design). The cost of designing a logo, setting up a Web site, preparing stationery, and so forth are all part of the office setup costs.

EDUCATION EXPENSES

You can deduct education expenses when they are related to your current expense. There are two ways to expense education: 1) as education that is required to maintain or improve skills; and 2) under an education assistance plan. Currently, the Internal Revenue Code under Section 127 allows up to $5,250 in annual tax-free assistance to each eligible employee. The education need not be job-related. Children of owners can qualify if they are over the age of twenty-one, are legitimate employees of the business, and are not dependents of the owners. You will need to have a separate written plan for this deduction and you cannot discriminate between employees (samples are provided in Appendix D). Note that there are two different ways to deduct education expenses. Education that is required to maintain or improve skills does not require a written plan and is not subject to the limits of $5,250 per employee. However, we recommend that you include a note in your minutes authorizing such expenditures.

ENTERTAINMENT EXPENSES

It's amazing to me how many clients fail to count their business and entertaining expenses. *Any* expense that is "directly related" to the business, and business is discussed or "associated with" the business, and the entertainment takes place immediately before or after a business decision, is deductible. Currently, 50 percent of the cost is deductible.

- The directly related test says that: 1) the main purpose of the combined business and entertainment was the active conduct of business; 2) you do conduct business with that person; and 3) you had more than a general expectation of getting income or other business benefit at some future time.

• Business that is held in a clear business setting and is for business purposes is considered directly related. Examples: 1) entertainment in a hospitality room at a convention where business goodwill is created through the display or discussion of business products; 2) entertainment that is mainly a price rebate on the sale of your products (such as a restaurant owner providing an occasional free meal to a loyal customer); and 3) entertainment of a clear business nature occurring under circumstances where there is no meaningful personal or social relationship between you and the persons entertained (such as entertainment of business and civic leaders at the opening of a new hotel or play when the purpose is to get business publicity rather than to create or maintain the goodwill of the persons entertained).

• If you don't meet the directly related test, you may still meet the associated test. You must show that the entertainment is associated with your trade or business and that it directly precedes or follows a substantial business discussion. In this case, you must show that you actively engaged in a discussion, meeting, negotiation, or other business transaction to get income or some other specific business benefit. The meeting does not have to be for any specified length of time, but you must show that the business discussion was substantial in relation to the meal or entertainment. It is not necessary that you devote more time to business than to entertainment.

• In some cases, though, 100 percent of the expense can be deductible. In this case, it needs to be provided for the "convenience of the employer."

• Occasional and sporadic meal reimbursements and supper money for overtime work are excludable from gross income.

• When a meal is provided so that employees are present for emergency work (emergency medical personnel who are on call, for instance), then the cost is 100 percent deductible.

• When a meal is provided because business operations require a short lunch period and employees don't have time to eat elsewhere (a short lunch period meal means less than one hour), then the cost is 100 percent deductible.

- If more than half the meals provided at the on-premises eating facility are provided for the employer's convenience, then the balance of the meals also are treated the same. In other words, if more than half of your employees eat for free (tax-free, that is), the rest do also.

LEGAL AND PROFESSIONAL FEES

Fees that you pay to attorneys, tax strategists, accountants, bookkeepers, or other consultants can be deducted in the year you pay them. If the work clearly relates to future years, such as patent work, the fees must be deducted over the life of the benefit.

TRAVEL EXPENSES

Deducting travel expenses has gotten more and more complex. Generally, when you travel for business, you can deduct many expenses such as the cost of the plane fare, costs of operating your car, taxi fare, lodging, meals, shipping, business meals, clothes cleaning, telephone calls, faxes, and tips. If you combine business and pleasure within the U.S., the trip is still deductible if the primary purpose is business. You can determine primary purpose by counting the number of days for business compared to the number of nonbusiness days. If there are more business days than nonbusiness days, then you have a deduction. What is a business day? It is a day in which you do business—any amount. Document what you have done by making a note in your organizer or calendar. Keep copies of any literature or business cards you collect as part of your business.

INTEREST

If you use credit to finance business purchases (like many start-up businesses), especially in the beginning, you can deduct the interest. If you take out a personal loan, such as a home equity loan, to fund business needs, then that interest is also deductible. You will need to keep good records showing how the money or purchases were used in your business.

MOVING EXPENSES

If you move your office, even if it is across the street, it is deductible. Many new business owners make the transition from home to executive suite to their own suite of offices. That's a lot of moves and they are all deductible. Many new business owners also get confused on this deduction and assume that the moving expense rules are the same for a business as they are for an individual. They are not. An individual can only take a moving expense if their new workplace is at least fifty miles farther from their old home than their old workplace was. A business is not subject to such restrictive rules.

SOFTWARE

What would a modern business do without software? Don't forget this common expense, especially in your first year of business when you transfer all the software you had previously purchased. The business should reimburse the cost to you, so it is a deduction.

CHARITABLE CONTRIBUTIONS/PROMOTION

If your business is formed under a flow-through entity (partnership or S corporation), your business can make a charitable contribution and pass the deduction through to you, to claim on your individual tax return. There are some limitations to how much in charitable deductions you will be able to take on your return. A C corporation can take deductions directly against their income, but is allowed in the current year only up to 10 percent of net profit. In many cases, there is actually a promotional aspect to what might be considered charitable contributions. For example, advertising in a program for an event sponsored for a local charity could actually be called a promotional expense. Wherever possible, look for promotional expenses within charitable deductions, so that you do not have problems with the limitation on charitable donations.

TAXES

There are many taxes that are deductible for your business. For example, sales tax paid on supplies and equipment for your business, excise taxes, fuel taxes, payroll tax, real estate taxes, personal property tax, city taxes, and state income tax are deductible for your federal income tax. Your federal income tax is never deductible. The state income tax is not deductible for your state tax return.

Hidden Business Deductions

"I saw some expenses in that list that I had forgotten—for example, we had bought the office furniture before. In fact, the office desk is really a table that we had before. Can we write that off?" asked Ellen.

"Yes, Ellen, you can," I answered. "You need to establish a fair market value and have the company pay you for that. There are a couple of different ways to do that. In this case, it will be Ted's company that purchases the furniture. So we will just have you make an invoice listing the furniture and the current fair market value. The company will write a check to Ted from its separate checking account. You could have also traded the furniture for stock in a company or set up a note, where the company owes you money in the future. The key is to get the expense on the company's books.

"Now, we're going to review your hidden business deductions," I continued. "As you know, one of my firm beliefs is that I never tell my clients to invest in something just for the simple fact that is a write-off. For example, if you buy something that you wouldn't buy anyway and get a tax deduction, you actually only get a return of your tax rate. If you buy something for $1,000 and get a write-off of 39.6 percent, you are getting $396 back for $1,000 invested. Does that sound like a good investment?" I asked them.

"Of course not," said Ted. "I think people hear the words 'tax write-off' and their eyes, or maybe mind, kind of glazes over."

"I'm glad you agree. So, what hidden business deductions means is looking for business deductions in the things you already pay for. You have already listed the expenses you incur each month," I said. "Let's go through the items one by one."

BOAT

If your boat has a rest room and a kitchen, then it can qualify as a second home. It's not a business deduction, but the interest on payments would be deductible. A boat could also be a deduction if, again, it is needed as "ordinary" and "necessary." In other words, if you had a business that required you to have a boat—such as a photographer or fisherman or boat seller—it would be a deduction. There is a famous story told by accountants of a man who went to his accountant and said he wanted to write off a new yacht. His accountant told him that he could not deduct it unless he had a business that needed it. That made the client angry enough to prove he could turn it into a business. So he started a business selling yachts . . . and made ten times more money than he ever had in his other business.

CHILDREN

There are many expenses associated with your children. The best plan is to have your children employed in your business so that they can pay for their own expenses. In this way, you are able to deduct the cost of their salary, and up to approximately $4,500 is not taxable to them (the amount changes each year). You may not want to stop there, though. If you are in a high tax bracket, it may make sense to have your child pay tax at their lower tax rate. See Chapter 10 and Chapter 17 for ideas on making your children employees and moving income from your high tax bracket to their lower tax bracket.

CLOTHING

The cost of items that are considered uniforms are deductible, as is the cost of cleaning such items. In other words, if you put a logo on your polo shirt, it is likely a business deduction, both for the cost of the shirt as well as the cleaning expense.

GIFTS

Many gifts are really promotional gifts—the flowers you send as a thank-you or the gift certificate to a restaurant. These are more properly considered promotional items and are deductible as such.

HOME OFFICE

This deduction has gone through some wild swings in the last decade. Currently, a home office is allowed for a self-employed person or a flow-through entity. In the case of a C corporation, it is a little easier. A C corporation can pay a fair market rental. Against that income, the individual recipient can deduct a pro rata portion of housing costs—such as mortgage interest, homeowners' dues, property tax, insurance, mortgage insurance, utilities, and so on. There is a question about whether taking the home office deduction puts a pro rata portion of the home at risk for the tax-free principal residence sale. In other words, under current law, if you live in your home for two of the past five years, then you can take up to $500,000 (for married filing jointly, $250,000 if single) of gain without paying taxes. But if you have determined that 10 percent of your home is used for business, then the argument is made that you have given up 10 percent of the tax-free gain. However, a careful reading of the law shows that the owner is allowed the tax-free gain if they have lived in the house for two out of the past five years. So, if you are considering a sale, just make sure that for two of the past five years your home has been solely for personal use.

MEDICAL REIMBURSEMENT

A medical reimbursement plan is one of the little used strategies that are available to businesses. With a plan in place (you can find a copy in Appendix D), you can deduct dental, vision, orthodontia, medical co-payments, therapeutic massage, and so on. These benefits are fully deductible for the business and are not income for the recipient. The plan cannot discriminate against other employees and must cover 70 percent or more of all employees. If there are more than 100 employees, a Form 5500 is required to be filed.

PERSONAL CARE

Remember the rule of "ordinary and necessary." An actress can deduct the cost of hair and nail care. In Nevada, a showgirl was allowed to deduct her augmentation expense. The question to ask is whether the cost really does help the business and even more importantly, does it pass the laugh test? In other words, can you write it down with a straight face?

PETS

The cost of pets can even be a business deduction. For example, the cost of keeping a watchdog is a deduction, as was proved in a tax court case in Hawaii, where a junkyard was allowed to deduct the cost of the dogs. Also, I have seen real estate brokers and land developers deduct the cost of keeping a horse when they use the animal to view property.

TRAVEL/VACATION

See earlier in this chapter for write-off rules regarding travel within the U.S. Of course, if you are in a business that has travel as an essential ingredient (for example, if you are a writer [especially travel writer] or photographer, you will have an easy time proving the business purpose of travel.) If your spouse and children are also legitimate employees, then their travel is deductible also. Finally, if you have a corporation, you are required to have an annual meeting of the board of directors. The costs of that meeting are a legitimate expense of the corporation. There are different rules if your travel is outside the U.S. If you stay away more than seven days, then you will have to allocate your expenses between time spent on business and time spent on pleasure.

Expenses That Pay in the Future

"The one exception to the rule of not incurring extra expenses just for the tax write-offs is when there is some other value to the expense," I said to Ted and Ellen. "Let's go through the following checklist of items that can have true future value."

GROUP TERM LIFE INSURANCE

Group term life insurance up to $50,000 of coverage is tax-free. Your company can also provide up to $2,000 of group term insurance for dependents. You can provide more than $50,000 in coverage, but there will be a slight amount of tax effect on the recipient.

RETIREMENT PLANS

A rose by any other name . . . There are many different names for retirement plans, and yet they all fall into one of two categories—the defined contribution and the defined benefit. These types of pension plans are tax-deferred, which means you are able to take a current deduction, but there is a day of reckoning when you pay the tax. At that time, you will pay tax on the then-current value of the pension. So the contribution, and the subsequent growth, is not tax-free—it is merely tax-deferred.

Defined Contribution Plans

Examples of the defined contribution plan are 401(k), SEP, Keogh, and SAR SEP, among others. The key issue is that the contributions are determined based solely on the salary—up to a maximum amount. However, there are significant limitations on the amount of contributions for owner-employees. For this reason, many small businesses that employ others have started to move away from the defined contribution plan. They are forced to give more away to others than they receive. That is a real disincentive to owners!

Defined Benefit Plans

Examples of defined benefit plans are the defined benefit plan and the age-weighted plan. In these types of plans, the contribution is calculated to determine what the future need is for each individual, based on their age and salary, and according to the plan agreement. In other words, let's say you start a defined benefit plan in your company when you are fifty-five years of age making $100,000 a year and define the agreement that all employees will have 100 percent of salary at retirement age of sixty-two. Your plan only has seven years to accumulate enough capital to guarantee you $100,000 for the rest of your life. That's a short period of time to accumulate a lot of money. On the other hand, assume you have an employee who is twenty-five years old and is making $30,000 per year. In this case, your company has thirty-seven years to accumulate enough capital to guarantee $30,000 per year. That's a much longer period of time, and with the time value of money, the required contribution would be small.

This plan works well where the owner-employee is older and the other employees are younger.

IRA

An IRA, otherwise known as an individual retirement account, is a pension plan for the individual. It would not be a deduction for the company. IRAs allow for tax-deferred growth, like the defined benefit and defined contribution plans, with pretax dollars. The money, when it is withdrawn from the IRA, is taxable. A Roth IRA, fairly new to the retirement planning arena, allows for tax-free growth with after-tax dollars. In other words, there is no deduction at the time the payment is made, but future withdrawals are tax-free. There are some good tax strategies available with the use of the Roth IRA. See Chapter 17 for more discussion regarding Roths.

VEBA

VEBA stands for voluntary employees' beneficiary association. A VEBA is sanctioned under the Internal Revenue Code Section 501(c)(9). It is an association of employees, formed for the purpose of providing welfare benefits to its members. Another definition of a VEBA is that it is a tax-exempt trust authorized by Section 501(c)(9) of the Internal Revenue Code, which is set up to provide certain types of benefits for employees of the sponsoring employer.

There are basically three different kinds of VEBAs: 1) corporate or single employer VEBAs (example, General Motors); 2) ten or more employer VEBAs; and 3) collectively bargained VEBAs.

Corporate or single employer VEBAs. These are VEBAs that are created for the use of the single employer. There are some restrictions to the benefits that can be offered. The general characteristics of these VEBAs are: tax-deductible contributions, tax-deferred accumulations, and taxable distributions. In a lot of ways, they work like pension plans. A company like General Motors would have this kind of VEBA.

Ten or more employer VEBAs. This type of VEBA is similar to the single employer VEBA, with a few more technical rules. Generally, all employees must be covered without discrimination.

Collectively bargained VEBAs. This type of VEBA is the most popular of the three types for small business owners. Through this organized VEBA, you can have an agreement that carves out certain groups of employees for special benefits.

A VEBA allows a current tax deduction, allows assets to accumulate on a tax-deferred basis, has no vesting requirements, allows early or late distributions, provides for flexible contributions, and can provide substantial benefit to key personnel, generally the owners. It also is protected from creditors and is frequently used as a vehicle in which to acquire tax-deductible life insurance.

Who Would Use a VEBA?
If you have:

- a highly profitable business seeking a large tax deduction
- a business that can no longer fund its retirement plan
- a business whose retirement plan is of little benefit to you
- a desire to protect assets from creditors
- a desire to reduce estate tax exposure

and you are comfortable with a higher level of risk, then a VEBA could be the right vehicle for you.

VEBAs have been used to pay for life insurance, education, disability coverage, medical benefits, and involuntary severance under some circumstances. The safest route is to apply for an IRS determination letter to solidify the deduction.

With the proper setup and good strategies in place, your company, with a VEBA, can take a deduction, allow benefits to accrue tax-deferred, and then allow employees to borrow against assets without ever paying it back during their lifetime. In other words, there is really tax-free growth *with* a deduction at the time of payment. That sounds like the best of all possible worlds!

VEBAs are considered a very aggressive area of the tax code, and so the rules must be meticulously followed. Also, they aren't for everyone. The contributions must be based on reasonableness. In one particular case, reasonableness was defined as a $1.1 million tax deduction for a VEBA that covered only certain employees.

History of VEBAs

The VEBA has actually been around since 1928. Before 1985, a VEBA was generally thought of as a plan that complied fully with the tax code. Prior to that time, many companies used a VEBA to obtain current deductions on future benefit expenses. But, as will happen, there were some significant abuses with VEBAs and new legislation came out in 1984 that limited the amount of contributions and added additional requirements for future tax years. The unfavorable rulings against the abusive companies have discouraged many people from using VEBAs, but in the right circumstances, and certainly not as a blanket answer for everyone, they are an excellent vehicle.

VEBA Warning

As with all aspects of tax planning, make sure you have a qualified tax strategist advising you. This is especially true when you venture into the more aggressive tax waters of a VEBA. The VEBA has been held both as legitimate expenditures in some circumstances and as disallowed deductions in other cases—the different results depend on how you do it.

There are also some plans on the marketplace currently that profess to be VEBA plans but in fact do not comply with VEBA rules. Be careful of plan promoters that tell you they do not have to comply with applicable tax rules because they have not filed with the IRS for a tax exemption. VEBAs work, and work well, in the right circumstances. Just make sure that you have the right circumstances.

LIFE INSURANCE

Another hotly debated area of tax planning is if and when to use life insurance and what kind of life insurance to use.

"Oh, yeah, I know about this. You should always buy term insurance and invest the difference in mutual funds," said Ted.

"In many cases, that is the correct answer, but not always," I responded. "Remember that life insurance, just like many other items you can buy (such as a corporation), is a product. The secret isn't to just buy a product, but instead to have a strategy first and then buy the products that support the strategy." Ted and Ellen quickly agreed.

"So let's explore a little first about the types of insurance and when you can use them," I said. "Just as with pension plans, there are many different names given to life insurance. But, basically, they fall under one of two categories—or a combination of the two—term life insurance and whole life (also known as cash value life or permanent life) insurance.

"Term insurance has premiums that only cover the insurance needs. It is used strictly as a way of providing life insurance proceeds in the event of the death of the insured.

"Whole life insurance has premiums that are greater than just the insurance portion. The excess is invested and can grow tax-advantaged to the recipient. That excess is known as the cash value of the policy.

"There are many different forms of both types of insurance. The difference in the form is a result of how the premium is calculated (in the case of the term insurance) or how the cash value is invested (in the case of permanent insurance)."

"So, should I have term insurance or cash value life insurance?" asked Ted.

"That's not a question you can easily answer," I said, "because the answer depends on what you want to accomplish with the insurance. You see, life insurance can potentially have two elements to it: 1) the life insurance portion, and 2) the financial and tax-planning element. The life insurance portion is needed where you have a family or business that depends on you. Right now, Ted, if something happens to you, Ellen will be the sole support for your family. You don't have passive income streams in place yet to help her out with the family obligations. So, the life insurance element is an important one. Also, if you have a business that relied on you as a celebrity, you would want to have 'key man' insurance to keep the business going without you.

"The second part—the cash value portion—depends on your personal income tax bracket, projected income tax bracket, assumed rate of return, and whether your current need for the insurance is short- or long-term."

"It sounds to me like you are answering the question with 'it depends,'" exclaimed Ellen.

"That's right, Ellen," I responded. "You understood exactly what I was saying. I want to put you in touch with a certified financial planner (CFP) to help you assess exactly what your needs are right now. I have someone I work with that I will refer you to. If you were looking on your own for such an advisor, my word of caution would be to make sure you aren't getting advice from someone who has the same pat answer for every question. That would be the person who always says, 'Buy term and invest the difference! or 'Never buy term insurance—you are wasting your money.' You want to make sure that you are having someone truly assess where you are, where you want to go, and determine a strategy to help you get there." I paused a moment. "But let's cover some of the basic strategies that can be used with life insurance, as an overview prior to your meeting with the CFP."

Cash Value Buildup—Tax Issues

The buildup portion of the policy's cash value is not taxable currently to the policy owner. Additionally, dividends generally are considered to be a "return of premium" and are not taxable to the policy owner. And, in most cases, life insurance death proceeds are also not taxable. If the insured has any elements of ownership in the policy at the time of his or her death, the proceeds are includable in the insured's gross estate for federal estate tax purposes. State inheritance taxes and federal gift taxes may also apply to life insurance policies/proceeds under specific circumstances.

Participating Whole Life Insurance

Participating (par) whole life insurance has been around for many years in the U.S. The participating feature allows for the payment of dividends to policy owners when actual experience justifies such payment. Participating whole life insurance is still very popular today.

Universal Life Insurance

Both traditional whole life and universal life products are examples of cash-value life insurance. However, there are several important differences between these two products. The whole life policies are set up to require the payment of fixed, level premiums, and provide for level death benefits and projectable cash values. On the other hand, universal life policies offer adjustable death benefits and flexible premiums that can be varied according to changing circumstances.

Roth for the Rich

One benefit of whole life insurance is the cash value that builds up, tax-advantaged. This cash value can be borrowed out with no requirement for repayment by the policy owner. One of the benefits of the Roth IRA plan is that it allows for tax-free growth. The disadvantage for many of my clients is that there is an income ceiling, and unfortunately, high-income individuals cannot qualify for a Roth. See Chapter 17 for further discussion of other ways to work with a Roth. The whole life insurance can be set up in conjunction with a C corporation using a form of insurance known as a "split dollar" or a "reverse split dollar" to let you use corporate funds to provide the insurance, and cash value that you can later borrow against, tax-free. It truly becomes a "Roth for the rich."

You can even take this one step further and combine the insurance with a VEBA plan. It is possible to set up a strategy that allows for tax-free growth with pretax dollars! That is truly the best of all possible worlds. There are costs involved in setting up these plans, and as discussed in the VEBA section, there can be significant risk if not done correctly.

What's Deductible?

Back to Ted and Ellen . . .

"We've covered a lot of information today and I know that you will want to review some of it again, but I hope that this begins to give you a better answer of what you can deduct," I said. Ted and Ellen looked a little overwhelmed as they nodded slightly. I thought it would be a good time to stop for the day.

"In a later meeting, we'll discuss what you need to do to *keep* the deductions you find," I concluded.

SUMMARY

Ordinary and necessary expenses. The IRS says, at Code Section 162(a), "There shall be allowed as a deduction, all the ordinary and necessary expenses paid or incurred during the taxable year in carrying on any trade or business." While other code sections, and case law, define specific instances of allowed and disallowed expenses, the primary question will be for all deductions whether the expense is truly an ordinary and necessary expense for that particular business. Ordinary expenses are defined as expenses that are normal, common, and accepted under the circumstances by the business community. Necessary expenses are expenses that are appropriate and helpful.

Most common overlooked business deductions. The most common overlooked business deductions are 1) auto expenses, 2) bad debts, 3) business start-up expenses, 4) education expenses, 5) entertainment expenses, 6) legal and professional fees, 7) travel expenses, 8) interest, 9) moving expenses, 10) software, 11) charitable contributions/promotion, and 12) taxes. These are not deductions for everyone, and in every circumstance. Use this list as a memory jog for your own circumstances.

Hidden business deductions. Examine the expenses you already have. After you have a budget of where your money already goes, look for the true business deductions you already have. Create and retain the proper documentation to keep the deductions you discover. You do not want to look for things you can buy just because you can take a deduction. Buying things of little value just for the deduction is a poor investment that just returns cents on the dollar.

Expenses that are really investments. There are expenses, some tax deductions and some not, that your business can have that will grow for you in the future. Examples of these are pension plans and permanent life insurance. These are really investments, not expenses.

VEBA. In some cases, you can take a current-year deduction for items that will grow tax-free in the future for you. An example of that is the VEBA plan. A VEBA (voluntary employees' beneficiary association) is a very aggressive tax planning tool that is not right in all circumstances. For a business that is highly profitable and seeking a large tax deduction that can no longer fund its retirement plan or whose plan is of little benefit to the owner and has a strong desire to protect the assets from creditors and to reduce estate tax exposure, the VEBA may be a good choice.

Life insurance. Life insurance can be either term, permanent, or some combination of both. Term insurance calls for premiums that cover the insurance cost. This is a good type of policy for a person with a family who is dependent on his income. In the case of his death, the insurance benefit will provide for his family. Permanent, or whole life, insurance has premiums that exceed the death benefit cost. The excess is invested and grows tax-advantaged to the recipient. At a future point, the cash value can be borrowed against, tax-free.

Chapter 10

Rate

Marginal Tax Rate

As we have seen, we have a graduated tax rate in the U.S. This means that there is a portion that is taxed at a lower rate, with the next layer then taxed at a higher rate, and so forth. You will likely hear accountants refer to tax rate by percentage—such as "You are in a 28 percent tax bracket." This means the marginal rate at which you are taxed. The first layer is still taxed at a lower rate.

These rates change each year and are readily available, so they are not reproduced here. For purposes of our example, we will use the year 2000 tax rates.

Using Tax Rates

"I don't think I really understood how the graduated tax rates worked before. It's interesting, but why do we care? It's pretty much just the way it is, right?" asked Ellen.

"You are right that the tax rate table is pretty firm," I answered, "but the tax planning comes about when you change *whose* tax rate table you use. We will cover the different business structures a little later but I want to review some basics of how taxation for businesses works now."

Business Structures

Businesses can operate in a variety of forms. The most common is the sole proprietorship, which requires filing of a Schedule C, and is, in fact, part of the tax return. This income is also subject to self-employment tax.

The other business structures—partnership, S corporation, limited liability company, and C corporation—require legal documentation and filing, with specific requirements for record keeping and accounting. Most business owners first operate as a sole proprietorship and then move on to other forms of business.

These three forms are illustrated in the diagram on page 130 (Fig. 10.1). The partnership, either a limited partnership or general partnership, is considered a flow-through entity. This means that the income (or loss) from the partnership flows through to the individual to be taxed at their personal income level. The form that reports the flow-through portion to the IRS is called a K-1. You might have heard people refer to K-1 income; this is what they were referring to. Partnership income can also be subject to self-employment tax, depending on the type of ownership—whether general or limited—and whether the partner is active in the business.

An S corporation also has income that flows through directly to the individual. Unlike the partnership, S corporation distributions are not subject to self-employment tax.

A limited liability company is taxed according to the state law in which it was formed. Most states now allow the LLC to determine how it is taxed at the time it is formed. This provision is called the "check the box" rule, because you can check a box to determine how it is taxed. The LLC will then follow the rules of whatever entity you chose. So, there are no specific LLC taxing rules—it will emulate the partnership or corporation structure.

Distribution Is Not Taxable Income

In the above cases of the S corporation and the partnership, income is reported on the individual owner's K-1. The K-1 reflects the income of the business multiplied by the ownership percentage of the individual. There is a common mistake made by many first-time owners in a flow-through company—distributions from the business do not equal the income from the company. It is possible to receive distributions from the company and have no taxable income at all.

It is also possible to have phantom income. This can be a potentially expensive lesson for an owner when they "receive" reported income, and must pay tax on it, but have no cash distributions to show for it.

I have seen investors in limited partnerships fall into this trap when they are in a minority position with no influence and continue to report taxable income with no cash to accompany it. A strong word of caution: Carefully read any limited partnership or limited liability company prospectus to make sure that the issue of phantom income has been adequately addressed. Some companies set up documents that call for mandatory distributions equal to a percentage of reported income so that their investors don't fall into this trap.

C Corporation

The C corporation is the only business structure that pays it own tax. All other business entities have income that is reported via the Schedule K-1 to the individual. The other business forms do not pay tax themselves. The C corporation, on the other hand, has its own tax table and pays it own tax.

Other Entities

"I understand now why you set up one of our businesses as a C corporation. You plan to have the income we make from that have its own tax rate table, so there is less tax," said Ellen.

"Ellen, you're exactly correct. Plus, I want to talk to you about another way we can move income from your own tax rate to another. That is very simply done by employing your children. That way you can move income from your higher rate to their lower rate. The amount changes each year, but you can count on roughly the first $4,550 paid to your children being tax-free," I explained. "In effect, you are moving the income from your higher rate into their tax rate, which actually might be zero."

Employing Dependents

Look for ways to take deductions for expenses you already have. Some of my clients support their elderly parents. Others have children that help out in the business, or are of the age that they could. If you decide to employ your children or other dependents, find a job that they could reasonably do. Many of my clients have children that are very good with computers. They employ them to set up and maintain Web sites, to enter data into databases, or do word processing or bookkeeping. Younger children can be employed to empty trash, clean out vehicles, straighten offices, and the like.

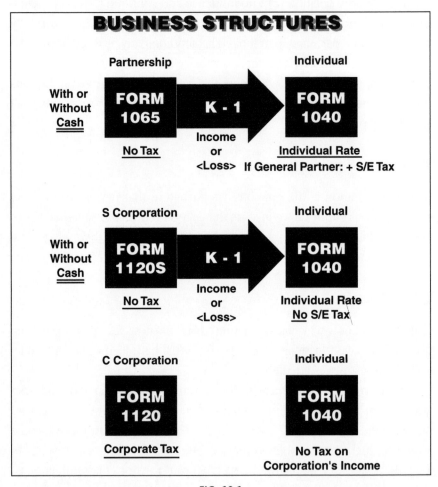

FIG. 10.1

There are a few rules to employing dependents. First, make sure you have a true job and job description for them. Pay them a reasonable wage for the work they do and make sure they keep track of the hours they work. In other words, treat your dependents as you would any other employee.

Some people have used their children as models for advertising on the annual calendar, business cards, or newsletter. This works, too! And it is a way to pay compensation to much younger children.

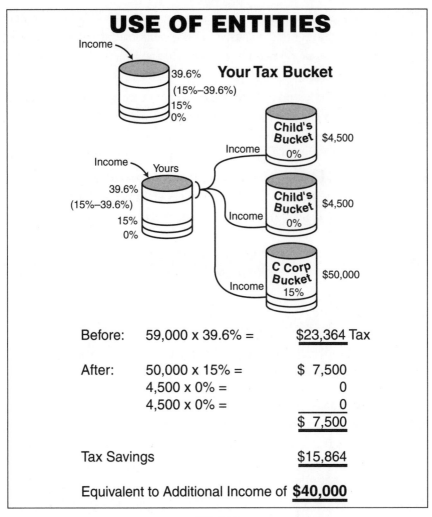

USE OF ENTITIES

Income

39.6% **Your Tax Bucket**
(15%–39.6%)
15%
0%

Income

Child's
Bucket $4,500
0%

Income — Yours

39.6%
(15%–39.6%)
15%
0%

Child's
Bucket $4,500
Income
0%

C Corp
Bucket $50,000
Income
15%

Before:	59,000 x 39.6% =	$23,364 Tax
After:	50,000 x 15% =	$ 7,500
	4,500 x 0% =	0
	4,500 x 0% =	0
		$ 7,500
Tax Savings		$15,864

Equivalent to Additional Income of **$40,000**

FIG. 10.2

If you pay less than $600 to a person in a year, it is not necessary to do any reporting to the IRS for the payment. For that reason, we recommend that clients pay their children less than $600 in a year for the modeling. It makes it much easier to do the paperwork—simply because there is none!

Of course, if the child is an employee, then you will need to set them up as a regular employee with payroll withholding and reporting.

Entities

"The idea, in summary, for making the best use of the tax rate is to look for the lowest possible rates available from the tax structures," I told Ted and

Ellen. "In your case, we are making use of the corporation's rate schedule, your children's rate schedule, and your own personal rate. Before we end this meeting today, we do need to discuss what you want to have your children do as employees."

Our meeting broke up after they had decided that Josh, the eleven-year-old, would be responsible for helping his father keep up his database. Josh had excellent computer skills, and on the open market that expertise was easily worth $15 an hour, which his father would pay him. Their daughter, Sarah, was only nine years old, but she helped her father with basic office work—emptying the trash, straightening his office, and general duties. Her limited skills were worth about $6 an hour and so they decided to pay her that amount.

SUMMARY

Marginal tax rate. The U.S. has a graduated tax in our country. In other words, there are layers of tax. The first bracket is 15 percent, the next bracket is 28 percent, and so forth. Everyone has the same brackets. Each year the bracket ceilings and floors for these rates are adjusted.

Distribution vs. income. A partnership and an S corporation have taxable income that is reported on the individual owner's tax returns. They do not pay federal tax. In some instances, there may be some state tax due. The income that is taxable to the owners is the amount of taxable income of these business structures. These companies may also provide distributions to the owners. The distribution is not taxable to the owner, but actually may represent income from the company.

C corporation. The C corporation (or limited liability company that has elected to be taxed as a C corporation) is the only business structure that pays tax at its own rate. The C corporation has a graduated tax rate with brackets, similar to an individual's.

Dependents. Your dependents also have their graduated tax rate with their own brackets. Legitimate jobs with job descriptions and time cards need to be created for these children, but this can be a very effective way to move income from a high-income taxpayer to their dependent children's lower tax bracket.

Part III

Picking the Right Business Structure

Chapter 11

Business Structures

What Is the Right Business Structure?

In Chapters 1–6, we saw how Ted and Ellen's business plan and tax strategy came together. They first completed the first step to determine where they are today financially, where their money goes, what their current and prospective business prospects are, and what their overall short-term and long-term goals are. From that we determined the right strategy and then designed the plan and path that Ted and Ellen would follow to reach their goal.

A large part of that strategy was determining what the best business structure would be for their businesses. In Ted and Ellen's case, they had a computer consulting company and a future multilevel marketing company. There were many factors that went into the decision of which type of business entity would be best. We took into account the following:

Ted and Ellen

1. Their current taxable income.
2. Source of current income and future projections of that income.
3. Hidden business deductions.
4. Dependents that can be employed (other entities).
5. Short-term financial goals.
6. Long-term financial goals.

Businesses

7. Current business and projection of income of that business.
8. Probability of projected business income.
9. Type of business.
10. Plan for proceeds from business and from saved taxes.
11. Plans for business continuation—exit strategies.
12. Funding needs for the business.

Asset Protection

13. Ted and Ellen's likely exposure to risk from personal acts.
14. Ted and Ellen's risk tolerance.
15. Exposure to risk from the business.
16. Ted and Ellen's net worth and projections of net worth.

I went through each step of the Five STEPS program thoroughly with Ted and Ellen. As part of that process, we examined and discussed each of the above sixteen factors, plus others as they came up.

Unfortunately, not everyone thoughtfully considers all the necessary factors to determine the correct entity. The following clients, Nick and Sue, came to me as a referral. They had already met with a company that specializes in setting up business entities—primarily C corporations—and, following the advice of one of the salesman, had purchased five corporations and five partnerships.

Nick and Sue: Product or Plan?

I was meeting for the first time with prospective clients Nick and Sue. We went through the normal evaluation process I go through with all my new clients. As I reviewed the information they had sent in, I knew immediately how they had gotten where they were. I noted their taxable income of $100,000 and that they had recently bought five corporations and five partnerships.

"One of the challenges my clients face is one I can really relate to. In fact, I have a piece of exercise equipment in the corner of our family room," I started out, noting their puzzled faces. "You see, I was mesmerized by an ad for the equipment that promised all kinds of benefits—health, weight loss, and it looked like I'd also get taller and grow long, blond hair. So I bought the equipment.

"The problem was I had bought a product with no plan. I don't know if this particular piece of equipment was the best one for me. I didn't have a plan for when or how often I was going to use the equipment," I continued. "Now it makes a great place to hang my jacket."

One look at their faces told me that I had really lost them, and so I came to my point.

"Something similar has happened to you. You see, you have bought product—five corporations and five partnerships. But I can see from your financial records," thinking that the real issue of "lack of financial records" was obvious, "that you don't have a plan for what to do with these structures."

"Oh, but we talked to this guy who knew all about corporations. He said that this was exactly what I needed," Sue interrupted.

"I am a strong proponent of operating in the right business structure, and for a lot of people a corporation is the right structure. I also frequently use the limited partnership structure for real estate investments. The problem is that you have five corporations with a controlled group issue, no plan for how to put assets into the corporation, and no plan on how to take assets out. Also, you have five partnerships and, right now, you have only one rental property. You see, these are all good ideas in the right circumstances. I'm not sure that you have the right circumstances. Plus, you need to have a plan on how to take advantage of what you have.

"The good news is that we know where you are," I continued. "Now, let's figure out where you are going and what you need. Finally, we'll design the path on how to get there."

"You sure talk a lot about having a plan," Sue interrupted again. "We don't need that, we've got these corporations and that guy knew a lot about corporations. He said this was the best way to go."

I knew right then that it was going to be a long discussion.

The Five Steps to Financial Freedom

As we have seen with Ted and Ellen, the easiest and most efficient way to reach your goal is to follow the Five STEPS: S—Starting Point, T—Team, E—Evaluation/Strategy, P—Plan and Path, and S—Starting point (Reevaluation). Nick and Sue had jumped immediately into action, trying to create their own plan and path, without assessing where they were, what their goals were, and without putting a strategy in place.

They did have some advisors, but they were attempting to use the advisors in the wrong areas. They had not assessed these advisors to determine whether they had the necessary education, credentials, and business and personal experience to truly advise them in pursuit of their personal goals.

There is an old adage that you never ask a salesman what you need, because whatever he sells is what he will tell you you need. It's not that he is wrong, he just firmly believes in his product and he will see everything through that filter. The salesman often believes that his product can solve all problems, when the sad fact is that an objective eye can see other answers that are more appropriate. And, of course, when you buy just product without a plan for its use, it often turns into a useless, expensive venture. It may turn out to be just like the piece of exercise equipment that I bought. The product could do everything promised—but without a plan, it's worthless.

That is the difference between having a plan and buying a product. When you just buy a product and expect it to create a plan, sometimes you might get lucky. And sometimes you might end up with a lot of product, like Nick and Sue, that you don't need!

The best advice is to follow each of the Five STEPS *first,* to get the best results with the least effort.

Nick and Sue's Plan

"I've drawn up a representation of your current plan with the various corporations and limited partnerships (Fig. 11.1). It looks pretty confusing, don't you agree?" I asked Nick and Sue.

"That's why we came to see you. We need to know how to work with this," said Sue.

"First, I'm going to need to examine what your purpose in all of this was and then we need to look at some of the areas where you have problems now," I began.

"Wait a minute! What problems? We haven't done much with this yet," interjected Nick.

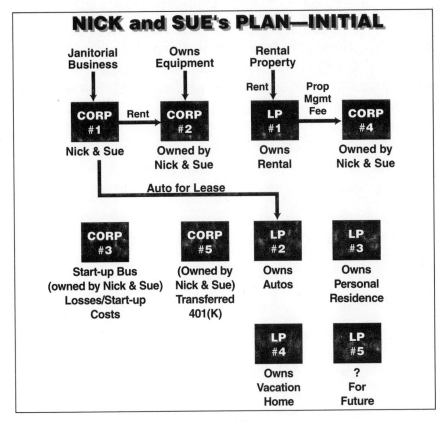

FIG. 11.1

"That's one thing you have in your favor. But your plan, as it is, falls into some of the traps of corporations. Now remember, I am a proponent of corporations when done correctly."

"We've heard from too many accountants that we shouldn't use corporations. I thought you liked them! That's why we came here!" said Sue, obviously getting emotional.

"I do like and work with C corporations, but *only* if they are the proper structure for what you want. There are rules regarding C corporations you must follow. Your plan does not follow those. Rather than just talk about them, let's go through them one by one," I said.

Sue calmed down a little, and we then went on to discuss the various corporate traps they had unwittingly stumbled into. We will discuss Nick and Sue further in Part V, where we learn what the traps of C corporations are and how to avoid them.

One Step at a Time

It is important to view all the factors when you design your own business structure. Seek good advisors who are experienced in a wide range of structures to help you make your choice. The first steps of the process may seem time-consuming, but the extra time planning for the right strategy and plan and path will amply reward you in reaching your goals faster and with more ease.

The following three chapters will discuss each of these factors in more detail. There are three primary areas to consider regarding business structure as you develop your strategy and plan for your business. These are:

1. Tax planning
2. Funding sources and exit strategies
3. Asset protection

Tax Planning

The focus of tax planning should start with you. How will the income from your business and investments impact the total amount of tax you pay? To start planning for the best tax plan for your business income, we start by assessing your current taxable income, the type of this current income, the future projections of that income, what hidden business deductions you have now, your family situation, and your short-term and long-term financial goals. It really is all about you at this point. You are unique and the cookie-cutter approach of our mass-producing economy will not give you the best result for your personal situation.

The purpose of these steps is to first identify how much your taxable income really is, after taking advantage of hidden business deductions and making use of extra entities such as your children or dependent parents. I have found that many new clients have great tax-saving potential without needing to make dramatic changes in their business structure. We first look for the simplest solutions to reducing your taxes by answering these questions.

The next step is to examine the type of income that you have. As we have seen, the concept of the three character types of income comes directly from the IRS tax code and has especially been important since the 1986 Tax Reform Act. Since that time, we have not been able to take advantage of losses or expenses in one area against income of a different type. For example, you cannot deduct investment expenses (portfolio) against earned income.

Finally, you will look at your short-term and long-term financial goals. Many of our clients have a primary goal of creating passive income. This goal can be planned by proper business structure setup.

Funding Sources and Exit Strategies

Most business owners are painfully aware in the beginning of their business of the need to find money for the business's operation. Funding sources are also an important issue as you go through growth spurts in your business. How will you fund your company's start and growth? You may wish to set it up to allow outside investors or to receive funding from the investments and businesses you already have. The structure you choose for your business can make receiving money easy . . . or hard.

As your business grows and becomes successful, your next question about money will be how will you get the money out? What is your exit strategy from the business? There are many different answers to that question. Some of my clients have a goal of setting up the business to create a passive flow of income to them in the future. It becomes a source of personal income with little or no involvement by them. Or they may want to take the company public, sell off a part to outside investors, merge with a larger company or sell the company as its value increases. Some clients want to build a business that will provide for the family into many future generations—truly creating a family business.

Asset Protection

The U.S. is the most litigious nation in the world. Most people today are waking up to the need to provide protection for the assets they have worked so hard to build. The business assets need to be protected from the individual owner and the owner wants to be protected from acts attributed to the business. I have found that most clients have very different points of view regarding the risk that they can tolerate. That is a very personal decision and there is no right or wrong answer. The answer is simply what is comfortable for the owner. Additionally, there are some types of professions, and types of people, that are viewed as more wealthy by the public. Some people are more visible in the public eye. You might have noticed that fact yourself if you peruse the *Forbes* list of the richest people. Some of the names you will recognize immediately, and there will likely be some of whom you have never heard. The more visible you are, the more risk you run of a lawsuit.

How to Work with the Sixteen Business Structure Factors

In Chapter 15, you will find a worksheet to use to compile your answers to each question concerning the sixteen factors listed at the beginning of this chapter. Use this completed worksheet to assess your own circumstances. You will likely find that there is some conflicting advice based on different goals. For example, the best structure for tax planning may not be the best structure for asset protection. Your own personal circumstances, situation, and goals will help your advisors weigh these factors to find the best answer for you.

SUMMARY

Product or plan? First, determine what your plan is by assessing where you are and where you want to go. The right products can then be added as required to set up the best result for you. There are many items that are products that can be disguised as plans. Examples of products are corporations, real estate programs, and insurance policies. I highly endorse all these products in the right instance. First, though, determine what your plan is. Jumping into products first can be expensive and time-consuming to unwind. It also can be discouraging as your attempts continue to fail.

Three considerations for business structures. There are three basic considerations for determining the correct structure for your business. First is tax planning. The focus and emphasis should be on you, the current or future business owner. You will want to examine the amount and type of income you currently have and what your goals are. Then, look at expenses your business has and tax planning you can immediately put in place—such as employing dependents. Second, examine how you will initially fund your company and how you will provide for anticipated future growth. Also, what is your business exit strategy? Third, consider what your asset protection needs and desires are. You will want to look at your own personal wealth and potential risk, as well as that of risk associated with your business.

Chapter 12

The Right Business Structure for Tax Planning

Considerations for Tax Planning

Of the sixteen business structure factors, it is important to look at the following items for tax-planning purposes:

1. Current taxable income.
2. Source of current income and future projections of that income.
3. Hidden business deductions.
4. Dependents that can be employed (other entities).
5. Short-term financial goals.
6. Long-term financial goals.

1. Current Taxable Income

A good tax plan must take into account current taxable income, from all sources, and its proper characterization. What tax bracket are you in now? Your tax bracket is defined as the marginal rate you pay on the next dollar that is earned.

Tax planning note: If personal income is high, is likely to continue at the same rate, and:

1. Business has income. Consider using a C corporation to contain income at the corporate level and pay tax at its own rate.
2. Business has initial losses. Consider a flow-through entity such as an S corporation to flow the losses through to your personal return and offset other income.

If personal income is at a lower rate now (15 percent–28 percent marginal tax rate) or if your personal income is expected to decrease to a lower tax rate and:

1. Business has low income. An S corporation will flow through income to your personal tax rate. This may be the easiest solution.
2. Business has initial losses. If loss would be lost to you personally, due to your own personally low taxable income, and you expect significantly more income in your business, you can consider forming a C corporation. The C corporation could then carry forward the initial losses to future years.

2. Source of Current Income and Future Projections of That Income

Where does your personal income come from now? Is it earned, passive, portfolio, or a combination of all three? (See Chapters 8 and 19 for discussion of these types of income.) Are there any passive losses or portfolio expenses that currently are not being allowed against other income? What are your future projections for the income of each category?

After you have reviewed the type of income and losses that you have, determine what changes you might want to make to the character of the income.

Tax planning note:

If your current income is all earned with no passive or portfolio losses or income, invest the proceeds from your business to create streams of passive and portfolio income. See Chapter 19 for ways that a C corporation can be used to change the character of the income.

If instead you have current income with lost passive or portfolio losses, it becomes more important to establish those types of income to offset the underused losses. If your lost passive losses are due to real estate, you may also be able to qualify as a real estate professional to take advantage of those losses.

A good tax plan should both take into account your immediate needs and allow for flexibility for your future needs. Assess your needs to change the character of the income. How will you do that if you need to?

Do you anticipate any changes in your income? For example, some clients start thinking about tax planning as they are preparing to leave their full-time employment to pursue their existing business full-time. How will that change the amount and type of income you receive?

3. Hidden Business Deductions

Go through the items of Chapter 9, "Expenses," as well as Appendix B, "300 + Business Deductions," to determine what hidden business deductions you have now. The purpose of this exercise is to determine what your actual taxable income will be. You may find that you can reduce your personal income tax liability merely by documenting and tracking expenses you already have.

There are also deductions that are only allowable for C corporations. Carefully consider the detailed list of corporate benefits in Chapter 20 to determine what benefits you can take if you are a C corporation. What is the total of those benefits? We don't recommend that you form a C corporation *only* because you will be able to deduct these expenses, but it is an important factor to consider.

4. Dependents That Can Be Employed (Other Entities)

Sometimes the simplest tax plan for using additional tax rates can be employing (and documenting) and paying your children. My experience has been that most children of entrepreneurs already help their parents. It often is just a case of paying them as an employee, which can greatly reduce the tax you pay, rather than paying a nondeductible allowance. Make sure you have a written job description, pay a reasonable amount for the work performed, and keep time cards. I have had clients employ their children as Web masters. Often they have as good or better skills than many computer experts that charge a lot of money for the same service. Why not pay your child to deduct the payment and reinforce a skill set for them?

Also remember that as your children become employees, they will also be able to take advantage of the pension plans that are available to any employee. For example, if you pay your child $6,000 in salary, you can also set up a SIMPLE pension plan in the amount of $6,000. If you are in a 39.6 percent tax bracket and pay your child $6,000, with $6,000 going into a SIMPLE pension plan, you will save $4,752 in taxes and your child will pay only $225—for a net savings of $4,527. This is done easily and relatively inexpensively without the need of any new elaborate tax structures.

5. and 6. Short-Term/Long-Term Financial Goals

As you and your advisors assess your current situation, following items 1–4, this should be done with an eye toward both your short-term and long-term financial goals.

Now look at the items that are applicable toward your business.

Businesses

7. Current business and projection of income for that business.
8. Probability of projected business income.
9. Type of business.
10. Plan for proceeds from business and from saved taxes.

7. Current Business and Projection of Income of That Business

What is the type of business you have or propose? What is the current income? Is it passive or earned income? Do you have self-employment tax currently? Do you project losses in the business? Would these losses be useful in offsetting current other income you have? Does the business provide tax credits? Will these be more useful for you or for the business?

In this step, compare the income you make from your business and its impact on your personal return. A few examples follow:

High Personal Income, High Business Income: The best structure, based on this step alone, could be a C corporation that allows you to pay tax using a separate tax rate structure. You may also look for ways to form additional C corporations, careful to avoid the controlled group status (Chapter 25). In this way, you can take advantage of multiple tax rates for each entity. It is also true that at the high income level, the tax-free benefits available only through a C corporation become especially important.

High Personal Income, Initial Business Losses: The best structure, based on this part of the analysis alone, could be an S corporation, which will allow the initial business losses to flow directly to your personal return, reducing the tax you pay on your personal level.

8. Probability of Projected Business Income

This may be the toughest question for you to objectively answer. But it is crucially important. You need to assess the probability of your business income projections. I recommend that clients do a worst-case, medium-case, and best-case projection of income. Then, assess a reasonable probability to the outcome. Typically, when you examine, in this much detail, the potential pitfalls of your business, you will actually receive much higher and better results. You have looked at the problems square on and many times that alone is your best defense against them. If you aren't sure of the probability, talk to experts in your field and have them assess your probability. The fact is that we all have great expectations in the beginning of any venture, or else we wouldn't even attempt it. And the fact also is that most businesses fail in the first three years. So, what is the realistic projection for your business?

9. Type of Business

There are some types of business that can be problematic if performed within a C corporation structure. Specifically, these are: 1) qualified personal service corporations; 2) real estate investments; and 3) investment companies.

If you have a concern that the income might make your corporation a qualified personal service corporation, you may decide to form an S corporation instead a C corporation. See Chapter 26 on the definition of a qualified personal service corporation and ways to overcome that potential problem first. If you provide services in the fields of architecture, engineering, health, law, accounting, actuarial sciences, the performing arts, or consulting, make sure you read Chapter 26.

You might also have a concern that the income would be considered a personal holding company. In that case, review Chapter 27. Typically the income that comes from a personal holding company, such as interest and dividends, can be attributed to appreciating assets. I never recommend that any potentially appreciating asset be put inside either a C corporation or an S corporation. If you have, or plan to have, appreciating assets such as stocks or real estate, the best structure might be a limited partnership with a corporation as partner.

Does your business fall within any of these categories?

10. Plan for Proceeds from Business and from Saved Taxes

What do you intend to do with the proceeds of your business? This can be an important element of your tax plan. It is much easier to take money out of an S corporation or partnership, for example, than a C corporation. The ease of distribution from these flow-through entities needs to be weighed against potential savings from the C corporation. Chapter 21, "Getting Your Money Out of a C Corporation," will deal specifically with some ways to set up a C corporation to do this. However, it remains much easier to withdraw money from the other entities. With all elements of a tax plan, you must determine the cost/benefit analysis. Does the potential benefit of tax savings outweigh the potential cost of the business structure?

You can then move on to evaluate the next two sections after you have analyzed the answers to the above questions, and determined the potential tax liability you really have and will have, based on the future projections of income, increased deductions from discovering your hidden business deductions, and making use of your dependents' lower tax rates.

SUMMARY

Tax planning factors. The six areas associated with tax planning are: 1) current taxable income, 2) source of current income and future projections of that income, 3) hidden business deductions, 4) dependents that can be employed (other entities), 5) short-term financial goals, and 6) long-term financial goals.

Current taxable income. The good tax plan will take into account current taxable income from all sources. You and your advisors will want to take into account the amount and impact of the business income on your personal tax return to determine if and how you want the business income to come to you.

Source of current income and future projections of that income. Examine the characterization of your income and losses. You are looking for previously lost deductions from passive and investment activities. The tax plan will look for ways to maximize any previously lost deductions.

Hidden business deductions. Look for deductions you may already have that could be business deductions.

Dependents that can be employed (other entities). I have found employing dependents to be the single most underutilized aspect of tax planning for prospective clients. In other words, they are not taking full advantage of this very simple tax-planning technique.

Short-term and long-term financial goals. The most important aspect of your financial and tax plan should be what your own personal goals are. I have seen many different goals, just as there are many different types of people. Don't assume that your advisors will know what you want. Make sure you communicate clearly what it is *you* want!

Business tax planning. There are four aspects to consider regarding your business income in your tax plan. The four aspects are 1) current business and projection of income of that business, 2) probability of projected business income, 3) type of business, and 4) plan for proceeds from business and from saved taxes.

Current business and projection of income of that business. Consider the amount and type of income you anticipate from your business. You will want to project that income so you can see what realistic trends will be for the income.

Probability of projected business income. After you have done your projections, consider what the realistic projections might be. This isn't "borrowing trouble"; instead, you are making intelligent plans for all eventualities.

Type of business. Before you finalize any plans for the choice of business structure, you will want to consider if your business would be under one of the potential C corporation problems. These are 1) qualified personal service corporations, 2) real estate investments, and 3) investment companies. In most cases, these should not be in the C corporation form.

Plans for proceeds from business and from saved taxes. This is a serious question, but probably one of the most fun. What do you plan to do with all the money you make?

Chapter 13

The Right Business Structure for Money In and Money Out

Money Goes In and Comes Out

The next two factors to consider are how the money goes into the business and how it will come out. These are two of the sixteen business structure factors:

11. Plans for business continuation—exit strategies.
12. Funding needs for the business.

Exit Strategies

When you plan for your business, this is one case where you truly begin with the end in mind. What do you want from the business? Do you want it to continue for your family to run someday? Are you looking for a short-term business to build other assets and then close the business? Do you want to sell the business? If you do sell, what would the likely value be? Would you sell stock through an IPO (initial public offering), to a competitor, to a larger company, or others? What would they be looking for? Or do you want to set up a true business that gives you cash flow for an extended period with little or no involvement by you?

There are many factors to consider as a result of the above questions. If you are running a business to create cash flow for other interests and plan to then close down the initial business at some point, you can probably move on from this section. But if you plan to sell the business or set it up to run a long time, then a great deal of thought needs to be given to possible tax and business structure considerations.

Following are some issues to consider if you plan to sell. Remember that these are just some of the possible factors that would go into making your decision. More than any other section of tax planning, this one needs the advice of a qualified expert and one experienced in the outcome you desire.

Selling a Business—Asset Sale vs. Sale of Stock

The issue of how you will sell, or distribute, assets, is primarily an issue within an S corporation or a C corporation. Partnerships can distribute assets at "basis." In other words, they can transfer out to partners (in partnerships) at the amount shown on the books, so there is no tax impact. This is why these types of structures are recommended for owning real estate or other appreciating assets. I cannot think of a single instance in which you would want to own real estate directly in your corporation. Of course, your corporation can be a partner in a partnership or your corporation can "pay for" real estate by paying rent that covers the payment for real estate owned by the partnership.

> Key: Hold real estate within a limited partnership. The corporation can pay for these by loans to the LP, by paying rent, or by being a partner in the LP.

If your plan includes the sale of your business, consider how that sale will occur. Will you sell the assets of the business (most likely) or sell to or merge stock into a larger company? In general, small companies that are purchased by someone wanting to run your company as it has been will want to buy the assets of the company. Larger companies are more likely to want to buy the stock, or to exchange some of their stock for yours.

If you have a C corporation and sell the stock, there can be great benefits through the 50 percent capital gain exclusion (shown below), and also the possibility of double taxation through liquidating dividends. The first is a good thing! The second is something you will need to plan to avoid. In Chapter 24, we will discuss strategies to eliminate double taxation. The answer is to plan ahead with a good strategy.

Small Business Capital Gain Exclusion—Selling Stock

A shareholder can exclude up to 50 percent of income from the gain or exchange of qualified small business stock—referred to as Section 1202 stock—that has been held for more than five years. The excluded gain is limited to the greater of $10 million or ten times the taxpayer's basis in stock. Stock must be issued after August 10, 1993, and have been acquired at original issue in exchange for money, property, or services. The corporation must have at least 80 percent of assets used in a qualified field. Businesses related to health, law, engineering, architecture, farming, insurance, financing, and hospitality are specifically excluded from the list of qualified fields.

> Key: To receive the small business capital gain exclusion, you must hold the stock five years or more, gain is limited by the greater of ten times your basis or $10 million, and the company must have been engaged in a qualified field.

Loss on Sale—Section 1244

What if the business doesn't turn out to be everything you want? If you have a corporation (either S corporation or C corporation), the amount of basis in stock that you have is now considered worthless. Normally, you are limited to $3,000 per year in capital losses that exceed capital gains. There is a way around this trap, if you plan ahead. If the business qualifies as a Section 1244 company, then you could take the loss against ordinary income. Well-drafted corporate documents should include a statement that the company is intended to be a Code Section 1244 company. To qualify, the company must have received less than $1 million in capital contributions.

In other words, a few simple lines in the initial documents, or in your minutes, will allow you the ability to take up to $75,000 per year in current-year losses in case your business venture fails.

Combine Sections 1202 and 1244

The best plan for a business that is anticipated to be held for over five years and then sold through a stock sale for a high price would be to set it up as a Section 1202 and 1244 qualified company. Then, if your plan succeeds, you will be able to legally avoid a tremendous amount of tax. And if your plan does not succeed, you will be able to take a substantial loss now against your current income. Note that a Section 1202 company must be a C corporation.

IPO—Initial Public Offering

Perhaps your plan is to take your company public. There are many different strategies you might take. In general, only a C corporation can be taken public by selling stock to the outside public. There are different ways to do this: 1) by selling the stock to accredited investors; 2) by selling shares in your company on U.S. stock exchanges; or 3) by selling shares in your company on another country's stock exchanges. There are separate requirements for each of the above options. Therefore, much forethought, along with specialists advising you, would be a recommended course of action.

One plan is to begin a company using an S corporation. Generally, a company will lose money in the first few years of existence. An S corporation allows you to take that loss against other income on your tax return. When the company begins to make money, or if you plan to take the company public, you can either change the status to a C corporation or dissolve the S corporation and begin a new C corporation.

Sometimes companies will buy an existing C corporation to merge their company into, in order to immediately begin trading.

As you can see, there are many ways to accomplish the goals you have. Set your goals, so you know where you are going!

ESOP—Employee Stock Ownership Plan

Another exit strategy can be to set up an ESOP (employee stock ownership plan), so that your employees buy the company from you. If this is your plan, you will again be selling stock, not assets, and most likely the employees will receive a loan from a financing institution in order to purchase the business. You will most likely want to have your business in the form of a C corporation.

Money Coming In

How will you fund the company? Initially, you will likely be putting your own money into the company. This can be done in one of two ways: 1) capital contribution; and 2) loan to the company. Additionally, you may have some resources (such as equipment and furniture) that you contribute into the company initially. These resources, the cash, and other assets, all need to be repaid in some form back to you by the corporation.

In general, most people try to contribute as little as possible in the form of capital contributions (i.e., stock), and maximize the amount of loans in the corporation. This way, there is a note payable booked on the corporation's records for the shareholder. The note can pay interest—creating portfolio income—to the recipient. It is a deduction for the corporation. This is one way that a corporation can change the character of income—by changing the earned income into portfolio income.

The IRS has challenged the undercapitalization of companies where the amount paid for stock is not reasonable for the company. The exact amount that is paid for the stock is something that you will need to discuss with your own advisor. You will want to consider what the worth of the company is. If you have a business that is providing income streams with little or no work from you, then it might be worth as much as eight to ten times the projected net income. On the other hand, if it is a risky beginning venture, the value might be simply cents per share, like a penny stock would be. Part of the assessment process in determining how much the capital stock you own is worth is trying to determine a reasonable value for it initially.

In some cases, you may not want to set up the majority of your funding in the form of a note payable. If you determine that you might want to exercise the small business exclusion under Section 1202 (see earlier in this chapter), for example, you would want to have a higher value in the common stock.

Potential Corporate Pitfall—Taxable Start-Up

Frequently, when you first begin your new corporation, you will find that you "contribute" time and property (furniture, computer equipment, and such) into the new venture. This reality of business could end up creating additional tax if you put your time and property into the new corporation unwittingly.

When there is an exchange for value going into a corporation (either S corporation or C corporation), you could run the risk of taxable gain without even knowing it. If you exchange services for stock, for example, and you have set a value on the stock already—then the stock received for services is taxable income to you. In other words, if you sold 1,000 shares of stock for $10,000 and then exchanged your services for an equal amount—1,000 shares—you have had $10,000 in attributed income. At this point, you have shares in a brand-new start-up company that has no ability to pay but at the same time have $10,000 you must pay personal income tax on! This can be a "buyer beware" if you put a company together and exchange your sweat equity for ownership.

There is some relief from this tax consequence, though, when property is contributed into a corporation. There are four available methods for transferring property to a corporation. These are:

1. Completely tax-free exchange. If you meet the requirements of this code section, you will be able to transfer property to a corporation solely in exchange for the stock of that corporation.

2. A partially tax-free transaction. In this case, you transfer property in exchange for the stock plus you receive other property.

3. A sales exchange. In this case, you sell the property to the corporation in a transaction completely independent of the actual formation of the corporation.

4. A lease. You would still have ownership of the property and would lease it to the corporation.

Potential Corporate Solution to a Taxable Start-Up

The IRS provides a solution to this potential taxable situation if you can meet the requirements of Section 351. This section provides that no gain or loss is recognized on the transfer of property by one or more persons to a corporation in exchange solely for stock in such corporation if, immediately after the exchange, the transferors control the corporation.

> Key: Define your initial sweat equity as know-how or trade secrets to avoid the tax on services that are exchanged.

"Property" is defined as real and personal property and includes cash, stocks and bonds, accounts receivable, installment obligations, treasury stock, leasehold improvements, patents, trade secrets, and know-how.

A corporation is considered "controlled" when the persons transferring property to the corporation own at least 80 percent of the voting power of all voting stock and 80 percent of the shares of all other classes immediately after the exchange is completed.

The exceptions of Section 351 are possible to be met, if properly addressed. A quick checklist for determining if the major requirements have been met follows at the end of the chapter. This checklist is designed to let you know if you are in the correct ballpark for passing the test. It should not be viewed as a substitute for good tax strategy advice.

Exit Strategy Considerations

There are two different considerations in determining how much you want to have in stock. These are determined based on your exit strategy. As noted above, there can be a significant reduction (50 percent!) in capital gains tax due upon sale in the case of small business stock sales. These discounts are limited to a multiple of the amount of your basis in the stock. In this case, you would want as much as possible shown as the value in the stock.

On the other hand, if you plan on continuing the business with a turnkey approach (business runs itself), then you would want to maximize the amount of loans to take advantage of the change in character of income available (changing the earned income into portfolio income). So, in this case, you would want as little as possible shown as the value in the stock.

Only S corporations and C corporations have capital stock. And only a C corporation has the distinction of being a separate taxing structure. If you form a partnership, then you have partner accounts and the issues of capital versus loans for initial funding are less significant. Of course, these entities do not have the ability to change the character of income or have the small business capital gains reduction.

Assets for a Note

You might want to contribute assets at fair market value in exchange for a note. This is especially true when you need to capitalize the new corporation with money. In this scenario, the corporation will promise to pay you back. That promise should be recorded both in the corporate minutes and in a properly executed note signed by a corporate officer. The note must have a reasonable interest rate. As the corporation pays the money back to the individual owner, there will also be interest paid on the note. This is one way in which a corporation can change the character of earned money (received by the corporation) into portfolio income (paper asset earning money) paid to you.

Here are a couple of guidelines that help ensure the notes are correctly set up:

1. Draw up a formal note and pay the interest when due. Be sure that the note has a maturity date.

2. Make sure that the note specifies at least the minimum rate required by the IRS.

3. Loan only enough funds to pay for the immediate needs of the corporation, and make it an amount that obviously can be paid back soon.

You might also want to own intellectual property within a separate business structure, thus employing the philosophy of not wanting to put all your eggs in one basket. Intellectual property might include patented or copyrighted information, as well as systems that you could charge rights or royalties for. There can be two significant reasons for doing this: 1) You move a valuable commodity away from the business and set it up for future franchising (more income streams). And: 2) The payments for the use of the intellectual property will be an expense to the operating corporation and income to the other company. When set up correctly, this can allow you to take advantage of multiple tax rates as discussed in Chapters 10, 22, and 29. This can also be an effective way to move income into a Nevada corporation. This method is discussed in more detail in Chapter 22.

In and Out of Partnerships

Most of this chapter has been devoted to the intricacies of corporate tax law. That is because the rules for partnerships are much easier in this area. Property can be distributed, for example, at basis to the owning partnerships without the need to deal with built-in appreciation that could occur. The same kind of distribution from a corporation to a shareholder must be done at fair market value.

SUMMARY

Money in and out. The next two of the sixteen business structure factors are 1) plans for business continuation—exit strategies—and 2) funding needs for the business.

Exit strategies. There are many different types of exit strategies to consider. The most common are 1) sell, 2) pass on to a family member, and 3) close the business down. The most lucrative may be to view your business as an asset that you will sell or continue on in the family.

Selling your business. You will want to determine what the most probable type of sale your business would have. A sale of business can take one of two forms—the sale of the assets or the sale of the stock of the business (if operated as a corporation). Also, consider who the potential buyer would be. It could be the employees, outside stockholders (through a public offering), or other company. Once you have determined your ultimate goal, you can set up your business to facilitate that sale by making it as attractive as possible to the potential buyers. Plus, you can set up your initial business structure to make that sale in the most tax-advantaged way.

Funding your business. At this step, determine how you are most likely to fund the company. You will need to plan for the source—whether they are loans, investments, or your own money. When you put money in the company, you will also need to decide whether it should be in the form of a loan to the company or a stock purchase.

Potential start-up problem. Be aware of a hidden tax consequence when you contribute time and property into your new start-up. Done correctly, this contribution can be considered a tax-free Section 351 contribution. Done incorrectly and this contribution could create tax for you!

Section 351 Exemption from Tax for Contribution into a New Corporation

Warning! The contribution of property into your new corporation could be considered taxable unless you can meet the exceptions under Code Section 351. This checklist walks you through the major requirements of this section.

	Yes	No
1. Was there an actual transfer of property?	____	____
2. Was the property transferred by one or more persons?	____	____
3. Were the transferors in control of the corporation immediately after the transfer?	____	____
4. Was the exchange solely for stock in the corporation?	____	____
5. Was the stock issued in proportion to the relative fair market value of the assets transferred?	____	____
6. Did the basis of the assets transferred exceed the liabilities assumed?	____	____
7. Did the corporation have a true business purpose for assuming the liabilities?	____	____

If you answered all of the above questions as yes, the transaction is tax-free. If your answer to any of the questions is no, there still may be a way to make part of the transaction tax-free. Do not take this lightly! There could be hidden tax in the most innocent of actions.

Chapter 14

The Right Business Structure for Asset Protection

Sue-Happy

Americans today are the most litigious people that have ever existed on the planet. As a culture, we seem to always be on the lookout for someone to blame for every mistake or unfortunate circumstance. The result is increasingly larger settlements awarded by juries. Successful people, aware of the danger of the bull's-eye on their back, will pay settlements to avoid jury trials, even if the person suing them has no possible grounds.

There is a better way. If you are concerned about lawsuits, you can set up your businesses and other investments to protect them.

Source of Danger

If the danger of a lawsuit comes about as a result of something related to the business, then a properly administrated corporation can protect you from that risk. If the danger comes about as a result of something from you personally, then a properly maintained limited partnership will protect your investments.

DANGER FROM YOUR BUSINESS

An S corporation, C corporation, and a limited liability company, when properly administered, have a corporate veil. That means that there is a "veil" between the risk that might come about as a result of daily business and your personal assets. For example, if your delivery driver hits someone while running errands for your business, the risk from that accident will be contained within the business. To protect against this risk, you can move the ownership of all tangible assets—such as personal property used in the business—into another business structure. This can also serve for tax planning as you create leasing income into another business structure and reduce earned income.

DANGER FROM YOU

In some cases, you may be concerned about danger that might result from you or your family. The public perception of you and your wealth can be quite distorted if you own a business or are a professional person. Having owned my own businesses for over twenty-five years, I am always amazed at how much non–business owners will overestimate the income and wealth generated by businesses. If you currently own your own business, I am sure you can agree that there have been lean years and times when you might not have known if you could pay the bills. Yet the public rarely sees that side of business ownership, and instead often views you as the pot of gold at the end of the rainbow.

I have had clients sued when their horse kicked another horse, six months after a supposed fall at an apartment building, and when someone stumbled over a sidewalk crack in front of their house. If you have a concern about liability that might result from your personal life, there is something that you can do to protect your assets.

A limited partnership or limited liability company can protect you against these suits. It should be noted that LLCs are not uniformly accepted among states and you should consult an expert in your state regarding the specifics of LLCs in your area.

How a Limited Partnership Works

An owner of a limited partnership share really does not have any say in the running of the partnership. By definition, a limited partner is not involved in the management. That function falls to the general partner. The general partner determines when and if distributions are made to the limited partner. In real life, if your personal assets are held within a limited partnership, of which you are merely a limited partner, you have no control over the distributions. If you were sued and a judgment was lodged against you, the most that the opposing side could receive would be a charging order. That means that the other side would stand in your place as a limited partner. Assuming the general partner is on your side, the other guy would know that distributions would not easily be forthcoming. Good attorneys know that. If they see a possible defendant who holds their assets in a limited partnership, they are much more likely to settle for cents on the dollar.

General Partner

When we discussed the asset protection available for your investments, note that we discussed how the limited partner was protected. The general partner has full liability. In this case, since the risk comes potentially from the business or investment, then the protection would come about by having a corporation (either S corporation or C corporation) serve as the general partner.

Other Ideas for Protection

Your mother might have told you not to put all your eggs in one basket. If you have businesses that could create liability, such as commercial buildings or apartments, you may want to separate these assets. In other words, if you own three apartment buildings, you might want to separate the three buildings into three separate limited partnerships to limit exposure. That way, if a lawsuit results from one of the buildings, they would not at all be at risk.

Can Insurance Provide the Protection?

Some clients prefer to carry large balances of umbrella policy insurance. These policies generally have limits of $1 million to $5 million. If you assess your risk as a slight, have a high level or risk tolerance, and there are no other reasons (such as tax savings) to have other business structures, it may be that an insurance policy is the best answer for you. Again, don't do anything without an overall plan and without examining the proposed plan using a cost/benefit analysis.

Assess Your Own Risk and Your Own Risk Tolerance

Before completing this section, take a moment and realistically assess your own risk potential. Typically, the more visible you are, the more at risk you are for lawsuits. Do you live in an upper-income neighborhood? Are you publicly visible? Are you in a profession that has a public perception of wealth—such as doctor or lawyer? If you answer yes to most of these questions, then you are more likely to be a target.

My experience has been that people tend to overestimate their risk tolerance. The best indication is your past experiences. Do you worry about loss? Do you worry about lost opportunities? If concern about loss keeps you up at night, then consider adding the extra protection of limited partnerships to contain risk that might come from your personal life. In almost all cases, I recommend that you have some sort of business structure—S corporation, C corporation, limited partnership, or limited liability company—for your business. These will be used both for tax advantage and for asset protection.

SUMMARY

Determine source of risk. The risk can come from two different directions. One is from you and your family's actions that would put your business and investments at risk. Some people lead more high-exposure and higher-risk lives—such as those in the public eye or professions like doctors. Other actions could be the inadvertent injury of another person through actions by you. Risk could also come from your business or investments themselves. For example, you might have an apartment building where a tenant is injured. There could then be danger from that investment toward your own personal assets.

Limited partnership for asset protection. A limited partnership can be used to protect the assets held within it from your personal actions. The limited partner is also protected from actions of the business. By definition, a limited partner can only have their personal investment at risk. A general partner would have risk from actions of the business.

Other sources of protection. Liability insurance can also provide protection; the policy would pay potential claims against you.

Assess your own risk and risk tolerance. Included at the end of this chapter is a test to help you determine your own risk tolerance. Most people overestimate their ability to tolerate risk, when in fact, the fear of risk is debilitating. By honestly assessing your own tolerance, you can take that into account in your own tax and asset protection planning.

ASSESS YOUR RISK TOLERANCE

The first part of this questionnaire, numbers 1–5, contains questions that are modeled after more traditional investment risk assessments. Although this test is not specifically designed to determine your risk tolerance for your investments, the way you approach investments is likely the way you approach a number of things in your life. The latter part of the test examines the psychological factors that determine how you approach risk. Together, the two parts of this questionnaire can provide an indicator of how comfortable you feel with decisions you make regarding tax planning, business strategy, and asset protection.

1. I would feel comfortable risking ——% of my investable money if the chance of doubling it was ——%:

    (a) 0% and 0%
    (b) 10% and 10%
    (c) 25% and 25%
    (d) 50% and 50%

2. What do you want your money to do for you?

    (a) Grow as fast as possible; current income is not important
    (b) Grow faster than inflation; produce some income
    (c) Grow slowly and provide a nice income
    (d) Preserve principal, no matter what

3. You have just heard that the stock market fell by 10 percent today. Your reaction is to:

    (a) Consider reducing the proportion of your portfolio that is invested in equities
    (b) Be concerned and continue to monitor the market
    (c) Not to worry because the market is likely to go up again at some time in the future

4. Which of the following best describes how you evaluate the performance of your investments?

    (a) My greatest concern is this quarter's performance.
    (b) The past twelve months are the most important to me.
    (c) I look at the performance over several years to help form an opinion about an investment's attractiveness.

5. What is the worst one-year performance you would tolerate for your portfolio?

    (a) –12%
    (b) –8%

(c) –4%

(d) Any loss is unacceptable to me.

Choose the response that most accurately reflects your feelings or behavior:

6. I generally prefer to stay in a familiar situation, rather than take a chance on a new situation.

    (a) Exactly like me

    (b) Somewhat like me

    (c) Not very much like me

    (d) Not at all like me

7. I am usually the one who gives in when my plans conflict with the plans of those around me.

    (a) Exactly like me

    (b) Somewhat like me

    (c) Not very much like me

    (d) Not at all like me

8. I often put off making financial decisions because I am afraid of making a mistake.

    (a) Exactly like me

    (b) Somewhat like me

    (c) Not very much like me

    (d) Not at all like me

9. I am optimistic about what the future holds for the economy.

    (a) Exactly like me

    (b) Somewhat like me

    (c) Not very much like me

    (d) Not at all like me

10. My lack of knowledge about investments keeps me from becoming more involved in financial planning activities.

    (a) Exactly like me

    (b) Somewhat like me

    (c) Not very much like me

    (d) Not at all like me

11. I often feel that I don't have enough control over the direction my life is taking.

    (a) Exactly like me

    (b) Somewhat like me

    (c) Not very much like me
    (d) Not at all like me

12. I would feel very embarrassed if anyone found out I made a major investment mistake.

    (a) Exactly like me
    (b) Somewhat like me
    (c) Not very much like me
    (d) Not at all like me

SCORING THE TEST:

For questions 1, 3, 4, 6, 7, 8, 10, 11, and 12 give yourself a 1 for every a, 2 for every b, 3 for every c, and 4 for every d.

For questions 2, 5, and 9 give yourself a 1 for every d, 2 for every c, 3 for every b, and 4 for every a.

12–23: You have a lower risk tolerance. Many times this is due to circumstances you might not even be aware of that are affecting you. Continue to get more information to correctly understand where real and imaginary risk occurs. Look for ways to reduce risk and contain the part that makes you uncomfortable.

24–36: You have a moderate risk tolerance. You can tolerate risk when you have a reasonable expectation that you will receive gain from taking the risk. Carefully assess possible gain and weigh it against the loss you might experience. This range is within the moderate category—you may be more comfortable with risk than the average person, but you will likely be the person who always wants information before you move.

37–48: You have a high tolerance for risk. Not only do you not mind taking risks, you get bored if you don't have a certain risk factor in everything you do. You are happiest when there is a potential for all or nothing. You will be able to handle risk in your financial life, but make sure you have done adequate homework to support your decisions. Don't jump in just because something sounds exciting.

Chapter 15

How to Identify Your Best Business Structure

What Is the Best Business Structure?

First, determine what your true taxable income will be from your businesses. Take into account the same things that Ted and Ellen did to evaluate their current status. Likely, your taxable income will be greatly reduced after you go through the hidden business deductions. Then, identify dependents that you can legitimately employ to spread the income around. After you have employed these techniques, move on to the next steps.

Where Are You?

1. Your current taxable income.
2. Source of current income and future projections of that income.
3. Hidden business deductions.
4. Dependents that can be employed (other entities).
5. Short-term financial goals.
6. Long-term financial goals.

Answer the following questions and review them with your personal tax strategist. You will want to select the best structure for your business in light of asset protection, taxable income (when added to your other sources of income), plans for income from the business, funding requirements, and your exit strategies. You will likely find that the best structure for some of your needs will not be what is best in meeting other needs. For example, the best plan for tax planning might not be the best plan for your funding requirements. The answer is to weigh the relative strengths and weaknesses of your plan. You are the only one who can assign the importance of the various items. How serious are you about your business? How realistic is your plan? What is the best, worst, and most likely case for your projected business plan?

Where Are Your Businesses?

7. Current business and projection of income of that business.
8. Probability of projected business income.
9. Type of business.
10. Plan for proceeds from business and from tax savings.
11. Plans for business continuation—exit strategies.
12. Funding needs for the business.

Asset Protection

13. Your likely exposure to risk from personal acts.
14. Your tolerance to risk.
15. Exposure to risk from the business.
16. Your net worth and projections of net worth.

Cost/Benefit Analysis

After you have determined the optimum business structure plan, calculate the amount of tax savings that it will generate. You will likely need some help doing this calculation—insist that your advisor do it. You will be comparing the amount of savings with the potential benefit. Some of the benefit, obviously, does not have an easily assessable value—such as the asset protection of a plan. But you want to make the determination with eyes wide open as to what the true cost is.

Determining Cost

There will be an initial and an ongoing cost to the business structure. Generally, there is a fee to set up a corporation, partnership, or limited liability company charged by your attorney. Additionally there will be fees charged by the state in which the entity is formed, generally on an annual basis. Also, there will be bookkeeping and tax preparation costs on an ongoing basis. Usually, the initial setup and consultation will be higher than the ongoing cost.

If you are considering setting up a corporation outside of your home state, such as in Nevada, make sure you consider all costs. It is important to weigh the cost/benefit of setting up a Nevada corporation, prior to taking advantage of the special provisions of Nevada law, including no state income tax.

Cost/Benefit

Now compare the initial and ongoing cost for your new business structures compared to the tax benefit you will gain. Is this a reasonable return on the amount invested? Are there other factors to consider, such as correcting past errors in structures or providing asset protection, that will influence your decision?

THE SIXTEEN FACTORS FOR BUSINESS STRUCTURE SETUP

Where Are You?

1. Your current taxable income (Line XX from Form 1040): _____

   Marginal tax rate: _____

2. Source of your current income and future projections of that income:

   % Earned Income _____% Passive Income _____% Portfolio Income _____

   Unused passive losses (annually): _____

   Unused investment expenses (annually): _____

3. Hidden business deductions: _____

   Amount of additional business deductions (after review of Chapter 9 and Appendix B):

   _____

   _____

   _____

   _____

   TOTAL   _____

Potential C corporation benefits (stated as annual total):

   Health insurance   _____

   Disability insurance   _____

   Annual medical checkup   _____

   Personal liability insurance _____

   Free housing/meals   _____

   Uniforms and small tools   _____

   Medical reimbursement   _____

   Recreation/health facility   _____

   Tuition reimbursement   _____

Child care   _____

Cost of $50,000 term insurance   _____

Qualified plan award   _____

Nonqualified plan award   _____

         TOTAL   _____

4. Dependents that can be employed (other entities):

   Name, age, job description, annual salary.

   _____

   _____

5. Short-term financial goals:

   _____

   _____

6. Long-term financial goals:

   _____

   _____

Recap:

(1) Taxable income   _____

Less: (3) Total hidden business deductions   (_____)

(4) Dependent salary   (_____)

New taxable total   _____

New marginal tax rate   _____

Total possible corporate benefits   _____

Reviewing 1–6 above, how important is:
(1 = least, 5 = most)

Reducing personal taxable income:	1	2	3	4	5
Changing character of income:	1	2	3	4	5
Investment of income for growth:	1	2	3	4	5
Investment of income for cash flow:	1	2	3	4	5

Businesses

7. Current business income and projection of income of that business:

   Current taxable business income (subtract hidden business deductions from total): _____

   Projected taxable business income for:

   One year from now: _____

   Two years from now: _____

   Three years from now: _____

8. Probability of projected business income: _____

9. Type of business: _____

10. Plan for proceeds from business and from saved taxes:

    _____

11. Plans for business continuation—exit strategies:

    What is your exit strategy for the business?

12. Funding needs for the business:

    Amount needed for funding and growth—when needed:

    _____

    _____

Reviewing 7–12 above, how important are the following:
(1 = least, 5 = most)

Current importance of business income not adding to personal:	1	2	3	4	5
Future importance of business income not adding to personal:	1	2	3	4	5
Likelihood of investors:	1	2	3	4	5
Necessity of personal funding:	1	2	3	4	5
Level of cash influx needed:	1	2	3	4	5
Likelihood of sale of business assets:	1	2	3	4	5
Likelihood of sale of stock of business:	1	2	3	4	5
Likelihood of public offering:	1	2	3	4	5
Real estate ownership in business:	Yes—1	No—2			
Unresolved personal service issue:	Yes—1	No—2			
Unresolved personal holding company:	Yes—1	No—2			

Asset Protection

13. Your likely exposure to risk from personal acts:

    Publically visible?   _____

    High-risk?   _____

14. Your risk tolerance:

    Your level of risk tolerance: 1   2   3   4   5

15. Exposure to risk from the business:

    How high is the exposure to risk from your business? _____

16. Your net worth and projections of net worth:

    What is your current net worth level?   _____

    Do you anticipate it significantly increasing?   _____

Review of 13–16 above:
(1 = least, 5 = most)

Level of risk from your personal acts:	1	2	3	4	5
Your risk tolerance:	1	2	3	4	5
Level of risk from business acts:	1	2	3	4	5
Level of net worth:	1	2	3	4	5

Note: Review this part with your tax advisor. You may have discovered as you went through the exercises in Chapters 11–15 that the structure that is best for tax savings is not the best for asset protection or that the structure that is best for your exit strategy is not the best for current taxes. Through the exercise in this chapter, you have hopefully pinpointed which parts are most important for your unique circumstances, needs, goals, and dreams.

Part IV

Tax Planning E-T-C

Chapter 16

Tax Planning E-T-C

E-T-C

"Finally, I want to talk about E-T-C," I said to Ted and Ellen. "It's a little bit of an accountant's joke—we've talked about most everything and now we'll talk about etc." I thought the joke was funnier than they did. Oh well.

There are three parts to E-T-C:

- E—Entity
- T—Timing
- C—Characterization

Entity

Since the U.S. has a graduated tax schedule per taxing entity, anytime you can employ income-splitting techniques to move income from one rate schedule to another, you are, in fact, moving from a higher rate to a lower rate. That makes a lot of sense!

The most common taxing entities are: you personally, your children, a C corporation, your pension plans, and whole life insurance.

Timing

Earlier we discussed the Small Change Principle and showed how a little bit of change, over time, can create big differences. The principle is probably best known when it comes to money. There is a time value to money. In other words, a dollar today is worth more than a dollar tomorrow. That can be one of the most important reasons to have a C corporation for your business. The C corporation is the only business structure currently allowed to have a business year end that is not a calendar year end. All other business structures—partnerships and S corporations (except in some unique situations)—require a calendar year end. You will learn in Chapter 18 how important that could be.

Characterization

In Chapter 8, "Income," we discussed the three types of income. In Chapter 19, "Characterization," you will discover specific ways that you can change the characterization of income. This is important because it will allow you to take full advantage of any portfolio expenses or passive losses that you might have.

Corporation E-T-C

Although we will discuss some different solutions other than a C corporation to make full use of E-T-C, the C corporation remains the best tool for its utilization. It is the concept of being a separate taxable entity that makes the C corporation so different from the others, and allows the magic of E-T-C (*En*tity, *T*iming and *C*haracterization) to work for you. The next three chapters will go into each of these concepts.

As you go through the reasons why E-T-C is so useful in tax planning, you will see that other structures can use some aspects of each. In fact, you might find a useful way to use E-T-C in a noncorporate way, but *only* a C corporation allows you to take advantage of all three tax saving strategies.

Chapter 17

Entity Selection

Corporate E for Entity—Back to Ted and Ellen

"You've mentioned this corporate E-T-C before," said Ellen. "I'm glad we're finally going to talk about it. I know that having a corporation is a good thing because it provides E-T-C, but I'm not sure what E-T-C is!"

"We're going to go through each of the sections of E-T-C separately," I told her. "First, let's talk about the E, which stands for entity.

"In this case, entity refers to a separate taxing structure. We discussed how a corporation was considered a legal person. Well, there are other taxing persons. It's necessary to identify what those are in each individual's situation, because it then allows you to do something called income splitting. Before I get too carried away with definitions, though, let's look at what the concept of income splitting really is."

Income Splitting

Income splitting allows you to move income from a higher tax bracket to a lower tax bracket. As we discussed earlier, the U.S. has a graduated tax system. Each level of income is taxed at a higher rate. Income splitting takes advantage of the graduated system, by moving income from a higher rate to a lower rate. For example, you can save $12,300 by simply moving $50,000 of income from the highest personal tax rate to the lowest corporate rate.

You can also move income from your personal taxing structure to your corporate taxing structure to your dependents (parents, children, siblings—anyone that you currently help support with after-tax dollars).

Employing Children

"One way that we've taken advantage of income splitting right away is by employing Josh and Sarah," said Ted. "We don't pay them a lot, but we do pay the going rate for office cleanup and computer support. Josh helps by keeping track of the computer updates. Sarah empties the office wastebaskets and, in general, provides help around the office. I'm paying her $6 an hour and Josh $15 an hour, which is how much I would have to pay someone else. But the thing I'm excited about is that Josh is getting very handy with the computer and Sarah is learning to be responsible. I'm looking forward to the day that Josh can help me with our Web page and with data entry. That's expensive to hire out."

"Ted, you're on the right track! The important thing is to make sure that you are paying Josh and Sarah a reasonable wage for what they are doing, that there are written job descriptions, and that they keep track of their hours. We've been able to move $5,000 to Josh and $3,000 to Sarah from your higher bracket to their lower tax brackets. After the standard deductions, Josh actually pays just a tiny bit of tax. Sarah doesn't pay any tax. You are saving a lot by taking advantage of income splitting. As Ellen's business takes off, she will be able to shelter that income from your higher bracket because of the way we have set up the C corporation. In fact, the concept of income splitting is a simple one that is frequently overlooked in tax planning. As long as you follow the guidelines, and the compensation is reasonable, there is no reason why you can't do it."

Looking for Income-Splitting Opportunities

One of the best ways to look for opportunities that you might have for income splitting with your business is to look where you are currently spending money. You might have dependent, or partially dependent, parents that you help support. Instead of paying for their expenses with after-tax dollars, pay them a legitimate salary for work they can perform. As long as you are moving the income from your higher tax bracket to their lower tax bracket, it makes a lot of tax savings sense to do so. And, in many cases, they may have no other income and so the income isn't even taxable.

Unfortunately, you can't practice income splitting with your wages from another company. The only way this system works is if you have a business and if your business is paying tax on income earned. You must first have a business making money in order to recognize tax savings from moving it to another person in a lower tax bracket.

Other Investment Structures

In some cases, other structures can be used for investments. For example, you might be familiar with pension plans such as 401(k) plans, SEPs, IRAs, and so forth. All of these allow for tax-deferred growth. There is actually a twofold benefit, in the right circumstances, to investing through these pension plans.

First, the contribution is tax-deductible in the year in which it is made. Even if the pension plan investments made no money at all, the theory is that the average American will make less money when they retire than they currently do. You are then moving income (via taking a deduction) from a higher current bracket to a future lower bracket. There are a couple of cautions regarding this strategy, however. You can never be sure what the tax brackets in the future might be. It could be that the tax rates have increased and you have either moved the money to a similar bracket, or even worse, moved it to a higher bracket. It also assumes that you will make less money in the future than you currently make. Many of my clients, like Ted and Ellen, are building assets that will generate passive income. This passive income will overtake their current earned income and will continue to increase as time works its magic on the investment.

There is a second benefit, though not often discussed, that outweighs the questionable benefit above. This is that as an asset increases in value, it is allowed to do so tax-deferred. This principle is the same as the Small Change Principle. If you don't pay tax on the increase each year, more of the investment is allowed to keep working. Given enough time, the difference between paying tax now and paying later adds up! It can be well worth the risk of a potentially higher tax bracket to make use of the tax deferral of income.

For example, if you put $2,000 per year into an investment that gives you 20 percent return and you are at the highest tax bracket, you will have a net amount at the end of twenty years, after the annual taxes, of $163,018. Now, if you put that same $2,000 per year into an investment that gives you 20 percent return and it is in a tax-deferred vehicle, you will have a total of $448,051 at the end of twenty years. Remember, you still have to pay taxes. If you still operated at the highest tax bracket, the net amount would be, after the taxes, $270,623. In other words, you will receive $107,605 more by deferring the taxes to the end. This is even though the tax rates are exactly the same!

Tax-Free

The above example is using a tax-deferred vehicle such as a pension plan. Tax-deferred means that there is tax due, but it is deferred, or put off, until some future date. As you have seen, the time value of the delayed tax can be huge.

It is also possible to have *tax-free* gains. There are primarily two different vehicles to use for this. One is by using a Roth IRA. This is a fairly new type of pension plan. Instead of getting a tax deduction when the contribution is made, you can take the money out at the end tax-free. The only challenge to setting up a Roth IRA is that you must have earned income, *plus* your income has to be below certain limits. Unfortunately, many of my clients make too much money to take advantage of a Roth IRA. However, many of them have been able to have their children set them up.

The ability of the Roth to grow tax-free is a significant benefit. For example, when Ted and Ellen's son, Josh, is a little older and drawing more salary, he can set up his own Roth account. Let's say that he is able to put $2,000 per year into his Roth account from age twelve to age twenty. If you assume 20 percent growth per year, at the age of retirement, if *he does nothing else,* he will have $83,808,020! And, that is tax-free!

That example might seem too much to grasp; a much more conservative return of 12 percent per year will get Josh $3,285,236 when he is sixty-two years old.

These are all examples of the time value of money. When you combine that concept with the ability to take that growth tax-free, the results are staggering.

The Roth IRA cannot invest in an active business, but it can hold a limited partnership interest. One tax-planning technique is to set up a limited partnership for investments such as real estate and allow the Roth IRA to hold the limited partnership share. That means that the income that flows through from the partnership to the Roth's interest is tax-free. Once the Roth's owner is age fifty-nine and a half or older (and the transferred assets into the Roth have been there for at least five years), the distributions can come out with no tax. That means the investment can continue to make money, and all income comes out with no tax.

Life Insurance

Another way for investments to grow tax-free is through the use of permanent life insurance. The cash value of the life insurance, which can grow at a good return with the advent of variable life insurance products, comes out tax-free. You can take out the cash value by borrowing against the amount held in the account. Those loans are not taxable. Life insurance investments are dictated by the various life insurance companies, so it isn't quite as easy to control the investments as it is with a Roth IRA. The main advantage for high-income clients is that there are no income restrictions for life insurance. Basically, anyone can buy such a policy.

Entities

Income splitting can be set up to: 1) move income from high rates to lower rates; 2) delay tax through deferred taxes in a pension plan; or 3) avoid tax completely through tax-free entities.

The C corporation is one of the key tools for tax planning. It works best in conjunction with other structures and, with the additional benefits they provide, can give you tremendous results.

SUMMARY

Entity. Your business can move income from your personal tax return in two ways: 1) as a deduction through the income-splitting method, and 2) through separate taxing structures.

Income splitting. You can utilize income-splitting techniques by moving income from your high bracket to other lower brackets. This can be done by employing dependents (children and other dependent relatives) who by performing legitimate jobs can draw salaries. This is a deduction from the business income and is often tax-free to the recipient (income limits set each year by the IRS). If the tax-free amount is exceeded, it still is generally beneficial, as taxpayers can take income from a higher tax bracket and move it to a lower bracket.

Roth IRA. There are limitations based on the individual's income regarding who can contribute to a Roth IRA. But for those who qualify (income below a certain level and possessing some earned income), the Roth IRA is a useful plan. The Roth grows tax-free and can invest in stocks, bonds, and mutual funds, as well as be a partner in a limited partnership.

Life insurance. A permanent life insurance policy has a cash value that is also allowed to build up tax-free. The cash value cannot be invested quite as easily as the Roth, but there are no limitations based on the individual's income.

C corporation. A C corporation is also a separate entity for taxing purposes. It is defined as a legal person under the law and is taxed under its own graduated tax rate schedule. By moving a business into a C corporation, you are often able to leave income in the C corporation at its lowest tax rate schedule and pull out some income in the form of taxable salary to you. Although this salary is taxable to you, it is a deduction for the corporation. In this way, you are able to take advantage of the lowest tax rate schedules for all entities.

Chapter 18

Timing

When Do You Want to Pay Your Taxes?

Only a C corporation can choose the year end for its business. All other business structures (S corporations and partnerships) must generally use the calendar year end of December 31. It should be noted that when a partnership is set up with the majority of the partners having a year end that is something other than calendar year end, the partnership must use the same year end. Of course, since only a C corporation can have a different year end, that means that the partner of the partnership must first be a C corporation.

"Why does it matter when my year end is?" asked Ellen.

"That's a great question, Ellen. In fact, sometimes I get so carried away with explaining why only a C corporation can do this I forget to explain why it's important. Let me clear that up right now.

"The answer is actually quite simple. Through the use of a different year end you can make use of the time value of money. If you can delay paying your taxes, you pick up the value of that extra cash. Plus, it allows for better planning opportunities when you have more than one year end. By default, we all as individuals have a year end of December 31. If our business also has a year end of December 31, everything is hitting at once. What if you discovered at December 15 that the income in your business was going to be more than you had anticipated? If your individual year end was the same, the only question would be where do you want to pay the tax? But if your business has a year end of June 30, and you discovered this extra income on June 15, you could choose to keep the income in the corporation and pay the extra tax there or bonus it to you as salary and take six more months to pay the tax.

"The main benefit is with flexibility of time," I went on. "You might notice that the planning that we do together is designed to make your good results as certain as possible. But the fact is that life is uncertain and you might have better than the good results you expected. When that happens, with the resulting extra income, it's good to know you have the flexibility to deal with the change."

"It seems like this is a pretty short explanation after all the others we've been through," Ted laughingly added.

"You're right," I replied. "But it doesn't mean that it is any less important than the other parts. Timing of when you pay your taxes is a valuable benefit to having a C corporation."

Other Timing

Pension plans also have a timing factor involved. They are set up to allow you to defer the tax until you take out the proceeds upon retirement. In general, pension plans are not a good solution for the wealthy. This is because the wealthy tend to have more wealth (in the form of passive and portfolio income—where business, real estate, and paper assets work for you) and income as they get older. It does not make sense to push off income into a future year for their circumstances, as it would with a typical wage earner.

However, with enough time and a high enough rate of return, the compounding principle of deferring tax can be significant. For example, say you put $1,000 per year in a pension plan for twenty years and have a blended federal and state tax rate of 30 percent now and when you retire. You will actually have over $15,000 more after taxes are paid at retirement if you defer the payment of taxes. That is because the amount of tax you pay is allowed to also earn in the pension fund. Given enough time, that can be significant.

Deferring Sometimes Means Never

Finally, there is the possibility of deferring tax, possibly forever. For example, you could do a like-kind exchange of real estate (see Chapter 8) and roll your basis into another property. What if you want to sell that property? You either have to again roll the gain into another property or pay the tax. Some people prefer to continue rolling their gains into other properties until they die, thus avoiding payment of taxes. The heirs inherit the property at a "stepped-up" basis, which means that they receive the property at the values as of that day. The rolled-over basis issue goes away.

SUMMARY

Timing issues. All business entities have a year end of December 31, with one exception. The C corporation can adopt year ends different than the calendar year end. This becomes more significant as you have multiple businesses so you can space out the time when you pay the tax. It is useful for a practical sense, too, to have different year ends for your business and for you. The business can then make bonuses and otherwise move income to you prior to their year end but well in advance of your own. Again, these principles demonstrate the time value of money.

Deferring income. Pension plans allow participants to defer income to a future retirement date. Section 1031 exchanges (like-kind exchanges) also allow owners to continually defer gain on property as they roll from one property to another.

Chapter 19

Characterization

Investing Through Your Corporation

"We're starting to see some of the profits that we had forecast in your C corporation. Congratulations!" I told Ted and Ellen as I looked over their financial statements.

"Yes, isn't it great! And, Ted has found a great apartment house with good cash flow. We're excited to be able to look at a big deal like this. What's next?" asked Ellen.

"We had discussed forming a limited partnership to hold real estate investments. We will probably do something like that and allow the corporation to start generating passive income through the new investment. Do you realize what you have been able to do regarding changing the type of income?" I asked.

Three Types of Income

Since the Tax Reform Act of 1986, income and losses have been characterized as one of three types—earned income, passive income, and portfolio income. Earned income comes from your job or from an active trade or business. Passive income comes from investments you have made such as rental properties. Portfolio income comes from income and dividends. Capital gains and losses are a subset of portfolio income. The significant aspect of portfolio income is that losses from one can generally not be used to offset income from another. In other words, your investment expenses (portfolio) can only offset portfolio income. If you have passive losses, they (generally) only offset passive income.

Part of a good evaluation of a taxpayer's position is to determine where there are losses that are not being utilized. Then, determine the way to take advantage of those losses. An advantage of a corporation is that it can generally change earned income into either passive income or portfolio income that can flow through to you.

In other words, the excess income that is being stockpiled in the C corporation (from earned income, and enhanced by good tax planning that reduces taxes) is invested in an apartment house that produces passive income. In the case of Ted and Ellen, they can be the other partners in the investment and, thus, receive the benefits of the passive income.

Benefits of Passive and Portfolio Income

Besides taking advantage of losses, passive and portfolio income are derived when your money works for you instead of the other way around. That is the dream of most people! The great thing about making full use of your C corporation is that the passive and portfolio income streams are built by the extra money that you receive because of good tax planning the C corporation makes available.

Changing the Type of Income

With the use of your business, and with proper investment strategies, you can change the character of income from your business. This is often done through the use of a C corporation.

For example, if you currently receive income from the sale of widgets and take out a salary from the business, all of your income is currently taken as earned income. Instead, you could buy real property through the use of the corporation's cash flow and create passive income. As you will learn in Chapter 20, you do not want to have a C corporation directly own real property, but there are ways to get money out of your C corporation (see Chapter 21) to create the investments.

You can also create paper assets with the use of your C corporation by loaning money to your corporation and taking back interest (portfolio income), or by investing through the corporation. In fact, your ownership in a

C corporation is actually a paper asset, since you own stock in the corporation. You can sell that stock, or additional stock in your C corporation, and, thus, actually create a paper asset out of your business itself.

Changing the character of income requires a sophisticated plan that must have good administrative controls and backup.

Additional ideas for investing through your C corporation are located in Chapter 21, "Getting Your Money Out of a C Corporation."

SUMMARY

Corporate investing. A C corporation allows you to change the character of earned income to passive and portfolio income by having the ability to invest the retained proceeds. As the C corporation begins to retain income, it can either invest directly or by becoming a partner in a limited partnership. This creates portfolio and passive income as the business invests.

Part V

C Corporations

Chapter 20

Special Rules for C Corporations

What Is a Corporation?

"We've been meeting for a few months now and you said that you would go over some of the advanced planning opportunities that we had available with the corporation," began Ted at our next meeting. "But first, I'm a little confused—I keep hearing about how everyone should be in a limited liability company."

"Ted, ten years ago, you might have said the same thing with one difference. Then you would have said that everyone was talking about being in an S corporation. Both an LLC and an S corporation are different from a C corporation. The tax plan we came up for you includes both a C corporation and an S corporation. I'm a proponent of the right structure in the right circumstances. But for now, we want to talk about just C corporations. And, to answer your question, remember that it can be very dangerous *anytime* to use a blanket answer for different circumstances. I would never agree that you should *always* use a C corporation any more than I agree with those who say that you should *always* use an LLC."

"First, let's talk a little bit about what a corporation is and why it is so unique."

The History of Corporations

The first recorded account of a corporate-like entity was England's Merchant Adventurers Company in 1407. The concerns of the businessman 600 years ago were not very different from the concerns of businessmen today. In that time, the merchant venturer was a shipowner. Ships didn't always come back from their trips. Cargos and men were frequently lost. But when they did come in the rewards were huge. The voyage could take several years to make, during which time the investor worried whether he would be fabulously wealthy or wiped out by the loss. It was in the best interest of England that these ventures continue, and so the king of England, along with a small group of powerful friends, formed the Merchant Adventurers Company.

By royal decree the investors (the king and his friends) could not be held liable for any losses of the venture. If the ship was lost or for any other reason the venture failed and went bankrupt, the shareholders lost only their invested money. The could not be sued by creditors, heirs of the ship's crew, or any other person with an interest in the ship, its contents, or its crew. All they could lose was their personal investment.

By the late sixteenth century, merchant traders had the possibility of huge gains, with risk that had now been limited by the corporate forebear, the Merchant Adventurers. Queen Elizabeth became an enthusiastic supporter in 1580, when her personal investment in Sir Francis Drake's ship, *The Golden Hind,* returned a 5,000 percent profit. If you could get 5,000 percent return, an investment of $1,000 would give you $50,000. Now that's a reason to support an industry!

With the powerful monarch now solidly in the merchants' corner, she further strengthened the limited liability provisions of the venture. It was later known as "Limited" in England and as "Corporation" in the U.S. Every country that has free trade has a version of this structure. For example, most Latin American countries use "Limitada," again deploying the concept of limiting liability for shareholders.

The corporation was the first type of business structure that was designed specifically to limit liability. Today it is found in any country that has a foundation from English law, and in many that do not.

The U.S. Corporation

In the U.S., the right to incorporate comes only from state government. You cannot incorporate under federal or city government, only under state law. That means that there are at least fifty different nuances to corporations because you have fifty governing bodies.

Corporate State

You can incorporate in any state, but may have to be "accepted" into other states as a "foreign" corporation. For example, if you incorporate your Colorado-based business under Nevada state law, you have a corporation formed under Nevada law. Then, if you do business in Colorado, it will have to be "accepted" to do business in Colorado. Colorado would consider it a "foreign" corporation, because it was incorporated in another state.

See more on Nevada corporations and how they can work with businesses based in other states in Chapter 22.

There are two primary differences in how states view corporations. First, they differ in how they impose tax. Some states (such as Nevada) have no state tax for corporations. Other states (such as California) not only have a state tax for corporations, they also use different tax law for determining how the tax is assessed than is used by the federal government. In essence, a California corporation must prepare two different tax returns, which are calculated using different amounts of income and expense.

Second, the states have different court cases that have determined how asset protection, shareholder disclosure, and other items are handled. In other words, corporations formed in Colorado and Nevada might have completely different statutes and liability protection for their shareholders.

Delaware has more corporations than any other state. The state of Nevada is a close second for companies looking for no state income tax and nondisclosure of shareholders.

Federal Tax

The ideas discussed throughout Chapter 10 are all based on federal tax law, which is applied the same throughout all of the states.

Who Do You Need for Your Corporation?

INCORPORATORS

The incorporators (called promoters in some states) do the preparatory work. They prepare and file the articles of incorporation. The articles of incorporation are actually the formal incorporation document. It is filed with a state office such as the secretary of state. Although several people can serve as incorporators and sign the articles of incorporation, only one incorporator is required by law, except in Arizona where two is the minimum. Once the articles of incorporation are filed, the incorporator's job is nearly done. The only things that remain to be completed are to select the first board of directors and to adopt the corporate bylaws (although in some states bylaws may be adopted by the directors).

SHAREHOLDERS

The shareholders own the stock of the corporation. One person can own 100 percent of the stock. Among the things that only shareholders can do are:

- Elect directors (although the initial board of directors is usually selected by the incorporator or promoter).
- Amend bylaws.
- Approve the sale of all or substantially all of the corporate assets.
- Approve mergers and reorganizations.
- Amend the articles of incorporation.
- Remove directors.
- Dissolve the corporation.

State law typically requires that shareholders hold an annual meeting.

DIRECTORS

The directors manage the corporation and make major policy decisions. Among other things, the directors authorize the issuance of stock; decide on whether to mortgage, sell, or lease real estate; and elect the corporate officers. Directors may hold regular or special meetings (or both).

The incorporators or shareholders decide how many directors the corporation will have. The number of directors is usually stated in the articles of incorporation or in the corporate bylaws. Most states specifically permit corporations to have just one director.

OFFICERS

The officers are normally responsible for the day-to-day operation of the corporation. State laws usually require that the corporation have at least a president, a secretary, and a treasurer. The president is usually the chief operating officer of the corporation. The secretary is responsible for the corporate records. The treasurer, of course, is responsible for the corporate finances, although it's common to hand day-to-day duties to a bookkeeper. The corporation can have other officers (such as a vice president) as well. In many states, one person can hold all the required offices.

EMPLOYEES

Employees work for the corporation in return for compensation. For the small corporations we're considering in this chapter, the owners (shareholders) are usually also employees of the corporation. It's through your salary and other compensation as a corporate employee that you'll receive most of your financial benefits from the business. Often, the person who runs the business on a day-to-day basis gets the most compensation. This may or may not be the president.

HOW IT ALL FITS TOGETHER

If you're new to all of this, the numerous components of a corporation may seem unduly complicated for a small business. Fortunately, it all fits together quite smoothly and easily.

A Great Idea Often Done Wrong

"I see now why you talk about corporations and I did understand that there were some real tax benefits to setting our structure up the way that we did. It seems that there are mainly two schools of thought regarding corporations—one group thinks you should never do it and the other group says you always should!" said Ted.

"Ted, you've hit the nail on the head. That's one of the biggest problems I see with some of the so-called advisors that I see potential clients rely upon. Often they do not have the complete background in business structures, including C corporations, and unless they have the credentials of CPA or tax attorney, they certainly do not have current information. The real answer is using the right structure for the right circumstance. The fact is that the C corporation is frequently the best structure, but the decision to form one should not be taken lightly. You must first know three things: 1) how you will put assets into the corporation; 2) how you will take assets out of the corporation; and 3) which elections you will make within the crucial first year."

How to Put Assets into Your Corporation

One of the first tasks to be done after you start your business is getting assets into the company so you can start doing business. If you have operated a company before under a different business structure, you will need to move company assets, such as computers, furniture, and so forth. If you are just starting a new company, you will likely need to also move assets that you might have used for personal use before. Plus, of course, you need to fund the company with cash.

There are many different ways to put assets into your new corporation. The key to finding the best way is to determine what is best for your specific case. You will see the two different ways that Ted and Ellen moved assets into their corporations. The methods and consequences were different because Ted had been operating a business before and he was moving to an S corporation. Ellen's business was new and she was moving into a C corporation.

"I had previously asked you to list all the business assets that you will use in your company," I said to them. "Ted, in your case, it was mainly a case of looking at the depreciation schedule that you had prepared previously for your Schedule C business (sole proprietorship). Ellen, your list took a little more thought. I know, for example, that you had your own computer that had not been a business asset for Ted's company. I also asked you to come up with the fair market value of those assets, based on their current valuation. Let's look at that list now."

Ted's List:

Computer, printer, scanner, software	$4,500
Fax machine	500
Desk	400
File cabinet	300

Ellen's List:

Computer, printer, scanner, software	$2,500
Desk	300

"In your case, Ellen," I explained, "based on your own circumstances, we will have Ted's company buy the assets from his Schedule C business at fair market value. The new S Corporation for Ted will owe Ted's previous business on a note for the amount. For Ellen, we will do something similar. The difference is that in Ted's case we are merely transferring assets from one business structure to another, so there really isn't much of a net gain in tax savings. However, Ellen is picking up true tax savings as she converts personal assets to business use."

"But I don't know when my company will have the money to pay for that," exclaimed Ellen. "Ted's business has steady income, but mine will take a little longer to get going."

"Ellen, that's fine. We're going to have your company draw up a note promising to pay you for the equipment. Plus, your company will have to pay a minimum amount of interest. Currently, the IRS tells us that we must charge a minimum of 7 percent on notes," I said reassuringly.

"Also, in Ted's case, he has a separate business checking account already. His new S corporation will have its own taxpayer identification number, so you will need to have a new checking account. But, basically, you can just transfer the amount in the account directly over to the new business account. Ted, when you talk to the bank they might tell you that they can just change the name on the account. I always recommend to clients that they set up new accounts. This is to avoid something called commingling, which we will talk about a little later. For now just know that it's a bad thing!" I finished with a smile.

"Ellen, you will need to open a new business account. I know that you will have to fund the business for a little bit so you can take all the deductions that we have identified for your business. That's okay. As expenses come in for your business, loan the money to your corporation and reimburse the expenses or pay them directly from the business.

"All the money that you are loaning and advancing to the corporation will be added to the loan, so you can take the maximum back out, tax-free, at a later date. Remember that there will be a minimum interest rate, in this case 7 percent, that the corporation will also need to pay you. Incidentally, that is one way that a corporation changes the characterization of income. That's another concept we're going to talk about again in just a little bit.

"Finally," I went on, "there is one more element to putting money into your corporations. Initially, you need to buy some stock. This can be a real stumbling block for new corporate owners, as they try to determine how much their new stock should be worth. There are actually many elements that go into that decision—don't go with a pat answer! In both of your cases, we can legitimately pay a minimum amount for the stock. You both had 25,000 shares of stock initially authorized through your articles of incorporation. We will issue 10,000 for each company, giving you the flexibility for later selling the remaining shares. At this point you have all the outstanding stock that has been issued. So, you are both 100 percent owners of the company.

"After calculating all of that, plus the relative value of the business at the beginning of your ultimate plans for the business, we determined that the shares should be worth 10 cents each. Each of you will need to pay $1,000 (10,000 shares times 10 cents) into the company for stock. After that, all other money you put into the company will be treated as a loan."

Warning

You just saw a representative calculation of beginning stock value that fits someone who is in *exactly* the same situation. This is a very critical calculation because you simply can't undo a bad decision. If an advisor tells you casually an amount to use as the initial stock purchase, it's time to talk to another advisor. If you're not sure how they determined the amount to use, ask.

Things to Consider When Valuing Stock

- Value of the company at the beginning.
- Value of contracts or other initial goodwill.
- Purpose of the company.
- Likelihood of selling the company (in which case you may want a *high* stock value).
- Other future shareholders and how they will buy shares.
- How the IRS would view the transaction.

- How you will dissolve the company.
- How you plan to take assets out of the corporation both during its use and at its dissolution.

How You Will Take Assets out of Your Corporation

"It might be simpler to view operating your business as a corporation like you would view taking a journey," I told them. "I do a lot of hiking and one of my favorite hikes is in a canyon in northern Nevada that is covered with ancient petroglyphs. The hike within the canyon isn't bad. The challenge is getting into the canyon and getting out of the canyon. If you take the wrong path in, it can take you literally hours more time and be a lot more treacherous as well. Once in the canyon, it's a wonderful hike. That is, until you reach the end, and try to pick up the path out of the canyon. The point of this story is that you need to know how you will get into your corporation and how you will get out of your corporation before you even start.

"The second point to consider as you begin your corporation is how you will take assets out. In both your cases, you will not be building a lot of assets initially. In fact, with the plan that Ted has for his business, he will not be building significant assets at all. The S corporation is not expected to grow much—just provide the income needed to support the family and grow some investments. For Ellen's corporation, however, we can see that income will continue to grow without much additional work. We'll eventually want to start taking advantage of the lower tax bracket for corporations for at least the first $50,000. The question now is what do you want to do with that money as it begins to stockpile in that corporation?"

Ellen answered, "I've thought about that, although it doesn't seem real yet. But I do know that we have a plan that we're following and constantly evaluating. That plan sets us to hit certain numbers in three years, but I keep looking beyond that. Wow! The income into my corporation starts really increasing then. Okay, so your question was what we want to do with the money. We've thought about it and want to use it to build our real estate investments. Is that possible?"

"Yes, it is possible," I answered her. "And that's a great goal. We're going to develop a plan for the corporation that specifically shows you how to take full advantage of all the benefits now. I'm glad you also know what you want to do once it really starts getting big. The simple truth is that you probably can't spend all the money that is generated by the company in the form of benefits. Knowing that you want to use that money for investments sets the stage for ultimately doing that in one of two ways. You can either take loans out of the company and use that to fund real estate investments, or, perhaps, the better way, have the corporation be a limited partner in a real estate venture and thus provide the funding for the investments."

"Good! We have a plan for all the money we're going to make. Wasn't there one more item to discuss at the beginning?" asked Ted.

Elections That Must Be Made Within the First Year

"Yes, Ted. Right on cue—there are some critical elections that must be made within the first year. We have made a number of these automatically, but I want to run through them with you just so you're aware of what is necessary in the beginning."

CRITICAL TIMING

One of the biggest problems that people encounter when they try to incorporate just using an incorporating service and without proper tax strategy planning is they miss the necessary initial elections. In most cases, the IRS chooses for you if you don't make a choice within the narrow time window. These initial elections are very costly and time-consuming to change if it is even possible to do so.

SELECTION OF ACCOUNTING PERIOD

In the case of a C corporation, you can choose a year end that is different from the standard December 31, or calendar year end. You saw in Chapter 18 why that can be so important to do.

You elect the year end by selecting it on Form SS-4, which you fill out when you apply for the employer ID Number (or taxpayer ID number). You can change it at a later date, but it will require additional accounting and a short-year tax return. The easiest way is to select it correctly in the beginning.

SELECTION OF ACCOUNTING METHOD

You select the accounting method when you file your first corporate tax return. As explained, there are two basic types of accounting methods—cash and accrual. There is also a hybrid method that combines elements of both.

CASH VS. ACCRUAL

There are two principal methods of keeping track of a business's income and expenses: cash method and accrual method (sometimes called cash basis and accrual basis). In a nutshell, these methods differ only in the timing of when you record income and expenses.

If you use the cash method, income is counted when cash (or a check) is actually received and expenses are counted when actually paid.

Under the accrual method, transactions are counted when they happen, regardless of when the money is actually received or paid. Thus, using the accrual method, income is counted when the sale occurs, and expenses are counted when you receive goods or services. You don't have to wait until you see the money, or until you actually pay money out of your checking account for entries to be made in your bookkeeping system.

The most significant way your business is affected by the accounting method you choose involves the tax year in which income and particular expense items will be counted. For instance, if you incur expenses in the 1999 tax year but don't pay them until the 2000 tax year, you won't be able to claim them in 1999 if you use the cash method. You would be able to claim them if you use the accrual method, since the very essence of that system is to record transactions when they occur, not when money actually changes hands.

Most businesses that have sales of less than $5 million per year are free to choose which accounting method to adopt. But if your business stocks an inventory of items that you will sell to the public, the IRS requires that the accrual accounting method be used. Inventory includes any merchandise you sell, as well as supplies that will physically become part of an item intended for sale.

Whichever method you use, it's important to realize that either one only gives you a partial picture of the financial status of your business. While the accrual method shows the ebb and flow of business income and debts more accurately, it may leave you in the dark as to what cash reserves are available, which could result in a serious cash flow problem. For instance, your income ledger may show thousands of dollars in sales, while in reality your bank account is empty because your customers haven't paid you yet.

And though the cash method will give you a truer idea of how much actual cash your business has, it may offer a misleading picture of longer-term profitability. Under the cash method, for instance, your books may show one month to be spectacularly profitable, when actually sales have been slow and, by coincidence, a lot of credit customers paid their bills in that month. To have a firm and true understanding of your business's finances, you need more than just a collection of monthly totals; you need to understand what your numbers mean and how to use them to answer specific financial questions.

For tax purposes, the accrual method can be devastating. This is true if you have a company that has a large amount of receivables (customers owe you money). You are required to consider that as income under the accrual method, and, thus, must pay tax on the amount invoiced. Yet you don't have the cash to pay the tax with.

ELECTION TO AMORTIZE START-UP EXPENSES AND ORGANIZATIONAL EXPENSES

This is a fairly automatic election for anyone familiar with corporate tax preparation. The problem comes about when a tax preparer who is not familiar with corporate taxes prepares the return. The election, although easy to do, can only be done with the initial return.

Organizational expenses are the costs of organizing any entity and include the cash outlays for legal fees, entity setup fees, and so on.

Start-up expenses are amounts incurred in connection with preopening expenses, initial legal services, organizational meetings, initial fees paid to state and local agencies, and other similar expenses.

An election is made with the first return to amortize the expenses ratably over sixty months, starting the first day that the business is actively engaged in business.

S CORPORATION ELECTION

If it is determined by your tax strategist that an S corporation is the best structure for you, you have a limited time in which to make your S corporation election. This is done by filing a statement with the IRS within the first two and a half months of operation (in some cases, extensions can be granted) that is signed by all shareholders and their spouses (if they reside in a community property state).

Why Is a Corporation So Different?

"One question I have, though," asked Ted, "is that it seems that a C corporation is dramatically different from the other types of business structures. Why is that?"

"That's the key to all of the rest of the benefits that we are going to discuss, Ted. You see, a C corporation is really considered a legal person under the law. A Schedule C, sole proprietorship, is really just an extension of you. A partnership is a group (generally) of individuals and is taxed as if they were individually operating. But a C corporation is unique in that it is considered a separate entity.

"Besides being the only business with its own taxing structure, the C corporation is also allowed deductions that no other business structure has," I told Ted and Ellen. "This is the part that is very exciting because there are many deductions that are available to the C corporation that can be provided tax-free to the owners. These are deductions that are different from the hidden business deductions we discussed earlier. Here, let me show you the list."

Corporate Benefits

Below you will find a list of benefits that are available to employees, tax-free, and are deductible by the corporations. These are deductions that are only available for the C corporation. Some of the benefits can be offered on a discriminatory basis, which means that you can pay these benefits only to yourself if you wish. Other benefits must be offered to all full-time (greater than 1,000 hours worked per year) employees.

CORPORATE FRINGE BENEFITS AVAILABLE ON A DISCRIMINATORY BASIS

Health insurance. Health insurance is a deduction for business formed in other types of structures (S corporations, partnerships), but the amount deductible is limited. It is deductible at 100 percent of the premium *only* in a C corporation.

Disability insurance. A C corporation can deduct the cost of disability insurance for their key employees. Frequently this insurance is wrapped with the health insurance package. When the insurance is paid through third-party insurance company (rather than through self-insurance) it can be provided to selected employees without violating IRS antidiscrimination rules.

Free parking. A C corporation can take a deduction for parking lot fees up to $175 per year provided for key employees. This is not taxable to the employee.

Annual medical checkups. The cost of annual medical checkups can be expensed by the C corporation and provided tax-free to the employee.

Personal liability insurance. Many companies furnish errors and omissions insurance for mistakes and errors done by their employees as well as directors insurance to cover acts by directors. These are deductions for the C corporation and are not taxable to the employee.

$5,000 death benefit. This, hopefully, is one deduction your corporation doesn't have the opportunity to take. But in case it is needed, your C corporation can take a deduction for up to $5,000 paid to the heirs of any employee.

Free housing and meals on company premises. A C corporation can provide tax-free meals and lodging for all employees where they are required to be on site for the benefit of the business. For example, businesses such as hotels, motels, farms, funeral parlors, mini-storage warehouses, wrecker's services, large apartment complexes, and boarding facilities may require that someone be on the premises at all times for the operation of the business. The code specifically says "for the convenience of the employer." When this is the case, all costs of meals furnished on the business premises are deductible at 100 percent of cost. (In other words, there is not a limitation of 50 percent for meals, as is normally the case for business meals.) The cost of lodging (rent, utilities, and other associated expenses) is also a 100 percent deduction for the C corporation and is furnished tax-free to the owner. There must be a written policy stating that it is a condition of employment that the employee is available at all times and that the employee is not allowed to reject the lodging. Note that the meals and lodging must be furnished in kind. In other words, you cannot reimburse or pay a per diem expense to the employee.

Small Christmas gifts. The C corporation can take as a deduction the cost of "small" Christmas gifts. This is one time where "small" doesn't refer to the old adage that "good things come in small packages." Instead, it refers to the cost of the package. It falls under the de minimis fringe definition, which says that the value is "so small as to make accounting for it unreasonable or administratively impracticable."

Subscriptions to business periodicals. The C corporation can pay for business magazine subscriptions provided to certain employees. These are not taxable to the employee.

Payment of professional and business club dues. There are so many no-no's in determining what is deductible (and what is not), that it is easy for an accountant to forget what still is deductible. The dues paid to professional or public service organizations (such as Kiwanis and Rotary clubs) are deductible if paid for business reasons, and the organization's principal purpose is not to conduct entertainment activities for members or their guests or to provide such persons with access to entertainment facilities. What is no longer deductible includes dues for entertainment facilities, such as yachts, hunting lodges, swimming pools, tennis courts, or bowling alleys, or social, athletic, luncheon, sporting, airline, and hotel clubs.

Cost of business conventions. The cost of business conventions, as well as the travel, hotel, and meals associated with the convention, are deductible for the C corporation and not taxable to the employee.

De minimis fringes. A C corporation can provide property or services without tax to the beneficial employee where the "value of which is (after taking into account the frequency with which similar fringes are provided to the employer's employees) so small as to make accounting for it unreasonable or administratively impracticable." Examples of this are Christmas gifts mentioned above, as well as Thanksgiving turkeys, occasional meals, and so forth.

Uniforms and small tools. Clothing is deductible if it is a uniform (with logo or other identifying corporate name), protective, or safety-related. This clothing, and the cleaning, can be deducted by the C corporation and are not taxable to the benefiting employee. The C corporation can also furnish small tools to employees that will help them in the completion of their work.

Nonqualified achievement awards. The "nonqualified" in the title of this deduction refers to the fact that the C corporation can discriminate in who receives this achievement award. The C corporation can give in-kind personal property (not cash) up to $400. The amount of $400 is the total amount per year that can be given by the C corporation.

CORPORATE FRINGE BENEFITS—CANNOT BE DISCRIMINATORY

Recreational and health facilities. Your C corporation can deduct all costs associated with an on-premise athletic facility (workout room) that is located on the premises of the employer, is operated by the employer, and that is used substantially by the employees, their spouses, and dependent children. This benefit is provided tax-free to the employees.

Prepaid legal assistance. The cost of a qualified group legal services plan is a deduction for a C corporation. A qualified group legal services plan is a separate written plan of an employer for the exclusive benefit of his employees or their spouses or dependents to provide such employees, spouses, or dependents with specified benefits consisting of personal legal services. These prepaid legal services can be paid by the employer through an outside-sourced prepaid legal assistance plan or through a separate plan self-funded by the employer.

Tuition reimbursement plans. The C corporation can provide up to $5,250 in annual tax-free assistance to each eligible employee. This education does not need to be job-related. The costs cannot include graduate-level courses and room and board is not covered. The educational assistance program (tuition reimbursement plan) must be stated in a separate written plan of the employer for the exclusive benefit of employees and cannot discriminate in favor of highly compensated employees or their dependents. The plan cannot offer a choice between educational assistance and other taxable forms of compensation. It also cannot be part of a Section 125 cafeteria benefit program. The program need not be funded and employees must be given reasonable notification of the availability of the program. (See sample forms in Appendix D.)

Meals expense provided to employees. A C corporation can provide meals to employees tax-free by providing occasional and sporadic meal reimbursements and supper money for overtime work. An employer can also provide tax-free meals to employees when the meals are for the employer's convenience. Examples of "for the employer's convenience" have been shown to be when there are insufficient eating facilities nearby and employees can't get adequate food within a reasonable period of time or the meal is provided to restaurant or other food service employees for each meal period during which the employees work. Additionally, if more than half of the meals provided at the on-premises eating facility are provided for the employer's convenience, then the balance of the meals also are treated as provided for the employer's convenience. All meals are then deemed to have been provided for the employer's convenience and are all then tax-free to the employees. In both of the above examples, the meals would qualify as a de minimis fringe and therefore will be 100 percent deductible (not subject to 50 percent meal limitation) to the C corporation. Note: This same deduction is allowed for an S corporation, but is not allowed for any shareholder who holds more than a 2 percent interest in the company.

Medical reimbursement plans. The C corporation can take a deduction for a medical reimbursement plan. This plan can cover all medical co-payments, prescribed drugs, dental, vision, orthodontia, and other employee medical expenses. It is tax-free for the employee and an expense for the corporation. There must be a written plan for the medical reimbursement program (see sample form in Appendix D) and it must benefit 70 percent or more of all employees, or 80 percent or more of all employees who are eligible to participate in the plan. Employees that may be excluded, legally, from the plan are: 1) those who have not completed three years of service, 2) those who are under age twenty-five, 3) nonresident alien employees, 4) employees covered by an agreement between employee representatives and the employer, and 5) part-time or seasonal employees (less than thirty-five hours per week or less than nine months per year). If a medical reimbursement plan has more than 100 or more participants it is also required to file an annual IRS Form 5500 series information return.

Child and dependent care up to $5,000 per year. The C corporation can provide dependent care payments up to $5,000 per employee that are tax-free to the employee for any dependent that is 1) a person the employee can claim as a dependent and who is under age thirteen; 2) a dependent of the employee who is physically or mentally incapable of self-care; and 3) the spouse of the employee if the spouse is physically or mentally incapable of self-care. The exclusion is limited to $5,000 or the employee's earned income, whichever is less.

$50,000 of group term life insurance. Group term life insurance up to $50,000 coverage is tax-free. Coverage over $50,000 is taxable to the employee. The benefit for the excess insurance is calculated using a uniform premium table established by the IRS and is very favorable to the employee. This amount is subject to FICA taxation.

$2,000 of group term life insurance for dependents. Group term life insurance up to $2,000 for an employee's dependents is tax-free. Any excess insurance is taxable to the employee, calculated using a uniform premium table established by the IRS.

Discounts on company products and services. It is not necessary for the employee to take into income any discounts provided by the employing company.

No additional cost services. A no additional cost service is a service provided by an employer to an employee where the service is regularly offered for sale to the customer and there is no substantial additional cost in providing it to employees. The entire value of a no additional cost service is excluded from income.

Qualified achievement awards. A qualified plan award is an employee achievement award (for longevity or safety) provided under an established written plan or program that does not discriminate in favor of highly compensated employees as to eligibility. A length of service award will not qualify if it is received during the employee's first five years of service. An award will not be considered a safety achievement award if made to a manager, administrator, clerical employee, or other professional employee or if, during the tax year, awards for safety achievement previously have been made to more than 10 percent of the employees, excluding managers, administrators, clerical employees, or other professional employees. A C corporation can give a total of $1,600 per year in qualified achievement awards.

One More C Corporation–Only Benefit

Finally, here's a C corporation tax advantage that defies accounting logic. A C corporation is able to deduct up to twice the basis of inventory or other ordinary income property that has been contributed to a qualifying charity.

What does this mean? If your corporation is in the business of selling books and tapes and a new version is out that makes your inventory obsolete, all is not lost! Your inventory of books and tapes can be contributed at *twice* the basis in inventory for a charitable deduction. In this case, a charity is defined as an organization exempt from tax under Section 501 (c)(3) and the use of the property is related to the purpose or function constituting the basis for its exemption, the property is not transferred in exchange for money, other property, or services, and the taxpayer receives a written statement representing that its use and disposition of the property will be in accordance with the provisions of the purpose of the charity. A qualifying charity is defined as a charity that serves the needy or disadvantaged.

SUMMARY

U.S. corporations. The history of corporations started over 600 years ago in Europe. In the U.S., the history, obviously, is a little bit more recent. Here, the incorporation is done at the state level. If you operate a business in all fifty states, you would incorporate your business in one state and then be recognized as a "foreign" corporation in the others. The law that governs the corporation is generally that of the state in which it is incorporated. However, there may be some special governing laws in the state in which the business operates that will prevail if there is litigation.

Components of a corporation. There are some roles that are commonly needed for all corporations. They are: 1) incorporators, who perform the preparatory work; 2) shareholders, who own the stock of the corporation; 3) directors, who manage the corporation and make major decisions; 4) officers, who are responsible for the day-to-day operation of the corporation.

Plan first. There are some key decisions that must be planned first thoughtfully. These are: 1) how you plan to put assets in your corporation; 2) value of the initial stock; 3) how to take assets out of the corporation; 4) whether to be an S corporation or C corporation; 5) what the accounting period will be; 6) what type of accounting method to use for the company's books; 7) election to amortize start-up and organizational expenses. These should be discussed with your tax strategist before you finalize any business structure decision.

Corporate fringe benefits—can be discriminatory. The following are benefits that are available on a discriminatory basis for employees of the C Corporation: 1) health insurance, 2) disability insurance, 3) free parking, 4) annual medical checkups, 5) personal liability insurance,

6) $5,000 death benefit, 7) free housing and meals on company premises, 8) small Christmas gifts, 9) subscriptions to business periodicals, 10) payment of professional and business club dues, 11) cost of business conventions, 12) de minimis fringes, 13) uniforms and small tools, and 14) nonqualified achievement awards.

Corporate fringe benefits—cannot be discriminatory. The following are benefits that are available to employees without discrimination: 1) recreational and health facilities, 2) prepaid legal assistance, 3) tuition reimbursement plans, 4) meals expense provided to employees, 5) medical reimbursement plans, 6) child and dependent care up to $5,000 per year, 7) $50,000 of group term life insurance, 8) $2,000 of group term life insurance for dependents, 9) no additional cost services, and 10) qualified achievement awards.

C corporation inventory deduction. A C corporation can also deduct up to twice the basis in inventory to a qualified charity.

Chapter 21

Getting Your Money Out of a C Corporation

How Do You Get the Money Out?

"We're making money in our C corporations now and we have some immediate plans for investments, but I'm worried about what happens when we make more money. Isn't it funny that we're starting to worry about that?" asked Ted.

"Ted, you'll often hear me say that there are just two problems that someone can have with money—not enough and too much. Most people are all to familiar with the problem of not having enough money. But have you considered what happens sometimes when people get too much money? That is when you see the tremendous crash and burns of the multimillionaire performers or the lottery winners. They did fine until they suddenly made a lot of money. Well, the same problem can happen with a business, and particularly a C corporation. That's why we discussed before the three things you had to decide before you started a C corporation: 1) how to put assets in; 2) how to take assets out; and 3) necessary elections of the corporation. Now, we're going to work a little bit more on the plan for taking money out."

How Did the Money Go In?

The first place to look when it's time to plan to take money out is how the money went in. For example, if you determined after carefully considering all the implications and strategies surrounding your exit strategy that you wanted to maximize the amount in the shareholder note, you would first repay this debt. In other words, in the beginning when the corporation needs funding, the contributions would show as notes from you. When you take the money out, you will be repaid on those notes. The amount of the note is really dictated by the reasonable value of the stock deducted from the amount contributed.

Benefits

The best way to take money out of your C corporation is by tax-free benefits that are deductible by the corporation. These were listed in Chapter 20.

Salaries

Salaries are an expense that the corporation can deduct from income before computing taxable income. However, salaries do have to be reasonable.

Directors Meetings

Every corporation must have one or more directors, depending on state law. The directors hold at least one annual meeting, at which time they elect the officers. Directors can be paid for their services. You can also deduct all of the cost of the meeting, including travel and meals. It is not unusual for busy, growing companies to need up to one board meeting per month—all tax-deductible.

Corporation Invests for You

FORM A PARTNERSHIP WITH YOUR C CORPORATION

As we observed with Ted and Ellen, they were planning to first take advantage of all the benefits available to them and then begin having their corporation invest for them. In one case, the corporation would become a limited partner, providing the funding for an apartment house. These are ways in which the corporation could invest in property that would provide a passive income stream.

CORPORATION PAYS RENT

A C corporation can also pay you rent for space that you own or, better still, that is held within your limited partnership. In this way the C corporation buys you assets, by providing the income stream that makes their purchase possible.

INVEST IN THE CORPORATION

The other way the corporation can invest for an owner for them is by purchasing split dollar life insurance. The cost of the insurance is not a deduction for the corporation, but reduces the problem of accumulated earnings tax and provides for tax-free growth for the shareholder/employee. The split dollar life insurance provides the benefits of tax-free growth and it doesn't discriminate against the high-income earner.

Start Planning Now on How You Will Take Money Out

Just as with every other element of proper tax planning, you must have a plan in place. Remember that this plan is likely to be fluid, and will change as your needs change. But begin thinking right away about how you will take money out.

SUMMARY

How did the money go in? The first question when determining how to get money out of a C corporation is determining how the money went in. If the money was first put in as a note, then payments back to the contributing shareholder will be a tax-free repayment.

Fringe benefits. The best possible way to take money out of your C corporation is by the use of deductible benefits that are tax-free to the recipient. In other words, the C corporation gets a deduction and there is no offsetting income. It is the absolute opposite of "double taxation." Here instead is "double deduction"!

Salaries. The C corporation can, and probably should, pay salaries to the shareholders. This is income to the recipient, but is a tax deduction for the C corporation.

Directors meetings. The C corporation should have regular directors meetings. They are also required to have an annual stockholders meeting. The expenses of these meetings—travel, accommodations, meals, and so forth—are all tax-deductible for the corporation.

Corporation invests for you. The C corporation can invest in a number of ways. It can form a partnership with you or others to provide funding for the purchase of income-producing assets. It can make loans to other business structures providing portfolio income (interest) to the C corporation. The C corporation can pay rent or lease income to you for the use of office and storage space or equipment use. The C corporation can also invest in life insurance, such as split dollar, that is for the benefit of its employees. The employee pays a small amount of tax based on the current value of the projected future value.

Chapter 22

Use of Nevada Corporations

NEXUS

"What is this I keep hearing about Nevada corporations?" asked Ted. "How come Ellen's corporation was a Nevada corporation, but mine had to be in my home state?"

"The state of Nevada has built an entire industry around supporting corporations that are headquartered within the state," I replied. "Nevada has no income tax, so corporations do not have to pay state income tax. Of course, they are subject to federal income tax, just as they would be in any other state. Additionally, the state of Nevada does not require disclosure of shareholders, so ownership is not readily apparent from state records. This all works to make Nevada the second largest incorporating state. The first is Delaware, which is more of the old-school Eastern U.S.'s state of choice. Delaware has good case law protecting the corporations, just like Nevada does. Delaware does have state income tax, but they have many more years of experience protecting the corporation, so for the person who is more concerned about asset protection, it is a good choice.

"You asked an important question, Ted," I continued. "Why did Ellen's corporation incorporate in Nevada and yours did not? The reason is because of something called nexus. What this refers to is where the income was earned. In the case of Ellen's corporation, a multilevel marketer, income cannot be attributed to any particular location or person. It is not earned by selling a product or service within a certain geographical area. However, in your case, Ted, you live in Arizona and provide all of your services in Arizona. You have nexus in Arizona and then must either incorporate in Arizona, or incorporate in Nevada and be admitted as a foreign corporation into Arizona.

"The first question when considering whether you should have a Nevada corporation is to determine where your business has nexus. Your computer consulting business has nexus in Arizona, but let's go into the next step and see if there's a way to make use of the Nevada corporation in another way."

Dual Corporations

"Another way for a corporation in another state, such as your Arizona corporation, to work with a Nevada corporation is by taking advantage of any of a number of 'dual corporate' strategies. First, the warning: These must be done correctly, or you could run into any of a number of problems. Some of the potential pitfalls to avoid include controlled group issues and the charge of being a sham corporation. The Nevada corporation that works with your home state corporation must have a business purpose that is something other than just saving on state income taxes.

"The basic premise," I went on, "is that you create an expense in your home state corporation that is offset by the income to your Nevada corporation. You then have less income in your home state upon which you pay state income tax, and the Nevada corporation, which now shows that income, has no state income tax. There are a number of ways that you could have the Nevada corporation set up to receive the income. One is by having the Nevada corporation provide some kind of service (such as marketing or accounting). Another way is by factoring accounts receivable, which we have used successfully with medical practices that have a large number of accounts receivable. The receivables are sold to the Nevada corporation at a discount of 5 percent per month. The customers pay the accounts receivable directly to the Nevada corporation."

Warning

"The biggest potential pitfall for someone who unknowingly sets up these dual corporations is to have the two corporations classified as a controlled group," I cautioned Ted. "As we have discussed previously, if the control for the two corporations falls within the definition of controlled group, then the two corporations are merged together and the whole tax plan is nullified.

"As with any tax strategy, you need to look at a cost/benefit comparison," I continued. "There is more of a cost to set up and run a Nevada corporation, as you need a Nevada address, Nevada business licensing, and other requirements. The question to ask is whether the potential tax benefit from saved state taxes outweighs that cost. In the case of your Arizona corporation, the state corporate rate is 8 percent. Assuming the additional cost for the other corporation is about $2,400 per year (cost of setup, business presence, additional bookkeeping, additional tax return, and the value of your time), you would need to be moving about $30,000 just to break even."

"I don't expect to make that kind of money!" exclaimed Ted.

"Right, so a Nevada corporation isn't really the best answer for your situation. However, for Ellen's corporation, it was a perfect solution. In general, Nevada corporations can work very well, but if your purpose is mainly tax savings, it is necessary to take a real look at the tax savings first. There is a lot of hype in the market about Nevada corporations that moves people to do things that aren't in their best interests."

How Can You Move Money into a Nevada Corporation?

FACTORING

Description

Two businesses are involved in factoring accounts receivable. They are the company (business) who has the receivables (Corporation A) and the company who buys the receivables (Corporation B).

In the first month, a portion of the accounts receivable is sold by Corporation A to Corporation B. The cost for that sale is 5 percent of the total. In other words, if $100,000 of accounts receivable is sold by Corporation A to Corporation B, Corporation A receives $95,000. The sold receivables (which need to be collected within thirty days in order to avoid additional costs being incurred) are now the property of Corporation B, which receives collection of these receivables.

In the second month, Corporation A pays Corporation B 5 percent of the uncollected balance of the previously sold accounts receivable. Also, Corporation A can again sell a new portion of accounts receivable as before.

In the third month, Corporation A again pays Corporation B 5 percent of the uncollected balance of the previously sold accounts receivable.

Procedure

1. Receive a list of accounts receivable from Corporation A's bookkeeper. This list of receivables should be an aging of the accounts receivable.
2. Determine dollar amount to be sold. This may be determined by the amount available in Corporation B to invest.
3. If amount is what Corporation B has to invest, divide this amount by 95 percent.
4. If amount given is what Corporation A will sell, use that amount.
5. Using number from Step No. 3 or Step No. 4 above, prepare a list of oldest accounts receivable, coming as close as possible to this number.
6. Corporation B writes a check to Corporation A for 95 percent of that total.
7. As money is received from these accounts receivable, it is sent to Corporation B.
8. Corporation B tracks receipt of the collected accounts receivable.
9. At month's end, a list of uncollected accounts receivable is given to Corporation A.

Second Month and Thereafter

10. Corporation A writes a check to Corporation B for 5 percent of the total shown on the list from Step No. 9.
11. Determine dollar amount to be sold. This may be determined by the amount available in Corporation B to invest.
12. If amount given is what Corporation B has to invest, divide this amount by 95 percent.
13. If amount given is what Corporation A will sell, use this number.
14. Using number from Step No. 12 or Step No. 13 above, prepare a list of oldest accounts receivable, coming as close as possible to this total.
15. Corporation B writes a check to Corporation A for 95 percent of that total.

16. As money is received from these accounts receivable, it is sent to Corporation B.
17. Corporation B tracks receipt of the collected accounts receivable.
18. At month's end, a list of uncollected accounts receivable is given to Corporation A.

LEASING PERSONAL PROPERTY

Another plan to move money into a Nevada Corporation is by leasing personal property from one company to another company. This actually serves two purposes: 1) it moves assets from a potentially vulnerable business, and 2) it moves income from a state subject to state tax to Nevada. In some states, there can be a sales tax required on the income for the home state.

PERSONAL PROPERTY LEASING

One way to achieve a flow of income to a Nevada corporation is by having personal property assets owned by the Nevada corporation (such as vehicles that are used in a business).

The personal property is sold to the Nevada corporation. The home state corporation then makes lease payments to the Nevada corporation. The amount of the lease needs to be reasonable, but this is one case where you shouldn't mind paying the high lease prices! You are moving income from the home state to the no-state-income-tax state of Nevada.

MANAGEMENT COMPANY

A Nevada corporation can be set up as a management company. A contract needs to be drawn that clearly states what duties will be performed by the management company and an employee needs to be shown in this corporation. The contractual fee could be a fixed amount on a periodic basis, or it could be based on a percentage of income or sales to ensure that the right percentage is going to the Nevada corporation.

LICENSING RIGHTS, ROYALTIES

A Nevada corporation could own intellectual property that would receive a fee for use by the home state company. This intellectual property could be a patented or copyrighted product or it could be a document system on which there are licensing rights paid. Make sure that there are good contractual documents substantiating the agreement and that the property is truly owned by the Nevada corporation.

SALE OF GOODS

In some cases, a Nevada corporation can be used to purchase raw material and add packaging or other value to the product to sell at an increased price to the home state company. The profit stays in the Nevada corporation and the home state's income is reduced by the increased price that is paid.

WEB SITE

In today's Web-based world, it can be difficult to say where nexus occurs. In fact, the Supreme Court has declined to address the question entirely by saying that they will not attempt to determine the flow of electrons. Generally, nexus is determined as occurring where a sale occurs—where the company takes the order, receives payment, and fulfills the order. In reality, many sales are now made to a Web site. The Web site receives the payment. An outside source fulfills the order. It doesn't take much to move such a company to Nevada.

Nevada Warning

Above all, there must be legitimate reason for having a Nevada corporation. You do not want to have the "tax tail wagging the business dog." In other words, there must truly be a business and a business purpose that is not merely a setup to avoid taxation. Additionally, read carefully about potential pitfalls in personal holding companies (Chapter 27) and controlled groups (Chapter 25). Finally, make sure that you have sufficient benefit to having a Nevada corporation.

Foreign Corporation

It is also possible to have a corporation formed under Nevada laws and then have it authorized to do business in your home state. This is called having foreign corporation status. It doesn't mean that the corporation comes from another country. As explained, the term foreign corporation refers merely to forming a corporation in one state and then authorizing it to do business in another state.

There can be some benefit to doing that, although you would not receive any tax benefit or privacy of shareholders. You would be subject to tax in your home state as if the corporation had been filed there. Also, at the time you applied for foreign corporation status, you would be required to file all paperwork as if the corporation had originally been filed in your state. The remaining advantage, therefore, is that you may be able to litigate in Nevada. Nevada has the reputation as being more pro-business with more case law supporting corporations. An example of this was when DuPont was sued in the huge product liability case regarding leaking breast implants. The nation wondered why the case was being conducted in Nevada. The reason was that DuPont had been formed as a corporation under Nevada law.

SUMMARY

Nexus. The nexus of income is determined based on where the sale took place. The sale is further defined as being where the order was taken, where the money was paid, and where the fulfillment of the service or product took place. This can be an important question when two states are involved that have differing tax rates.

Dual corporations. A part of your tax planning strategy is determining how businesses will work together through separate business structures. Provided that the issue of controlled groups (Chapter 25) is correctly handled, it is possible for one company to pay for the services and products of another company. This in effect will "upstream" income from one state to another. This needs to be done with the utmost care and for truly legitimate purposes so that there is no risk of sham transactions. A sham transaction is one where there is no economic purpose for an action—it is merely done for tax purposes.

Cost/Benefit. There is a cost to setting up and running separate business structures. This is especially true if you intend to set up a Nevada corporation. There can be significant ongoing costs to running these additional structures. Make sure that you have enough benefit to justify these costs.

Possible Nevada corporate functions. A Nevada corporation can be set up to do factoring, as a leasing company, providing management services, holding licensing rights and royalties, selling goods from Nevada, or providing Web site services for products and services.

Chapter 23

Traps of C Corporations

Nick and Sue

We first met Nick and Sue in Chapter 11. At that meeting I found out that they had just purchased five corporations and five partnerships, but had no plan or education on how to work with these structures. We had designed a new strategy for them, but before we moved into the implementation, I wanted to go over some of the fundamental traps of C corporations. (A diagram of their new tax plan is in Chapter 25.)

"Well," Sue said, "the new structure looks a lot simpler than what we had before. Is there any other reason to make that change?"

"There were some of the common C corporation pitfalls in your old plan," I answered. "You can avoid the traps by properly planning around them, but you first need to identify them."

"What are these traps you talk about?" asked Nick.

I began to review the potential pitfalls of C corporations, and the ways to plan around them.

Traps of Corporations

There are some potential traps that you must plan to avoid with your corporation(s). Each of these will be discussed in more detail in the following five chapters.

DOUBLE TAXATION

Double taxation occurs when income is first taxed at the corporate level and then at the personal level, with no offsetting deduction for the corporation. In other words, the income is taxed twice.

CONTROLLED GROUP

A controlled group issue comes about when the same person, or persons, controls multiple corporations. The definition of control, and how to calculate it, follows in Chapter 25. When a controlled group issue occurs, the corporations are collapsed into just one corporation. There is only one tax rate table. There is only one Section 179 deduction. The benefits of multiple corporations goes away.

PERSONAL SERVICE CORPORATION

A personal service corporation is subject to a flat tax of 35 percent and has a lower threshold for accumulated earnings tax. A personal service corporation is defined as a specific type of company where the shareholder/employer provides his own services for the corporation.

PERSONAL HOLDING COMPANY

A personal holding company is a corporation that has been established for the main purpose of collecting dividends, interest, and other solely passive investment income. The income for a personal holding company is taxed at a higher rate (39.6 percent), and special corporate tax breaks—such as the dividend exclusion—do not exist.

ACCUMULATED EARNINGS

When a corporation has exceeded a certain amount in earnings that have been retained within the corporation, an additional tax is assessed on the corporation.

Dissolving the Corporation

"Well, if these aren't right, let's just dissolve these old corporations and get the right type of corporations. We've been messing around with this for far too long," said Nick.

"Yes, we are going to end up needing to dissolve some of these corporations," I answered. "And I certainly agree that we need some action on moving forward on a new plan. Unfortunately, dissolving a corporation isn't quite as easy as it might seem. There are some specific steps that you must follow. Let's go through them so you see what is involved and we can then move forward."

Plan of Liquidation

The ending of a corporation for tax purposes is called a liquidation. A dissolution occurs at the state level and will require that paperwork be filed at the state level. It is necessary to both dissolve and liquidate a corporation.

In a complete liquidation, the existence of the corporation terminates and all remaining assets are distributed to the shareholders. A corporation is considered in complete liquidation when it ceases to be a going concern and its activities consist merely of winding up its affairs, paying its debts, and distributing any remaining assets to its shareholders.

In a straight liquidation, where the corporation sells its assets and then immediately distributes the money to the shareholders, double taxation will occur. The money distributed to the shareholder is considered as payment for the shareholder's stock.

Corporations are required to report the adoption of a plan of liquidation within thirty days on IRS Form 966, together with a certified copy of the plan. Corporations can also submit a request for prompt assessment with the IRS. Typically, the IRS has three years after the filing date of the tax return to assess additional tax. With a request for prompt assessment, that time is shortened to eighteen months.

A sample copy of a "Certified Copy of Resolutions to Liquidate the Corporation" is found in Appendix D.

The final corporate tax return is due by the fifteenth day of the third full month following the liquidation of the corporation. The final tax return must have the following attached: 1) a certified copy of the plan of liquidation and related minutes adopting the plan; 2) the fair market value of any assets distributed to the shareholders; 3) information as to the date of the final liquidating distribution; and 4) a statement of the assets retained to pay liabilities and the nature of the liabilities.

The liquidating corporation is required to report the fair market value of the property distributed to the shareholders on Form 1099-DIV.

Liquidation Is a Serious Matter

Liquidation of a corporation is a serious matter, and should be well thought out first, just as beginning a corporation should also first be well thought out. Done wrong, you can incur serious penalties and double taxation. Done correctly, the corporation can simply unwind without dire consequences to the shareholders. This is a unique part of tax law. More so than perhaps any other part of tax planning, plan implementation, and tax compliance, make sure your advisor is well versed in all of the ramifications of corporate liquidation.

SUMMARY

Traps of C corporations. There are some potential traps of C corporations that should be recognized and discussed in depth with your tax advisors. These are: 1) double taxation, 2) controlled group status, 3) personal service corporation status, 4) personal holding company status, and 5) accumulated earnings tax.

Dissolving the corporation. Do not make the decision to form a corporation lightly. If you decide later to get rid of the corporation, there will be significant work involved in dissolving and liquidating the corporation. Dissolution occurs at the state level and usually requires paperwork that must be filed at the state level. The corporation must also be liquidated for tax purposes. A plan must be filed with the IRS for the liquidation of the corporation, a final return must be filed, and a Form 1099-DIV must be completed for the shareholders.

Double Taxation

"By now I know that I have to be careful about the advisors I choose to listen to, but I do have one question," Nick began. "I read something the other day that said you should never form a C corporation, because you would then have double taxation. What are they talking about? Do I have double taxation in my corporation?" he asked, a little hesitant to bring up another commonly heard objection at this late date.

"Nick, I've heard that before," I answered. "In fact, I use it as a way to gauge the sophistication of advisors that my clients have talked to. You see, double taxation is one of the easier problems there is to avoid. I'd like to go over a number of problems that you might hear can happen with a C corporation. First, though, let's talk about what double taxation really means."

What Is Double Taxation?

The term double taxation refers to tax that is paid by both the corporation and the individual owner on the same income. In other words, there is double tax paid.

When Does Double Taxation Occur?

Double taxation occurs only in a few select cases. *Most* expenses that a corporation pays are *deducted* against the income of the corporation, so there is no double taxation.

There is one notable exception—when dividends are paid to the shareholder(s). Dividends are *not* deducted against the corporation's income and they are taxable to the shareholder.

Liquidating Dividends

Double taxation can also occur when a corporation is liquidated. For example, if you sell off all the assets of your corporation and then dissolve the corporation, you receive something the IRS calls a "liquidating dividend." There is no deduction for the corporation because it doesn't exist anymore and you have to pay tax on the income.

How to Avoid Double Taxation

In the first case, the way to avoid double taxation is to *not pay dividends.* Instead, find other ways to compensate owners through salary and benefits. See Chapter 21 for ways to get money out of your C corporation.

In the second case: Don't sell off the assets and immediately dissolve the corporation. In fact, if you are selling your qualifying small business corporation, there can be tremendous exclusions from capital gains if you do it the right way. Those exclusions do not occur for any other form of business entity but a C corporation. So you would want to have a C corporation if selling the stock in your company is your projected exit strategy.

If you do sell the assets from the corporation, you probably should not dissolve the company. Keep a small portion of the business still going so that you can take out the remaining income through salary and benefits. This creates expenses in the company that offset the gain realized from the sales. This is one way to stop double taxation from occurring.

As explained, double taxation occurs when dividends are paid, which are not deducted from the income of the corporation. When salaries are paid, they are deducted from the corporate income. When nontaxable benefits are paid, they are deducted from the corporate income and there is no income tax consequence to the shareholder. The best scenario is to pay benefits so there is *no* taxation. The worst scenario is to pay dividends so there is *double* taxation.

Why Is Only a C Corporation Subject to Double Taxation?

Double taxation starts with the fact that a C corporation pays tax on its own net income. It is not a pass-through entity such as a limited partnership, S corporation, or limited liability company. After income is received, there are many choices as to how the money (income) can be spent within the corporation (expenses, benefits, salaries, retirement plans, or other tax-deductible expenses for the corporation), or it can be paid out in dividends.

All but one of these expenses are deductions for the corporation. That means if your corporation has taxable income in year one, and resulting cash left in the account, the corporation can pay the expenses that are deductions against year two's income. And, if there is no income next year, the loss can be carried back to the previous year for a refund. Double taxation does not occur here, because while tax is paid initially, there is a deduction against income as expenses are paid.

How to Always Take Advantage of Deductions

Following are two examples. In example one, salary is paid to the owner in the second year and there is income to offset in that year. The salary income is taxable to the owner and a deduction to the corporation.

Example One:

YEAR ONE

Taxable Income	**$50,000**
Federal Income Tax @ 15%	$7,500

	YEAR TWO			YEAR TWO	
	Corporation			Individual	
Income	$50,000				
Salary	($30,000)	→	Income	$30,000	
Taxable Income	$20,000		Taxable Income	$30,000	

Salary paid to the owner is a deduction to the corporation and income to the owner—no double taxation here!

In example two, there is no income in the second year, but salary is paid to the owner. The net loss is carried back to the previous year, resulting in a deduction to the corporation, *even though there was no income.*

Example Two:

YEAR ONE

Taxable Income	$50,000
Federal Income Tax @ 15%	$7,500

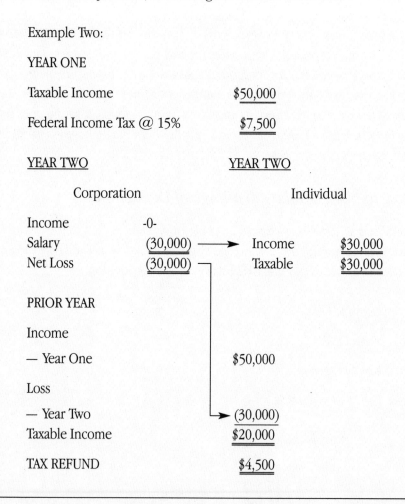

YEAR TWO		YEAR TWO	
Corporation		Individual	
Income	-0-		
Salary	(30,000) ⟶	Income	$30,000
Net Loss	(30,000)	Taxable	$30,000

PRIOR YEAR

Income	
— Year One	$50,000
Loss	
— Year Two	(30,000)
Taxable Income	$20,000
TAX REFUND	$4,500

Salary paid to the owner is a deduction to the corporation that is taken in a previous year when there is income—no double taxation here!

Plan Now to Avoid Double Taxation

The previous examples demonstrate—one with continuing business income and one without business income—how the double taxation issue does not have to occur. In fact, it only occurs when there is improper or complete lack of planning.

There are many other ways to compensate owners with benefits that are not taxable to the owner and, in effect, become double deductions! The key point regarding double taxation is that you need to plan at the beginning of each tax year to avoid this issue.

Double Taxation by Default

You have seen how double taxation can occur by improper planning. It can also occur when the corporation doesn't have proper documentation. If benefits are paid on behalf of the shareholder without the proper plans in place and without the proper documentation (such as resolutions, filing systems, and so on), the IRS will determine that the benefits are really dividends. This is also easy to avoid by having the proper administration. This will be covered in greater detail in Chapters 30–31.

SUMMARY

Double taxation. The term double taxation refers to the condition that can occur in a C corporation. It occurs when dividends are paid by the C corporation to a shareholder. The dividends paid are not a deduction for the corporation, but they are income to the shareholder. Double taxation does not occur when salary is paid to a shareholder because the salary paid is a deduction against the income of the corporation.

Liquidating dividends. Double taxation also occurs if a C corporation sells off its assets and then immediately liquidates and dissolves the corporation. A good exit strategy for the C corporation will eliminate this risk.

Chapter 25

Controlled Group

Multiple Corporations, Not Multiple Tax Tables

"The whole reason that we set up these corporations in the beginning was to take advantage of the fact that we could make $50,000 a year in income and only pay 15 percent," Nick said as our meeting continued. "So Sue and I estimated our income from the business at $200,000. We thought we could just set up four corporations. That way each corporation would only have tax at 15 percent on the $50,000 in each one. I don't understand why you don't think that is a good idea."

It was obvious that he was upset as he was learning about some of the problems with his current tax plan.

"Isn't it true that a corporation only pays 15 percent tax?" asked Sue, supporting her husband.

I thought for a moment before replying. I've always found it difficult when people come to me after they have begun their own tax planning and have been relying on questionable or misguided advice. The challenge is always how to undo the misconceptions they might have. Unfortunately, the intricacies of tax law don't always make logical sense, and frequently change. The advice they had gotten before might be very logical, as it seemed with Nick and Sue.

"As you know, we have a graduated income tax rate. That means that the rate goes up incrementally. In the case of a corporation, the first $50,000 is taxed at 15 percent, the next $25,000 is taxed at 25 percent, and so forth. So if your business was all in one corporation, the total tax on $200,000 would be," I paused a moment, running the calculator, ". . . let's see . . . a total of $61,250. So, instead of paying four times $7,500, or $30,000, you would have to pay $61,250."

"Right, but we don't have just *one* corporation!" exclaimed Sue.

"Let me show you a worksheet that we use to determine something called controlled groups. That might help make the problem more evident," I offered, wondering how many issues were going to come up as the appointment continued.

What Is a Controlled Group?

The IRS caught on pretty quickly to the trick of using multiple corporations in order to take advantage of the graduated tax rates for each corporation. That is why they came up with the concept of controlled groups. In essence, if one or more of the same people maintain control of a group of corporations, they are considered to be just one corporation. This has become a significant problem for many people when they simply buy the product of a corporation, without the overview of their entire plan. It is also an issue with upstreaming, a concept discussed more extensively in Chapter 22. With upstreaming, a fee is paid from one corporation to another corporation. The main point is to remove income from a higher-taxing state to a state that has no tax, such as Nevada. However, this plan must be done correctly, or there is a danger of having the entire plan collapse by application of the controlled group rules.

Two Types of Controlled Groups

There are two types of controlled groups—parent-subsidiary and brother-sister. Following are abbreviated definitions of the two types. There are more steps involved in determining controlled groups, but the purpose here is not to make you a complete expert. Rather, use this information to see if there could be an issue and then seek the right advisors. (See also the worksheets in Appendix D.)

PARENT-SUBSIDIARY
This exists if one corporation owns 80 percent or more of the stock of another corporation. This is a very straightforward calculation, but of course

made more complicated by human nature. If Corporation A owns a partnership that owns 80 percent of the stock of Corporation B, then a parent-subsidiary relationship exists. The determining factor isn't ownership as much as it is one of control. Who controls the corporation? If a corporation owns a trust or a partnership or a similar entity, it still is the corporation who is behind it all controlling it. If that other business entity, controlled by a corporation, owns 80 percent or more of another corporation, then a parent-subsidiary relationship exists and it is a controlled group.

BROTHER-SISTER

This exists when five or fewer persons own at least 80 percent of the voting stock of two or more corporations and these same people own more than 50 percent of each corporation. Both conditions must be met for a brother-sister relationship to occur. See Appendix D for the "Brother-Sister Controlled Group Test."

What Controlled Group Status Means

When two or more companies are determined to have controlled group status, their income must be consolidated—as if there was only one company.

That means that there is only one graduated tax rate table, one Section 179 deduction, a limit on foreign tax credits, and one accumulated earnings credit. All intercompany transfers of income and expenses must be eliminated. In other words, if one company sells a product or service to another company within the group, that transaction must be wiped out for both companies.

In some cases, it is beneficial, though, to be under controlled group status. That is because the earnings of one company can be used to offset the losses of another.

Multiple Corporation Plus Multiple Tax Rates

In the case of Nick and Sue, they had based their plan on future goals not relevant to their current status. Their income was currently $100,000, not $200,000. Also, they had not taken full advantage of all the tax-free benefits available to them. When they had done that, they discovered that they only needed one C corporation. Their start-up business was moved to an S corporation, to take advantages of the losses. A limited partnership whose ownership was comprised of Nick and Sue as limited partners and a C corporation as a general partner owned the equipment used by the janitorial business. Rent was paid by C Corporation #1 to Limited Partnership #1. This reduced the income from the first C corporation and actually changed the type of income from earned income to passive income.

This simplified their tax plan from the initial five C corporations and five limited partnerships to the new plan, showing two C corporations, one S corporation, and one limited partnership.

You will want to review the cost of having multiple business structures against the possible benefit. There are additional paperwork and time requirements that increase with every business structure you add.

See Fig. 25.1 for Nick and Sue's corrected plan.

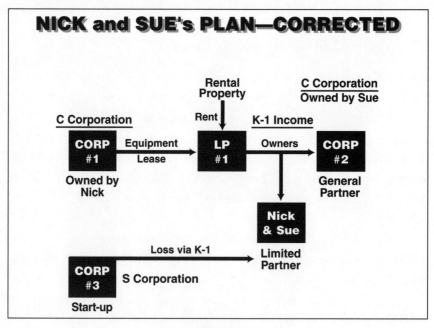

FIG. 25.1

How to Avoid Controlled Group Status

The key with controlled group status is to avoid having control with any small group of people. One way to avoid that is to have unrelated persons (unrelated by blood or marriage) own a portion of the corporation. You will need to have different people in each corporation. You cannot avoid the controlled group status by giving shares that have no voting rights. The main question is who has the control. With each idea, work the ownership through on the "Brother-Sister Controlled Group Test" in Appendix D. This is a test you want to fail!

SUMMARY

What is a controlled group? A controlled group issue occurs when one or more of the same group of people maintain control of a group of corporations. In this case, the corporations will be collapsed into one corporation. This in effect does away with all the benefits of multiple corporations such as multiple tax rates. This can also become an issue with upstreaming, where income is moved from one state to another. If the corporations are collapsed into one corporation, then there is no benefit.

Two types of controlled groups. There are two types of controlled groups—parent-subsidiary and brother-sister. A parent-subsidiary controlled group occurs if one corporation owns 80 percent or more of the stock of another corporation. A brother-sister controlled group occurs when five or fewer persons own at least 80 percent of the voting stock of two or more corporations and these same people own more than 50 percent of each corporation.

Avoiding controlled group status. The easiest way to avoid controlled group status is by having other ownership in the company. An unrelated (by blood or marriage) person can own 21 percent or more of the company to avoid the status. Use the worksheets in Appendix D to help you determine if you should be concerned about controlled group status.

Chapter 26

Personal Service Corporation

A Change in Plans

We leave the story of Nick and Sue to return to Ted and Ellen.

"We've been meeting for six months now and it's amazing how much progress we've made," Ted informed me happily at one of our scheduled meetings. "Ellen's multilevel business is taking off better than we expected and we've already started investing in real estate. Now suddenly my plans are changing. As you know, I had planned on just using my computer consulting business as a way to cover some expenses and I would continue with my job with the state for a while longer. Well, we found out last week that the state is going to start having some cutbacks in my department. The amazing thing is that the computer work that I provide now is going out to contract and I bid on it. It looks like I will get the contract. So that means I'll leave my W-2 job and start receiving four times the money for doing the same work!"

"What does this do for our plan now?" asked Ellen.

"You've heard me say this before—this is why we meet monthly. The plan is always going to be undergoing changes as your circumstances change. That's the beauty of the STEPS program. The final step, Starting Point (Reevaluation), takes all of that into account. Now, though, we need to discuss a couple of other issues.

"First, we will probably need to change your current S corporation into a C corporation. But that will create another issue we need to discuss."

"Oh, you mean controlled group issue," interrupted Ted. "Well, I'll own that corporation by myself, 100 percent, and Ellen has hers, 100 percent by herself. We had talked about that before. That means that we won't have the controlled group issue."

"Actually, I was thinking of another issue—personal service corporation. Let's review what that is," I said.

Professional Corporations

In many states, professionals who want to incorporate their practices must create what's called a professional corporation.

The list of professionals required to incorporate as a professional corporation is different in each state. Usually, though, mandatory incorporation requirements apply to these professionals:

- accountants
- engineers
- health care professionals such as audiologists, dentists, nurses, opticians, optometrists, pharmacists, physical therapists, physicians, and speech pathologists
- lawyers
- psychologists
- social workers
- veterinarians

Personal Service Corporations

The designation of professional corporation is important because the IRS also considers that professional corporations are generally also personal service corporations. Additionally, the IRS has recently expanded the description of "personal service" to include consulting or any other type of work that requires the personal service of the owner-shareholder.

Why Not a Personal Service Corporation?

A personal service corporation incorporated as a C corporation is subject to a flat tax of 35 percent. Additionally, the ceiling for accumulated earnings tax is lower at $150,000. More on that in Chapter 28.

How to Avoid Being Designated a Qualified Personal Service Corporation

First, see if you qualify as a personal service corporation. Take the test on page 249.

If you do qualify as a personal service corporation, is there any way to purposely fail any of the steps? For example, can you include other businesses into your corporation so that less than 95 percent of your and your employee's time is spent on non–personal service corporation activities?

An example of that is a medical professional who also operates a health food store. If the ownership of that store is held within the same corporation (and state law permits it to be), and more than 5 percent of the total time spent on all employees is spent with the store, you do not have a personal service corporation even if it is incorporated as a professional corporation.

Or, can the ownership of 5 percent or more of the stock be held by someone who is not an employee and clearly removed from the operation of the business? Caution: State law may require that ownership be 100 percent with the professional.

What if You Must Be a Qualified Personal Service Corporation?

Many professionals who are stuck with the personal service corporation designation have taken S corporation status. That way, the income flows through to the individual shareholder's personal tax rate and, thus, is not subject to the flat tax.

In some cases, with two high-income people married to each other, the flat tax of 35 percent might be desirable as the other's income puts the couple in the higher 39.6 percent tax bracket.

A professional with a personal service corporation may take most of the income out in the form of wages and benefits. Beware of unreasonable compensation, however. Unreasonable compensation means that the amount paid to the shareholder-owner is too much. It isn't reasonable to pay someone in that capacity that much in wages.

To protect against the claim of unreasonable compensation: 1) establish a higher salary at the beginning of the year and thus decrease the amount of bonuses paid near year end; 2) document the amount of the salaries and the reasons for any unusual changes from the prior year in the corporation's minutes; 3) establish measurable performance goals at the beginning of the year for owner-employees and provide specific bonuses for the achievement of these goals (reflect the plan in the minutes); 4) establish bonuses based on productivity or some other measure, rather than on stock ownership; 5) document in the minutes the various criteria used to establish an employee's salary, including the employee's education, special skills, contribution to the firm's profit, training, professional reputation, time spent on company business during the year, and other similar factors; and 6) review the compensation levels for comparable professionals in the area, and if the compensation you are paying is higher than normal, document the reason for the difference in the corporate minutes.

QUALIFIED PERSONAL SERVICE CORPORATION STATUS

Instructions: If your business qualifies as a personal service corporation (PSC) due to the type of work performed, use this checklist to determine if you are subject to the qualified PSC rules. If you answer yes to questions 1–3 below, you have a qualified PSC and are subject to the 35% flat tax rate as well as subject to the lower accumulated earnings threshold.

	YES	NO
1. Is the corporation a C corporation?	____	____
2. Is 95% or more of all employee time spent in the performance of services in one or more of the listed fields? See Section I below.	____	____
3. Is 95% or more of the value of the stock of the corporation owned by employees involved in qualifying personal service activity? See Section II below.	____	____

SECTION I. Function.

1-1. Total hours worked for all employees in the year.	____	____
1-2. Hours worked in personal service activity.	____	____
1-3. Divide Line 1-2 by Line 1-1 (If 95% or more, answer yes on Line 2 above.)	____	____

SECTION II. Stock Ownership.

2-1. Value of shares owned by employees.	____	____
2-2. Value of shares owned by non-employees.	____	____
2-3. Add Lines 2-1 and 2-2.	____	____
2-4. Divide Line 2-1 by Line 2-3. (If 95% or more, answer yes on Line 3 above.)	____	____

SUMMARY

Personal service corporation. Most states require that professionals incorporate their practices and create what's called a professional corporation. These mandatory professional incorporation requirements also make them personal service corporations. Additionally, the IRS code says that work performed in the following fields is required to be a personal service corporation: accounting, engineering, medical, legal, veterinary medicine, and consulting.

Qualified personal service corporation. The code also further defines some personal service corporations as qualified personal service corporations. If your corporation is considered a qualified personal service corporation, the tax rate is set at 35 percent, the corporation must have a calendar year end, and the limit for accumulated earnings tax is reduced. However, you can fail the qualified test if either the ownership of people working in the field or total hours of all employees fall below 95 percent for the entirety. (A test is included in this chapter to help determine if you can fail the qualified personal service corporation designation.)

Chapter 27

Personal Holding Company

Special Dividend Tax Rate for Corporations

Joann was a successful real estate developer. She loved to speculate in real estate. Yet, for financial security, she would maintain a fairly conservative stock portfolio with plenty of blue-chip stocks paying dividends to her. She was very excited to learn that her significant dividend income (and the resulting tax) could be lowered drastically through a C corporation structure. In fact, only 30 percent of the dividends received in a C corporation are subject to income tax.

What a C Corporation Could Mean for Her

Joann's dividend income was $20,000 per year and was being added to her already high income. She paid the highest possible federal and state tax rate on that income.

BEFORE:

Federal income tax	$7,920
State income tax	1,740
	$9,660

PROPOSED:

Income	$20,000
C corporation dividend	(14,000)
Taxable dividend income	$6,000
Federal income tax	$900
State income tax	$480

Personal Holding Company

But if Joann creates a C corporation only to hold her investments, then it is deemed to be a personal holding company. A personal holding company *cannot* take the special dividend reduction and, even worse, there is a tax on undistributed personal holding company income of 39.6 percent.

How can Joann avoid being designated a personal holding company?

What Is a Personal Holding Company?

The IRS defines a personal holdling company as a corporation:

(1) in which 60 percent or more of the corporate income was personal holding company income;

AND

(2) has five or fewer individuals who own 50 percent or more of outstanding stock.

Personal Holding Company Income

Personal holding company income includes dividends, interest, royalties, annuities, rents (unless they constitute 50 percent or more of the adjusted income of the corporation), and personal service contracts where the person performing the work is specified.

All other forms of income (including rent where 50 percent or more of the income comes from rent) are *not* personal holding company income.

How to Avoid Personal Holding Company Status

If Joann put only her dividend paying stock into the corporation, she would have a personal holding company because 60 percent or more of the corporate income was personal holding company income and she was the only shareholder. She then met both definitions of the qualifications for a personal holding company. But this is one test she didn't want to pass!

In Joann's case, the question was how she could flunk the personal holding company status on purpose.

One way to fail was by having more than five people hold 50 percent of the stock.

She could also fail the test based on the income portion. She knew that her dividend income would be roughly $20,000 per year and the income she earned was clearly considered personal holding company income. So how could she create net income of at least $14,000 per year that was not portfolio income? (Adding $14,000 personal income would mean total income of $34,000, of which only $20,000 would be dividend income (58.8 percent—less than the 60 percent requirement).)

Joann could easily do that by putting a portion of her real estate business into her C corporation. In fact, she saved even more taxes by moving that business into her C corporation.

Note: Personal holding company tests can be more complicated than in Joann's case. It is always advised that you have an experienced tax strategist helping you with this element of your plan.

SUMMARY

Dividend reduction. A C corporation pays tax on only 30 percent of the dividends received.

Personal holding company. A C corporation is defined as a personal holding company if 60 percent or more of the corporate income is personal holding company income and five or fewer individuals own 50 percent or more of the outstanding stock. If your C corporation is deemed to be a personal holding company, the special dividend reduction is not allowed and there is a flat tax rate of 39.6 percent.

Personal holding company income. Personal holding income is defined as dividends, interest, royalties, annuities, rents (unless they constitute 50 percent or more of the adjusted ordinary income), and personal service contracts where the person who will be performing the work is specified.

Avoiding personal holding company status. If more than five people hold 50 percent of the stock, a personal holding company would not be formed. Another way to fail this test would be to have income that was not personal holding income comprise 41 percent or more of the total income.

Chapter 28

Accumulated Earnings Tax

Ted and Ellen—The Price of Profit

"I am glad to see how well both of your businesses are going," I said at the start of my next meeting with Ted and Ellen. "Plus, the real estate business looks to be a good source of passive income. It's probably time to start thinking about what the price of this profit might be."

"Right—you mean tax, don't you?" said Ellen. "We're doing a good job, I think, of planning for that tax through our monthly meetings."

"Actually, there is another tax to be concerned about—it's called the accumulated earnings tax. You might consider this another tax that is the price of success. To explain this, let me tell you the story of another company."

Life was looking great to the ten owners of ABC Inc. (A Big Company). In the beginning, they spent a few years struggling to create income, but the past five years had been profitable. After paying all their benefits and salaries, they still had $50,000 of income from each of the previous years. Maximizing the tax rate tables, they left the $50,000 of taxable income in the company at the low 15 percent tax rate.

Well, life had looked great until they learned about the accumulated earnings tax.

What Is Accumulated Earnings Tax?

Every C corporation runs the risk of being subject to this additional tax of 39.6 percent assessed on accumulated earnings in excess of $250,000 ($150,000 for personal service corporations). *This tax is in addition to the regular income tax paid by the corporation.*

ABC Inc. had just reached the $250,000 threshold ($50,000 × 5 years) and now had to face this tax. But first their board wanted to find out more about what accumulated earnings was and, more importantly, how to avoid it.

What Is Accumulated Earnings?

This is a much litigated portion of tax law and, interestingly, the case law does not mirror the IRS code and regulations. The simple definition, from the IRS code and regulations, states that accumulated earnings are the previously taxed income in the corporation reduced by any net capital gain. In other words, they are the retained earnings held by the corporation without any capital gains reflected.

There has been significant case law supporting the Bardahl formula, which basically says that accumulated earnings is actually the *working capital* of the company.

The working capital, or Bardahl formula, approach defines working capital as the amount necessary to run your company. There is a form at the end of this chapter that will help you determine your company's working capital needs.

The necessary working capital for your business can be used to reduce the accumulated earnings. For example, if you discover that you have a total of $350,000 in accumulated earnings in your company for a potential 39.6 percent tax on $100,000, you may also find that your working capital needs of $100,000 will allow you to avoid this tax. But as your company makes more money each year, the accumulated earnings will increase, increasing the risk of this problem.

Besides the working capital reduction, your company can also withhold a certain amount for projected growth and investment in the business. Your corporation can also take a deduction for life insurance paid on the life of key men and officers of the company.

You do not actually report the reduction for accumulated earnings. If your retained earnings are over $250,000, your corporation may get a letter from the IRS that asks about the accumulated earnings. You will be a long way ahead of the game if you can immediately offer copies of your working capital calculation, additional forecasted needs for the company, and corporate minutes that substantiate all of it.

ABC's Solution

ABC actually had a number of solutions to their issue. First, the IRS makes a specific exclusion for an amount necessary for the running of the business. So the accumulated earnings (however calculated) can be reduced by capital necessary for the business cycle. Examples of this would be additional inventory, down cycles in the business, additional equipment, and even future construction—as long as it relates to the business. A statement needs to be attached to the corporation's tax return that explains the purpose of the accumulated earnings.

Another potential solution, and one especially favorable for owners, is the purchase of a split dollar life insurance policy on the life of the owner by the corporation. (See below and Chapter 9.) The insurance premium reduces the accumulated earnings and allows cash to grow tax-free on behalf of the owner.

There are many issues surrounding split dollar life insurance, so it is important that you have a very knowledgeable insurance agent involved in the development of this plan.

Ted and Ellen's Plan

"I'm glad you told us about this potential tax," said Ellen. "My business is doing so well that I think we'll be looking at accumulated earnings tax sooner than later!"

"Let's talk about your plan for addressing that. What future expansion do you foresee?" I asked them.

Ted answered, "Actually, I don't see the business needing much more capital. To be honest, I'm intrigued with the split dollar life insurance. I remember when we talked about tax-free money growth and how powerful that was. Couldn't this split dollar life insurance grow tax free for me?"

"Ted, you're absolutely correct! One of the benefits of split dollar life insurance is that the corporation pays the premium, and a portion, based on the present value of a future income stream, is attributed to the employee. The employee will pay taxes on that amount, but, as you know, present value of future money is generally a small amount. So you are taking full advantage of the time value of money with this plan. I should note that there are many types of split dollar plans, including reverse split dollar plans. It depends on your and your corporation's specific situation. I'd be glad to talk to your insurance agent to help set up the best plan for you. It's great to get so much benefit *and* avoid a problem at the same time."

Split Dollar Life Insurance Plan

Ted and Ellen decided to get a split dollar life insurance plan. In their case, based on their own personal circumstances, they were able to pay less than $30,000 per year into a plan that would then grow into tax-free benefits upon retirement of $175,000 per year. They had to pay a small amount of tax each year, based on the PS58 costs of the plan. This is an actuarially based number that reflects what the present-day value of a future benefit is. The $30,000 per year paid into this plan was not a deduction for income tax, but was a reduction in the amount accumulating under the calculation for accumulated earnings tax. The split dollar plan was also a good solution for their personal-wealth-building plan, as their income was planned to increase as they got older. A traditional pension plan, which assumes that your tax rate will decrease upon your retirement, would not fit their needs.

SUMMARY

Accumulated earnings tax. The accumulated earnings tax of 39.6 percent is assessed on a C corporation's accumulated earnings in excess of $250,000.

Accumulated earnings. Accumulated earnings is defined as the previously taxed income reduced by any net capital gain. The IRS has allowed that the amount of accumulated earnings can be reduced by the necessary working capital of the business as well as reasonable amounts (which are substantiated) necessary for the projected growth and investments of the business. A form is included at the end of this chapter to help you determine the amount of accumulated earnings you have and whether you should be concerned about this additional tax.

ACCUMULATED EARNINGS TAX
SHORTCUT CALCULATION

Calculated at year end of   _____

Number of years operating   _____

1. Retained earnings per tax return   _____

ADD:

2. Dividends-received deduction (70%–80%
   reduction previously allowed)—all years
   in operation   _____

LESS:

3. Federal income tax—all years in operation   (_____)

4. Carry forward charitable contributions
   in current year   (_____)

5. Capital loss disallowed in current year   (_____)

6. Total accumulated earnings $_____

7. Credit ($150,000 for qualified personal service
   corporation; $250,000 for other corporations) (_____)

8. Excess accumulated earnings $_____

Note: The amount shown on Line 8 is potentially subject to 39.6 percent accumulated earnings tax. This is in addition to any federal and state income tax. The next form will show you ways to prepare for and avoid this tax.

WORKING CAPITAL NEEDS— BARDAHL FORMULA REDUCTION OF ACCUMULATED EARNINGS

Operating Business Cycle

1. Average inventory held $ _____

2. Total cost of goods sold $ _____

3. Inventory needed (Line 1 ÷ Line 2)   _____%

4. Average accounts receivable $ _____

5. Total sales $ _____

6. Accounts receivable float (Line 4 ÷ Line 5)   _____%

7. Average accounts payable $ _____

8. Material purchased $ _____

9. Accounts payable float (Line 7 ÷ Line 8)   _____%

10. Net percent (Line 3 + Line 6 – Line 9)   _____%

Working Capital Requirements

11. Operating expenses for a full year $ _____

12. Less depreciation expense   ($ _____)

13. Plus estimated income taxes $ _____

14. Adjusted operating expense $ _____

15. Necessary working capital (Line 10 × Line 14) $ _____

The working capital amount can be used to reduce the excess accumulated earnings amount.

Part VI

Keeping It Legal
and Safe

Chapter 29

Protect What You Have

Protect What You Have

"You've been operating your corporations for about six months now. How are you doing with keeping up with the paper and filing requirements?" I asked Ted and Ellen.

"I have to be honest, paperwork is just a strong point for either of us. Do we really have to do all of this?" asked Ellen, somewhat sheepishly.

"After putting together your corporations and then actually running your businesses, it probably seems that the paperwork is just one more boring and time-consuming task, and since it doesn't put any money in your pocket, might not even seem that important. Trust me, it is vitally important! You see, that is where you either succeed or fail in *keeping* what you've built. You want to keep it safe from lawsuits and from IRS judgments. Many people have felt like you have. Now is a good time to reinforce why this paperwork is so necessary."

Operating Like a Business

"Just like in the very beginning, when we examined if you truly had a business in order to take potential losses outside of the hobby loss rule, you must always make sure you truly have a business," I said.

"Many of these things become automatic once you have established the pattern. Here is an easy list of things to be done."

Make Sure Your Corporation Is Treated Like a Legal Entity

The risk is that a court may decide that you have operated your corporation as an "alter ego." In other words, there really wasn't a separate business that gave you protection from potential lawsuits. To make sure your assets are protected from risk, *always* do the following for your corporation:

1. Open a separate bank account(s) in the name of the corporation.
2. Do not commingle personal and business income or expenses.
3. Sign all documents as a corporation officer.
4. All advertising, stationery, signs, and so forth should reflect the corporation name.
5. Draw up employment contracts between the owner-employees and the corporation.
6. Key decisions should be approved in the minutes of the corporation.

Each of these will be discussed below. Why is all this required? The simple truth is that if you do not follow good business practices you must be prepared to stand personally liable for all debts and liabilities of the corporation, plus you might sacrifice all tax benefits that you planned on receiving from your corporation. Those seem like pretty good reasons to keep the necessary documentation!

OPEN A SEPARATE BANK ACCOUNT

The corporation must have a bank account that is separate from your personal account. Banks will frequently offer to just change the name on an existing sole proprietorship business to a corporation. I do not recommend this. It is much easier and cleaner to start with a new account.

You will need a copy of your articles of incorporation, your corporation's taxpayer ID number, and a resolution to open the bank account. The bank will probably provide you a blank corporate resolution for the bank account. This should be signed by a corporate officer. Usually the bank requires the signature of the corporate president and secretary.

DO NOT COMMINGLE FUNDS

What is commingling? It is mixing up your personal expenses with those of the corporation. *Never do this!* If you need to pay some corporate expenses and there isn't enough money in the corporate account, loan the corporation the money from your personal account so that the expenses are paid from the corporate account. If you do pay for items that require an expense reimbursement, use a standard expense reimbursement form, just like you would for any other business. In other words, leave a good trail.

Conversely, don't pay personal expenses from the corporate checking account. If you need the money, consult with your tax strategist for the best way to take money out of the corporation. Then pay those personal expenses from your personal account.

Commingling Is Dangerous!

Early in my career, I met with a new client who had just finally completed paying for a devastating judgment. Prior to becoming my client, he had operated a large strip mall under a corporation. However, he ran the corporation very loosely. He received Social Security checks and deposited those into the corporate account. At the end of the year, his prior tax preparer would credit those checks into a loan that the corporation owed to him.

Then, tragedy struck. Someone slipped on uneven pavement in the parking lot and was seriously injured. A lawsuit ensued. My new client had had liability insurance that capped at a certain level. The person was willing to settle for that amount until his attorney discovered that my client had been depositing his personal Social Security checks into the business. It didn't matter that at year end the accountant had made the proper adjustments, the fact was that these were personal income items that had been deposited directly into the business.

As a result, he was found to have commingled funds, and the court awarded a judgment against all of my new client's personal assets.

He had learned a very hard lesson about commingling and it is a lesson I never forgot. More than anything else, I strongly caution and watchdog clients against commingling funds.

SIGN ALL DOCUMENTS AS A CORPORATE OFFICER

Always sign as a corporate officer on any contracts, agreements, or correspondence. Some advisors also recommend that you sign as corporate officer on all checks that are written. It is a good rule of thumb to always use your corporate title whenever it could possibly be misconstrued as to whom you are representing—yourself or the corporation.

This is simple to do. Indicate the company name, and "By:", then sign your name, followed by your title. For example: "ABC Inc. By: Jane Doe, President." This reflects the company name, the signatory's name, and the title.

ADVERTISE UNDER YOUR CORPORATE NAME

Make sure your corporate name is used prominently in any literature for your business. This would include letterhead, business cards, telephone number in the phone book, and the sign outside the business office.

Again, this all goes to support that you have a separate corporate business, that this business is not merely a reflection of you personally.

DRAW UP EMPLOYMENT CONTRACTS

Clarify what your position is with the company by clearly outlining tasks, responsibilities, and compensation in an employment contract between the corporation and the employee. Frequently, new businesses don't have the revenue initially to pay the owner-shareholder. That's okay. Set up the contract and then in your annual minutes reflect that you have delayed compensation.

KEEP MINUTES THAT REFLECT KEY DECISIONS

Minutes of meetings are easy to prepare. First, of course, you need to convene a shareholders or directors meeting in accordance with the requirements in your corporate bylaws. Fortunately, this is easy to do. Next, clearly write out the decisions approved by your board of directors or shareholders by majority vote (the usual vote requirement for most corporate decisions). It is often easiest to do this using fill-in-the-blanks forms, since this is one legal area where using standard boilerplate legal language works well. Finally, place a copy of the minutes in your corporate record book.

You don't need to document routine business decisions—only those that require formal board of directors or shareholders approval. In other words, you are not required to clutter up your corporate record book with day-to-day business records, such as those for purchasing supplies or products, hiring or firing low- or mid-level employees, deciding to launch new services or products, or any of a host of other ongoing business decisions. All key legal, tax, and financial decisions, however, should be acted on by your board of directors and, occasionally, your shareholders.

What kinds of decisions should be considered key? Here are some examples:

1. Proceedings of annual meetings of directors and shareholders.
2. Issuance of stock to new or existing shareholders.
3. Purchase of real property.
4. Approval of a long-term lease.
5. Authorization of a significant loan amount or substantial line of credit.
6. Adoption of a stock option or retirement plan.
7. Important federal or state tax elections.
8. Other important decisions that have been made by your board of directors or shareholders.

Tax Tail Wagging the Economic Dog

One of the overriding concerns of courts has been that there should truly be a business purpose to the corporation. They have used the example of the "tax tail wagging the economic dog" to describe the type of sham business that is set up only for tax purposes. Obviously, you are allowed, in fact encouraged, to take advantage of the most optimum tax structures and tax planning. But there must also be a business purpose, and that business purpose can't be merely to pay less taxes. This is an area in which you will need good, experienced tax strategy advice.

Corporate Veil

"I heard the other day someone say you were completely protected for everything if you had a corporation. How does that work?" asked Ted.

"Ted, that's partially true. A corporation, when run correctly with all of the proper controls and documentation, has what is called a corporate veil. That means that lawsuits that might come about as a result of the business of the corporation can't get to your personal assets. For example, if an employee in your business got in a car accident while running errands for you, and it was determined that he was working for the business at the time, you could have risk from the results of that accident. But that risk would only go to the corporation and its assets. The person suing can't attach to any of your other assets, if your corporation has been properly set up and administered.

"There is one more point, though," I continued. "If there is a lawsuit that comes about as a result of something you, Ellen, or your children do, then the assets of the corporation could be at risk. For example, let's pick on Josh. When he's old enough to drive, let's assume that he gets in an accident. If there is a lawsuit against you, then the other side has the right to discovery of all of the assets that you own. One of those assets would be stock in the corporation. So you see the corporation veil really only works one way for asset protection."

"But there is a way to protect your assets, and that is through the use of a limited partnership. If your assets are held as a limited partner, and this could include the stock in your corporation, then the limited partnership can provide asset protection. In real life, if you were sued as a result of the hypothetical accident created by Josh, then the most that a successful judgment could get would be your rights as a limited partner. As you know, the control for a limited partnership rests with the general partner, not the limited partner. So the judgment doesn't have any assurance as to when or if the party suing you will get any assets. The reality is that as soon as a suing party sees a limited partnership interest they will likely try to attack the limited partnership. If all of the paperwork is correct, and they are not successful, they generally either go away or settle for a smaller amount."

SUMMARY

Operate like a business. One common mistake that owners of closely held corporations often make is that they try to run their corporations just like an offshoot of themselves. Do not fall into this trap! Run the business like a business. Make sure it is treated as a separate, legal entity. Do not commingle personal and business income and expenses. Sign all documents as an officer of your company. All advertising, stationery, and signs should reflect the corporate name. Draw up employment contracts between the owner-employees and the corporation. Key decisions should be approved by the board and documented in the minutes of the corporation. There must be a business purpose to the corporation.

Corporate veil. The corporate veil protects shareholders against liability that occurs from within the corporation. The corporation veil works just one way, though. A corporation will not protect the assets held within the structure from liability that arises from your personal actions. The asset that shareholders hold is the stock of the corporation, which can be attached by court judgment.

Chapter 30

How to Reduce Risk of an IRS Audit

IRS Audit Risk

"Ted, we're finally getting to an issue you had a while back—the concern about an IRS audit," I said as an introduction to the next subject with Ted and Ellen.

"I'm glad we're covering this. I know my fear is irrational at times, but I've heard such horror stories about the IRS," said Ted.

"Actually, a lot of those stories are blown out of proportion. Those things do happen to some people, but the fact is they don't happen to that many people. You just don't want to be one that they happen to! There are basically two ways to reduce IRS risk: 1) reduce the likelihood of an audit; and 2) reduce the damage that an audit can do. First, I want to discuss how to reduce the likelihood of an audit."

Reduce the Likelihood of an Audit

The IRS uses patterns and statistics in deciding which taxpayers to audit. By decreasing the red flags on your tax return, you can significantly reduce your chances of being audited. Here are some of the ways to avoid red flags:

1. Make sure there are no math errors on your return.

2. If at all possible, don't put down round numbers such as $10,000 or $4,000 on your tax return.

3. Make sure you put down on the tax forms the exact amount reported to you from the following forms—*even if they are wrong* (write the correct amount in a separate entry on the form):

- W-2 (wages and salaries)
- W-2G (gambling winnings)
- 1098 (mortgage interest paid)
- 1099-INT (interest earned)
- 1099-DIV (dividends earned)
- 1099-B (proceeds of sale)—allocating basis
- 1099-MISC (rents, royalties, prizes and awards, nonemployee compensation)
- 1099-R (pensions and IRA withdrawals)
- Form 5498 (IRA contribution information)

4. Attach all required schedules. For example, if you give noncash gifts having a value in excess of $500 to charity, you are required to attach a schedule.

5. Make sure you have the correct principal business or professional activity code on your business return. The wrong code will result in your return being compared to dissimilar businesses. See Appendix A for a list of the business codes.

Special Circumstances

One of the other things the IRS will look for will be that there is inventory and uniform capitalization of costs where there are sales of products. Many retailers don't properly record their inventory and many businesses that also happen to sell products don't even show inventory. The IRS is on to them!

Uniform capitalization has been around for a number of years now, but I am amazed at how many tax preparers either don't understand how to apply this principle or ignore it. You don't need to know how to do the calculation, but make sure your tax preparer does!

Uniform capitalization (called UNICAP) requires certain taxpayers to capitalize direct costs and an allocable portion of indirect costs. UNICAP covers any reseller who does not alter the form of the property, self-constructors who produce property for use in their own trade or business, and producers who acquire inventory and then change the form of the inventory before selling it. Resellers who have less than $10 million in gross sales price per year are exempt. If you manufacture products, your gross sales exemption is much lower. Check out the current law with your tax preparer.

Business Form

Although you don't want to make economic decisions simply based on audit statistics, the fact is that a Schedule C business (sole proprietor) has the highest likelihood of audit.

Following are the percentage of audits performed by the IRS, by year:

	1997	1998	1999
Individuals	0.61%	0.46%	0.31%
Schedule C			
$25,000–$100,000 in income	2.04	1.44	1.01
$100,000–above in income	3.44	2.85	2.08
Corporations			
Less than $250,000 in assets	1.16	0.75	0.44
$250,000–$1 million in assets	3.49	2.49	1.65

The other fact you see from studying this chart is that the number of audits is going down. The IRS is concentrating on certain pockets of known problems and is reducing the number of face-to-face audits.

What Is an Audit?

The other thing to remember when you hear the statistics on how many Americans are audited each year is how the IRS counts audits. Any letter sent questioning or changing a tax amount is considered an audit. Many audits today are conducted as desk audits. That means they do not come to your home or your business. In fact, many times you don't even go to their office, but simply mail in proof of whatever they are questioning.

Final Comments

- File on time (or with timely extension)
- Be thorough
- Be neat
- Be sure math is correct
- Be consistent
- Fill in all blanks that should be filled in
- Balance out deductions to reasonable amount compared to income
- Sign your return
- Mail return receipt requested

SUMMARY

IRS audit risk. There are two ways to reduce IRS risk. First, reduce the likelihood of an audit and, second, reduce the damage that an audit can do.

Ways to reduce risk of an audit. In order to reduce the risk of an IRS audit, make sure there are no math errors on the return. Don't put down round numbers. Make sure your return reflects any tax forms that report income, even if the forms are incorrect. Attach all required schedules. Make sure you have the correct principal business or professional activity code on your business return. If you have a targeted business, be prepared for an IRS audit. Make sure you are in compliance with special circumstances such as recording inventory if you sell products.

Chapter 31

How to Reduce Risk from an IRS Audit

What to Do if You Get a Letter from the IRS

First of all, you are not going to jail! But don't ignore the letter either. Action is needed. It just needs to be reasoned and logical action. I always instruct my clients to immediately fax to me any correspondence they receive from the IRS. That serves two purposes: 1) gets it out of their hands, so they can stop worrying; and 2) serves notice to someone who knows how to deal with the notice.

You Get a Letter

There are three general types of IRS audits:

1. Mail audit
2. Office audit
3. Field audit

The mail audit typically occurs when there is a discrepancy within the return (such as a calculation error) or with third-party information (such as 1099s). Usually, these audits merely require submitting backup information, documents, and an explanation.

An office audit normally is for W-2 wage earners and some small business owners. The taxpayer is required to bring substantiating documentation for the return to the local IRS office for analysis. The office audit typically lasts one day or less. Immediately upon receipt of an office audit notice, the taxpayer should consult their tax preparer.

Field audits, where one or more IRS revenue agents come to a taxpayer's office, are usually reserved for corporations, partnerships, and limited liability companies, although complex sole proprietorships are also subject to field audits. The auditor has to go to the office of the taxpayer because the documentation and legal issues are voluminous and complex. The taxpayer should expect to obtain proper representation, as well as further accounting assistance to prepare for the audit.

Maybe They Made a Mistake

Don't assume that the IRS is right if you get a notice. There are some common areas where the IRS's technologies have not kept up and they consistently make errors. Some common errors by the IRS:

• Mismatching information on W-2 forms with information on Form 1040.

• Employers can currently file W-2 returns on their employees using either a standardized W-2 form or via magnetic media (tapes). In some cases, with large employers, they must file using the magnetic media. When they do, they can use a nonstandardized W-2 form, which will not always be readily apparent to the temporary IRS worker who is working on the crunch of mail that arrives during tax time. There are simply too many forms to look at, and they might miss one, which kicks the return out for a letter. Nothing was done incorrectly, it is simply a case of human error and a system that doesn't support the IRS worker.

• Total the IRS key-punches from Form 1099 is more than the gross income actually reported.

What if You Get an Incorrect 1099?

You may occasionally get an incorrect Form 1099. What you do about it will depend on what the error is.

- Social Security number is incorrect: Contact the issuer to have them send a corrected Form 1099 with correct number.
- Income is stated incorrectly: Contact the issuer to have them send a corrected Form 1099. If they refuse, include the amount shown (if more) on your return and then subtract the difference with a note that the Form 1099 was issued incorrectly.

What if the IRS Is Wrong?

The IRS is incorrect more often than they probably want to admit. If they are, always follow these three steps: 1) promptly answer their correspondence; 2) send copies of documentation proving your point; and 3) always mail return receipt requested.

Before the Letter Arrives

Reduce the risk from an IRS audit before you even get a letter by always having proper documentation, corporate minutes, properly executed agreements, and copies of invoices and canceled checks neatly filed.

The IRS will expect you to produce the following documents:

- Bank statements, canceled checks, and receipts.
- Books and records. A good accounting software program such as Qbooks Pro will provide the necessary information, as long as the information has all been accurately and competently entered.
- Appointment books, logs, and diaries. Businesses generally track appointments using calendars, business diaries, or appointment books that are shown either manually or on computer programs. These can provide excellent additional proof for business expenses.
- Automobile records. A log is the best way to track business use of an automobile, but it is not strictly required by the tax code. Another plan would be to keep all gas and repair receipts in an orderly fashion with notations of trips showing how the car was used for business. A less accurate way is to simply add up the gas bills and divide the number of miles per gallon that your car averages.
- Travel and entertainment records. You must have a written record of the specific business purpose for the travel or entertainment expense, as

well as a receipt for it. For entertainment, the amount of each separate expenditure must be substantiated.

How Long Do You Need to Keep Records?

Following is a snapshot look at various records and the recommended time to retain them. (See also "Suggested Record Retention List" in Appendix D.) The major categories are:

• Supporting records. You must keep records until the statute of limitations for the return expires. Ordinarily, the statute of limitations for an income tax return expires three years after the return is due to be filed or is filed, or two years from the date that tax is paid, whichever is later. In some cases, you must keep records indefinitely. For example, if you change your method of accounting, records supporting the necessary adjustments may remain applicable for an indefinite time.

• Employment tax records. You must keep all employment tax records for at least four years after the date on which a tax return becomes due or the tax is paid, whichever is later.

• Tax returns. You should keep all copies of your filed tax returns for all years. They will help you in preparing your future tax returns, and in making computations if you later file a claim for a refund. They may also be helpful to the executor or administrator of your estate, or to an IRS examiner if your original return is not available.

Good Records

The law requires that you keep good records so that you can prepare complete and accurate tax returns. You must be able to substantiate items of income, deductions, and credits. (See also "Suggested Record Retention List" in Appendix D.)

Review the following:

• Identify sources of income. You may receive money or property from a variety of sources. Your records should identify the sources of your income. You need this information to separate taxable income from non-taxable deposits.

• Keep track of expenses. You may forget an expense unless you record it when it occurs. You can use your records to identify expenses for which you can claim a deduction.

• Keep track of the basis of property. You need to keep records that show the basis of your property. This includes the original cost or other basis of the property and any improvements you made.

• Prepare tax returns. You need records to prepare your tax return. Good records help you file quickly and accurately.

• Support items reported on tax returns. You must keep records in case the IRS has a question about an item on your return. If the IRS examines your tax return, you may be asked to explain the items reported. Good records will help you explain any item and arrive at the correct tax with minimum effort. If you do not have records, you may have to spend time getting statements and receipts from various sources. If you cannot produce the correct documents, you may have to pay additional tax and be subject to penalties.

Targeted Businesses

There are some types of businesses that the IRS has specifically targeted as being poor record-keepers. If you have one of these businesses, make sure you have good records to stop a problem before it begins. These following targeted businesses and business-related issues are directly out of the IRS agents manual:

Air charters
Attorneys
Bed-and-breakfasts
Gas retailers
Mortuaries
Entertainment
Independent used car dealers
Taxicabs
Trucking
Employment tax—Classification of workers as independent vs.
    employee
Alaska commercial fishing

Architects

Bars and restaurants

Foreign athletes and entertainers

Entertainers

Ministers

Mobile food vendors

Rehabilitation tax credit

Resolution Corporation (RTC) Trust—cancellation of indebtedness

Wine industry

Beauty and barber shops

Auto body and repair

Reforestation

Pizza restaurants

The Port Project

Grain farmers

Passive activity losses

Oil and gas

Tobacco

Cattle

Entertainment—music

Garment contractors

Artists and art galleries

Bail bond industry

Coal excise tax

Commercial banking

Commercial printing

Computers, electronics, and high-tech

Farming—specific income issues and farm cooperatives

Furniture manufacturing

Garment manufacturing

Hardwood timber

Retail liquor

Tour bus

Tip reporting—hairstyling

Tip reporting—gaming

Tip reporting—food service

Prepare

The single answer for how to reduce risk from IRS audit is to properly prepare for the audit. With good, neat, and easily accessible records, the concern will be reduced. If keeping good records is not your strongest suit, then turn that function over to a competent bookkeeper. Bookkeepers are trained in how to keep track of documentation. Follow their lead!

Common Errors for Businesses

If you are audited by the IRS, the agent's handbook will direct them to look at specific items. These follow:

• **IRS Code Section 7872—Imputed interest rules.** The IRS agent is looking for loans to and from stockholders and their corporations that have been made at below-market interest rates. They also will look to see that the property interest income or expense has been recorded. The answer to this is to make sure you have proper documentation for loans and that interest has been recorded. The IRS publishes a list each year of minimum interest for loans. For 2000, interest at 7 percent or more would be safe.

• **IRS Section 3121—Disguised compensation.** The agent is looking for payments that have been made in lieu of wages, such as management fees or contract fees. Be careful that you do not mix nonemployee compensation with personal compensation.

• **IRS Section 162—Trade or business expenses.** The IRS is looking for inappropriate or clearly personal expenses that have been expensed in the corporation. Above all, look for reasonableness in the expenses you show on your return. Don't put huge amounts as "miscellaneous" or lump amounts together that would look more normal when separated out.

• **IRS Section 3509—Employer's liability for employment taxes.** The IRS is looking for the failure of employers to classify workers correctly and thus avoiding employment taxes.

• **IRS Section 1101—Adjusted basis for determining gain or loss.** The IRS is checking here to make sure that the totals shown on your depreciation schedule match the numbers shown on your balance sheet.

• **IRS Section 301—Distributions of property.** The IRS makes sure that assets that have been distributed to shareholders have been reported at the property's fair market value. They will specifically examine below-market sales to related parties. Of course, the answer to this problem is to never put potentially appreciating property into a C corporation. These should instead be held within a structure that can be taxed as a partnership.

- **IRS Section 1231—Sales of trade or business property.** The IRS Form 4797 is used to report these sales and it is extremely complex. The IRS has also discovered that many tax preparers make math errors on this report.

- **IRS Section 531—Accumulated earnings tax.** The best way to handle this potential problem is to prepare for it as discussed in Chapter 28.

- **IRS Section 61—Gross income.** The IRS will look for the gross profit margins (gross profit equal sales less cost of goods) that are out of alignment with other similar businesses.

- **IRS Section 471—Inventories.** The IRS is looking for inventory that has been understated (increasing cost of goods sold). To protect against this challenge, take an actual physical inventory each year and keep records of how this is done and calculated.

- **IRS Section 3121—S corporation shareholders.** In this case, the IRS is looking for 2 percent or more shareholders within an S corporation that receive distributions or excessive rent payments in lieu of a reasonable salary.

- **IRS Section 1366—Pass through to shareholders.** The IRS requires that certain benefits paid to shareholders be reported separately to shareholders and that these shareholders adequately track basis and correctly calculate debt basis.

Targeted Business Forms

The IRS has categorized certain types of business structures as subject to fraud and are specifically targeting them for audit. These are:

- Business trusts
- Equipment or service trusts
- Family residence trusts
- Charitable trusts
- Foreign trusts

For more information regarding the IRS's view of these types of businesses, see www.irs.gov for Publication 2193, "Too Good to Be True Trusts."

SUMMARY

What to do if you get a letter from the IRS. First of all, you are not going to jail! The best response is to send the letter to your tax preparer and follow the advice given.

Three types of IRS audit. There are three general types of IRS audit: 1) mail audit, 2) office audit, and 3) field audit. A mail audit occurs when there is a discrepancy within the return or between the return and third-party information. An office audit occurs for W-2 wage earners and small business owners. The office audit typically lasts one day or less and is performed in the IRS office. A field audit occurs when IRS revenue agents come to a taxpayer's office to review documents.

The IRS can be wrong. The IRS is frequently incorrect. If that is the case, do not ignore the notice. Instead promptly respond and make sure you always mail your response return receipt requested.

Keep good records. The key to surviving an IRS audit is to have good records. These include copies of invoices, canceled checks, bank statements, general ledgers, and other supporting computer and accounting records. In the case of a corporation, make sure you have supporting minutes authorizing all major acts of the directors.

A Final Word

Tax planning, above all, must make sound economic sense. Don't make the ends (less tax) justify the means (all that it takes to get there). For one thing, that means may be much more expensive than the benefit. Weigh carefully the decisions you make for your own tax strategies. Assess your goals, the skill of your assembled team, and look at the cost/benefit of any changes. The costs can be seen in many areas—lost sleep, more team needed, unease, and, of course, the actual hard cost of operations.

Are You Planning to Be Rich?

You *can* make the decision today to make significant changes in your financial life. Follow the Five STEPS, learn the Three Step Tax Formula, and carefully consider the other elements of tax planning. Loopholes do exist. They are there for you, too. Make the most of what is available to create the financial life you've always dreamed of. Live rich!

Appendix A
IRS Principal Business and Professional Activity Codes

The IRS compares businesses, their income, and expenses based on the type of business activity they have. Following is the list of business codes that the IRS recognizes. You or your tax preparer will have to select from the following list when you file your corporate or partnership return. Take the time to check the list to find the best fit for your type of business. Careful selection can be the single most powerful way to avoid unnecessary IRS audits.

Agriculture, Forestry, Fishing and Hunting

CROP PRODUCTION

111100	Oilseed & Grain Farming
111210	Vegetable & Melon Farming (including potatoes & yams)
111300	Fruit & Tree Nut Farming
111400	Greenhouse, Nursery & Floriculture Production
111900	Other Crop Farming (including tobacco, cotton, sugarcane, hay, peanut, sugar beet & all other crop farming)

ANIMAL PRODUCTION

112111	Beef Cattle Ranching & Farming
112112	Cattle Feedlots
112120	Dairy Cattle & Milk Production
112210	Hog & Pig Farming
112300	Poultry & Egg Production
112400	Sheep & Goat Farming
112510	Animal Aquaculture (including shellfish & finfish farms & hatcheries)
112900	Other Animal Production

FORESTRY AND LOGGING

113100   Timber Tract Operation

113210   Forest Nurseries & Gathering of Forest Products

113310   Logging

FISHING, HUNTING, AND TRAPPING

114110   Fishing

114210   Hunting & Trapping

SUPPORT ACTIVITIES FOR AGRICULTURE AND FORESTRY

11510   Support Activities for Crop Production (including cotton ginning, soil preparation, planting, & cultivating)

115210   Support Activities for Animal Production

115310   Support Activities for Forestry

Mining

21110   Oil & Gas Extraction

212110   Coal Mining

212200   Metal Ore Mining

212310   Stone Mining & Quarrying

212320   Sand, Gravel, Clay & Ceramic, & Refractory Minerals Mining & Quarrying

212390   Other Nonmetallic Mineral Mining & Quarrying

213110   Support Activities for Mining

Utilities

221100   Electric Power Generation, Transmission, & Distribution

221210   Natural Gas Distribution

221300   Water, Sewage, & Other Systems

Construction

BUILDING, DEVELOPING AND GENERAL CONTRACTING

233110   Land Subdivision & Land Development

233200   Residential Building Construction

233300   Nonresidential Building Construction

HEAVY CONSTRUCTION

234100   Highway, Street, Bridge & Tunnel Construction
234900   Other Heavy Construction

SPECIAL TRADE CONTRACTORS

235110   Plumbing, Heating & Air-Conditioning Contractors
235210   Painting & Wall Covering Contractors
235310   Electrical Contractors
235400   Masonry, Drywall, Insulation & Tile Contractors
235500   Carpentry & Floor Contractors
235610   Roofing, Siding & Sheet Metal Contractors
235710   Concrete Contractors
235810   Water Well Drilling Contractors
235900   Other Special Trade Contractors

Manufacturing

FOOD MANUFACTURING

311110   Animal Food Mfg
311200   Grain & Oilseed Milling
311300   Sugar & Confectionery Product Mfg
311300   Sugar & Vegetable Preserving & Specialty Food Mfg
311500   Dairy Product Mfg
311610   Animal Slaughtering and Processing
311710   Seafood Product Preparation & Packaging
311800   Bakeries & Tortilla Mfg
311900   Other Food Mfg (including coffee, tea, flavorings & seasonings)

BEVERAGE AND TOBACCO PRODUCT MANUFACTURING

312110   Soft Drink & Ice Mfg
312120   Breweries
312130   Wineries
312140   Distilleries
312200   Tobacco Mfg

TEXTILE MILLS AND TEXTILE PRODUCT MILLS

313000   Textile Mills
314000   Textile Product Mills

APPAREL MANUFACTURING

315100	Apparel Knitting Mills
315210	Cut & Sew Apparel Contractors
315220	Men's & Boys' Cut & Sew Apparel Mfg
315230	Women's & Girls' Cut & Sew Apparel Mfg
315290	Other Cut & Sew Apparel Mfg
315990	Apparel Accessories & Other Apparel Mfg

LEATHER AND ALLIED PRODUCT MANUFACTURING

316110	Leather & Hide Tanning & Finishing
316210	Footwear Mfg (including rubber & plastics)
316990	Other Leather & Allied Product Mfg

WOOD PRODUCT MANUFACTURING

321110	Sawmills & Wood Preservations
321210	Veneer, Plywood & Engineered Wood Product Mfg
321900	Other Wood Product Mfg

PAPER MANUFACTURING

322100	Pulp, Paper & Paperboard Mills
322200	Converted Paper Product Mfg

PRINTING AND RELATED SUPPORT ACTIVITIES

323100	Printing & Related Support Activities

PETROLEUM AND COAL PRODUCTS MANUFACTURING

324110	Petroleum Refineries (including integrated)
324120	Asphalt Paving, Roofing, & Saturated Materials Mfg
324190	Other Petroleum & Coal Products Mfg

CHEMICAL MANUFACTURING

325100	Basic Chemical Mfg
325200	Resin, Synthetic Rubber & Artificial & Synthetic Fibers & Filaments Mfg
325300	Pesticide, Fertilizer & Other Agricultural Chemical Mfg
325410	Pharmaceutical & Medicine Mfg

325500   Paint, Coating & Adhesive Mfg

325600   Soap, Cleaning Compound & Toilet Preparation Mfg

325900   Other Chemical Product & Preparation Mfg

PLASTICS AND RUBBER PRODUCTS MANUFACTURING

326100   Plastics Product Mfg

326200   Rubber Products Mfg

NONMETALLIC MINERAL PRODUCT MANUFACTURING

327100   Clay Product & Refractory Mfg

327210   Glass & Glass Product Mfg

327300   Cement & Concrete Product Mfg

327400   Lime & Gypsum Product Mfg

327900   Other Nonmetallic Mineral Product Mfg

PRIMARY METAL MANUFACTURING

331110   Iron & Steel Mills & Ferroalloy Mfg

331200   Steel Product Mfg from Purchased Steel

331310   Alumina & Aluminum Production & Processing

331400   Nonferrous Metal (except Aluminum) Production & Processing

331500   Foundries

FABRICATED METAL PRODUCT MANUFACTURING

332110   Forging & Stamping

332210   Cutlery & Handtool Mfg

332300   Architectural & Structural Metals Mfg

332400   Boiler, Tank & Shipping Container Mfg

332510   Hardware Mfg

332610   Spring & Wire Product Mfg

332700   Machine Shops; Turned Product; & Screw, Nut & Bolt Mfg

332810   Coating, Engraving, Heat Treating & Allied Activities

332900   Other Fabricated Metal Product Mfg

MACHINERY MANUFACTURING

333100   Agriculture, Construction & Mining Machinery Mfg

333200   Industrial Machinery Mfg

333310 Commercial & Service Industry Machinery Mfg

333410 Ventilation, Heating, Air-Conditioning & Commercial Refrigeration Equipment Mfg

333510 Metalworking Machinery Mfg

333610 Engine, Turbine & Power Transmission Equipment Mfg

333900 Other General Purpose Machinery Mfg

COMPUTER AND ELECTRONIC PRODUCT MANUFACTURING

334110 Computer & Peripheral Equipment Mfg

334200 Communications Equipment Mfg

334310 Audio & Video Equipment Mfg

334410 Semiconductor & Other Electronic Component Mfg

334500 Navigational Measuring, Electromedical & Control Instruments Mfg

334610 Manufacturing & Reproducing Magnetic & Optical Media

ELECTRICAL EQUIPMENT, APPLIANCE AND COMPONENT MANUFACTURING

335100 Electrical Lighting Equipment Mfg

335200 Household Appliance Mfg

335310 Electrical Equipment Mfg

335900 Other Electrical Equipment & Component Mfg

TRANSPORTATION EQUIPMENT MANUFACTURING

336100 Motor Vehicle Mfg

336210 Motor Vehicle Body & Trailer Mfg

336300 Motor Vehicle Parts Mfg

336410 Aerospace Product & Parts Mfg

336510 Railroad Rolling Stock Mfg

336610 Ship & Boat Building

336990 Other Transportation Equipment Mfg

FURNITURE AND RELATED PRODUCT MANUFACTURING

337000 Furniture & Related Product Mfg

MISCELLANEOUS MANUFACTURING

339110 Medical Equipment & Supplies Mfg

339900 Other Miscellaneous Mfg

Wholesale Trade

421100	Motor Vehicles & Motor Vehicle Parts & Supplies Wholesalers
421200	Furniture & Home Furnishings Wholesalers
421300	Lumber & Other Construction Materials Wholesalers
421400	Professional & Commercial Equipment & Supplies Wholesalers
421500	Metal & Mineral (except petroleum) Wholesalers
421600	Electrical Good Wholesalers
421700	Hardware & Plumbing & Heating Equipment Supplies Wholesalers
421800	Machinery, Equipment & Supplies Wholesalers
421910	Sporting & Recreational Goods & Supplies Wholesalers
421920	Toy & Hobby Goods & Supplies Wholesalers
421930	Recyclable Material Wholesalers
421940	Jewelry, Watch, Precious Stone & Precious Metal Wholesalers
421990	Other Miscellaneous Durable Goods Wholesalers

Wholesale Trade, Nondurable Goods

422100	Paper & Paper Product Wholesalers
422210	Drugs & Druggists' Sundries Wholesalers
422300	Apparel, Piece Goods & Notions Wholesalers
422400	Grocery & Related Product Wholesalers
422500	Farm Product Raw Material Wholesalers
422600	Chemical & Allied Products Wholesalers
422700	Petroleum & Petroleum Products Wholesalers
422800	Beer, Wine & Distilled Alcoholic Beverage Wholesalers
422910	Farm Supplies Wholesalers
422920	Book, Periodical & Newspaper Wholesalers
422930	Flower, Nursery Stock & Florists' Supplies Wholesalers
422940	Tobacco & Tobacco Product Wholesalers
422950	Paint, Varnish & Supplies Wholesalers
422990	Other Miscellaneous Nondurable Goods Wholesalers

Retail Trade

Motor Vehicle and Parts Dealers

441110	New Car Dealers
441120	Used Car Dealers

441210   Recreational Vehicle Dealers
441221   Motorcycle Dealers
441222   Boat Dealers
441229   All Other Motor Vehicle Dealers
441300   Automotive Parts, Accessories & Tire Stores

FURNITURE AND HOME FURNISHINGS STORES
442110   Furniture Stores
442210   Floor Covering Stores
442291   Window Treatment Stores
442299   All Other Home Furnishings Stores

ELECTRONICS AND APPLIANCE STORES
443111   Household Appliance Stores
443112   Radio, Television & Other Electronics Stores
443120   Computer & Software Stores
443130   Camera & Photographic Supplies Stores

BUILDING MATERIAL AND GARDEN EQUIPMENT AND SUPPLIES DEALERS
444110   Home Centers
444120   Paint & Wallpaper Stores
444130   Hardware Stores
444190   Other Building Material Dealers
444200   Lawn & Garden Equipment & Supplies Stores

FOOD AND BEVERAGE STORES
445110   Supermarkets and Other Grocery (except convenience)
           Stores
445120   Convenience Stores
445210   Meat Markets
445220   Fish & Seafood Markets
445230   Fruit & Vegetable Markets
445291   Baked Goods Stores
445292   Confectionery & Nut Stores
445299   All Other Specialty Food Stores
445310   Beer, Wine & Liquor Stores

Health and Personal Care Stores

446110	Pharmacies & Drug Stores
446120	Cosmetics, Beauty Supplies & Perfume Stores
446130	Optical Goods Stores
446190	Other Health & Personal Care Stores

Gasoline Stations

447100	Gasoline Stations (including convenience stores with gas)

Clothing and Clothing Accessories Stores

448110	Men's Clothing Stores
448120	Women's Clothing Stores
448130	Children's & Infants' Clothing Stores
448140	Family Clothing Stores
448150	Clothing Accessories Stores
448190	Other Clothing Stores
448210	Shoe Stores
448310	Jewelry Stores
448320	Luggage & Leather Goods Stores

Sporting Goods, Hobby, Book and Music Stores

451110	Sporting Goods Stores
451120	Hobby, Toy & Game Stores
451130	Sewing, Needlework & Piece Goods Stores
451140	Musical Instrument & Supplies Stores
451211	Book Stores
451212	News Dealers & Newsstands
451220	Prerecorded Tape, Compact Disc & Record Stores

General Merchandise Stores

452110	Department Stores
452900	Other General Merchandise Stores

Miscellaneous Store Retailers

453110	Florists
453210	Office Supplies & Stationery Stores

453220   Gift, Novelty & Souvenir Stores
453310   Used Merchandise Stores
453910   Pet & Pet Supplies Stores
453920   Art Dealers
453930   Manufactured (Mobile) Home Dealers
453990   All Other Miscellaneous Store Retailers (including tobacco, candle & trophy shops)

NONSTORE RETAILERS
454110   Electronic Shopping & Mail-Order Houses
454210   Vending Machine Operators
454311   Heating Oil Dealers
454312   Liquefied Petroleum Gas (bottled gas) Dealers
454319   Other Fuel Dealers
454390   Other Direct Selling Establishments (including door-to-door retailing, frozen food plan providers, party plan merchandisers & coffee-break service providers)

Transportation and Warehousing

AIR, RAIL AND WATER TRANSPORTATION
481000   Air Transportation
482000   Rail Transportation
483000   Water Transportation

TRUCK TRANSPORTATION
484110   General Freight Trucking, Local
484120   General Freight Trucking, Long-distance
484200   Specialized Freight Trucking

TRANSIT AND GROUND PASSENGER TRANSPORTATION
485110   Urban Transit Systems
485210   Interurban & Rural Bus Transportation
485310   Taxi Service
485320   Limousine Service

485410   School & Employee Bus Transportation
458510   Charter Bus Industry
485990   Other Transit & Ground Passenger Transportation

PIPELINE TRANSPORTATION
486000   Pipeline Transportation

SCENIC AND SIGHTSEEING TRANSPORTATION
487000   Scenic & Sightseeing Transportation

SUPPORT ACTIVITIES FOR TRANSPORTATION
488100   Support Activities for Air Transportation
488210   Support Activities for Rail Transportation
488300   Support Activities for Water Transportation
488410   Motor Vehicle Towing
488490   Other Support Activities for Road Transportation
488510   Freight Transportation Arrangement
488990   Other Support Activities for Transportation

COURIERS AND MESSENGERS
492110   Couriers
492210   Local Messengers & Local Delivery

WAREHOUSING AND STORAGE
493100   Warehousing & Storage Facilities (except lessors of miniwarehouses & self-storage units)

Information

PUBLISHING INDUSTRIES
511110   Newspaper Publishers
511120   Periodical Publishers
511130   Book Publishers
511140   Database & Directory Publishers
511190   Other Publishers
511210   Software Publishers

MOTION PICTURE AND SOUND RECORDING INDUSTRIES

512100	Motion Picture & Video Industries (except video rental)
51220	Sound Recording Industries

BROADCASTING AND TELECOMMUNICATIONS

513100	Radio & Television Broadcasting
513200	Cable Networks & Program Distribution
513300	Telecommunications (including paging, cellular, satellite & other telecommunications)

INFORMATION SERVICES AND DATA PROCESSING SERVICES

514100	Information Services (including news syndicates, libraries & on-line information services)
514210	Data Processing Services

Finance and Insurance

DEPOSITORY CREDIT INTERMEDIATION

522110	Commercial Banking
522120	Savings Institutions
522130	Credit Unions
522190	Other Depository Credit Intermediation

NONDEPOSITORY CREDIT INTERMEDIATION

522210	Credit Card Issuing
522220	Sales Financing
522291	Consumer Lending
522292	Real Estate Credit (including mortgage bankers & originators)
522293	International Trade Financing
522294	Secondary Market Financing
522298	All Other Nondepository Credit Intermediation

ACTIVITIES RELATED TO CREDIT INTERMEDIATION

522300	Activities Related to Credit Intermediation (including loan brokers)

Securities, Commodity Contracts and Other Financial Investments and Related Activities

523110	Investment Banking & Securities Dealing
523120	Securities Brokerage
523130	Commodity Contracts Dealing
523140	Commodity Contracts Brokerage
523210	Securities & Commodity Exchanges
523900	Other Financial Investment Activities (including portfolio management & investment advice)

Insurance Carriers and Related Activities

524140	Direct Life, Health & Medical Insurance & Reinsurance Carriers
524150	Direct Insurance & Reinsurance (except life, health & medical) Carriers
524210	Insurance Agencies & Brokerages
524290	Other Insurance Related Activities

Funds, Trusts and Other Financial Vehicles

525100	Insurance & Employee Benefit Funds
525910	Open-End Investment Funds (Form 1120-RIC)
525920	Trusts, Estates & Agency Accounts
525930	Real Estate Investment Trusts (Form 1120-REIT)
525990	Other Financial Vehicles

Real Estate and Rental and Leasing

Real Estate

531110	Lessors of Residential Buildings & Dwellings
531120	Lessors of Nonresidential Buildings (except miniwarehouses)
531130	Lessors of Miniwarehouses & Self-Storage Units
531190	Lessors of Other Real Estate Property
531210	Offices of Real Estate Agents & Brokers
531310	Real Estate Property Managers
531320	Offices of Real Estate Appraisers
531390	Other Activities Related to Real Estate

RENTAL AND LEASING SERVICES

532100	Automotive Equipment Rental & Leasing
532210	Consumer Electronics & Appliances Rental
532220	Formal Wear & Costume Rental
532230	Video Tape & Disc Rental
532290	Other Consumer Goods Rental
532310	General Rental Centers
532400	Commercial & Industrial Machinery & Equipment Rental & Leasing

LESSORS OF NONFINANCIAL INTANGIBLE ASSETS (EXCEPT COPYRIGHTED WORKS)

533110	Lessors of Nonfinancial Intangible Assets (except copyrighted works)

Professional, Scientific and Technical Services

LEGAL SERVICES

541110	Offices of Lawyers
541190	Other Legal Services

ACCOUNTING, TAX PREPARATION, BOOKKEEPING AND PAYROLL SERVICES

541211	Offices of Certified Public Accountants
541213	Tax Preparation Services
541214	Payroll Services
541219	Other Accounting Services

ARCHITECTURAL, ENGINEERING AND RELATED SERVICES

541310	Architectural Services
541320	Landscape Architecture Services
541330	Engineering Services
541340	Drafting Services
541350	Building Inspection Services
541360	Geophysical Surveying & Mapping Services
541370	Surveying & Mapping (except geophysical) Services
541380	Testing Laboratories

SPECIALIZED DESIGN SERVICES

541400   Specialized Design Services (including interior, industrial, graphic & fashion design)

COMPUTER SYSTEMS DESIGN AND RELATED SERVICES

541511   Custom Computer Programming Services
541512   Computer Systems Design Services
541513   Computer Facilities Management Services
541519   Other Computer Related Services

OTHER PROFESSIONAL, SCIENTIFIC AND TECHNICAL SERVICES

541600   Management, Scientific & Technical Consulting Services
541700   Scientific Research & Development Services
541800   Advertising & Related Services
541910   Marketing Research & Public Opinion Polling
541920   Photographic Services
541930   Translation & Interpretation Services
541940   Veterinary Services
541990   All Other Professional, Scientific & Technical Services

MANAGEMENT OF COMPANIES (HOLDING COMPANIES)

551111   Offices of Bank Holding Companies
551112   Offices of Other Holding Companies

Administrative and Support and Waste Management and Remediation Services

ADMINISTRATIVE AND SUPPORT SERVICES

561110   Office Administrative Services
561210   Facilities Support Services
561300   Employment Services
561410   Document Preparation Services
561420   Telephone Call Centers
561430   Business Service Centers (including private mail centers & copy shops)

561440   Collection Agencies

561450   Credit Bureaus

561490   Other Business Support Services (including repossession services, court reporting and stenotype services)

561500   Travel Arrangement & Reservation Services

561600   Investigation & Security Services

561710   Exterminating & Pest Control Services

561720   Janitorial Services

561730   Landscaping Services

561740   Carpet & Upholstery Cleaning Services

561790   Other Services to Buildings & Dwellings

561900   Other Support Services (including packaging & labeling services & convention & trade show organizers)

WASTE MANAGEMENT AND REMEDIATION SERVICES

562000   Waste Management & Remediation Services

Educational Services

EDUCATIONAL SERVICES

611000   Educational Services (including schools, colleges & universities)

Health Care and Social Assistance

OFFICES OF PHYSICIANS AND DENTISTS

621111   Offices of Physicians (except mental health specialists)

621112   Offices of Physicians, Mental Health Specialists

621210   Offices of Dentists

OFFICES OF OTHER HEALTH PRACTITIONERS

621310   Offices of Chiropractors

621320   Offices of Optometrists

621330   Offices of Mental Health Practitioners (except physicians)

621340   Offices of Physical, Occupational & Speech Therapists & Audiologists

621391   Offices of Podiatrists

621399   Offices of All Other Miscellaneous Health Practitioners

Outpatient Care Centers

621410   Family Planning Centers

621420   Outpatient Mental Health & Substance Abuse Centers

621491   HMO Medical Centers

621492   Kidney Dialysis Centers

621493   Freestanding Ambulatory Surgical & Emergency Centers

621498   All Other Outpatient Care Centers

Medical and Diagnostic Laboratories

621510   Medical & Diagnostic Laboratories

Home Health Care Services

621610   Home Health Care Services

Other Ambulatory Health Care Services

621900   Other Ambulatory Health Care Services (including ambulance services & blood & organ banks)

Hospitals

622000   Hospitals

Nursing and Residential Care Facilities

623000   Nursing & Residential Care Facilities

Social Assistance

624100   Individual & Family Services

624200   Community Food & Housing & Emergency & Other Relief Services

624310   Vocational Rehabilitation Services

624410   Child Day Care Services

Arts, Entertainment and Recreation

Performing Arts, Spectator Sports and Related Industries

711100   Performing Arts Companies

711210   Spectator Sports (including sports clubs & racetracks)

711300   Promoters of Performing Arts, Sports & Similar Events

711410   Agents & Managers for Artists, Athletes, Entertainers & Other Public Figures
711510   Independent Artists, Writers & Performers

MUSEUMS, HISTORICAL SITES AND SIMILAR INSTITUTIONS
712100   Museums, Historical Sites and Similar Institutions

AMUSEMENT, GAMBLING AND RECREATION INDUSTRIES
713100   Amusement Parks & Arcades
713200   Gambling Industries
713900   Other Amusement & Recreation Industries (including golf courses, skiing facilities, marinas, fitness centers & bowling centers)

Accommodation and Food Services

ACCOMMODATION
721110   Hotels (except casino hotels) & Motels
721120   Casino Hotels
721191   Bed & Breakfast Inns
721199   All Other Traveler Accommodation
721210   RV (Recreational Vehicle) Parks & Recreational Camps
721310   Rooming & Boarding Houses

FOOD SERVICES AND DRINKING PLACES
722110   Full-Service Restaurants
722210   Limited-Service Eating Places
722300   Special Food Services (including food service contractors & caterers)
722410   Drinking Places (Alcoholic Beverages)

Other Services

REPAIR AND MAINTENANCE
811110   Automotive Mechanical & Electrical Repair & Maintenance
811120   Automotive Body, Paint, Interior & Glass Repair
811190   Other Automotive Repair & Maintenance (including oil change & lubrication shops & car washes)

811210	Electronic & Precision Equipment Repair & Maintenance
811310	Commercial & Industrial Machinery & Equipment (except automotive & electronic) Repair & Maintenance
811410	Home & Garden Equipment & Appliance Repair & Maintenance
811420	Reupholstery & Furniture Repair
811430	Footwear & Leather Goods Repair
811490	Other Personal & Household Goods Repair & Maintenance

Personal and Laundry Services

812111	Barber Shops
812112	Beauty Salons
812113	Nail Salons
812190	Other Personal Care Services (including diet & weight reducing centers)
812210	Funeral Homes & Funeral Services
812220	Cemeteries & Crematories
812310	Coin-Operated Laundries & Dry-cleaners
812320	Dry-cleaning & Laundry Services (except coin-operated)
812330	Linen & Uniform Supply
812910	Pet Care (except veterinary) Services
812920	Photofinishing
812930	Parking Lots & Garages
812990	All Other Personal Services

Religious, Grantmaking, Civic, Professional and Similar Organizations

813000	Religious, Grantmaking, Civic, Professional & Similar Organizations

Appendix B
300+ Business Deductions

Business Tax Deductions

Instructions: Check each tax deduction that applies to your business.

A

	Abandonment of property used for business purposes
	Accounting and auditing expenses, such as:
	Auditing of your books and accounts
	Costs of bookkeeping
	Costs of tax strategy preparation
	Costs of preparing and filing any tax returns
	Costs of investigation of any tax returns
	Costs of defense against any IRS or state agency audits or challenges
	Accounts receivable, worthless
	Achievement awards—requires plan
	Longevity award
	Safety award
	Sales award
	Advances made to employees or salespeople where repayment is not expected
	Advances to employees canceled as bonus
	Advertising expenses, such as:
	Premiums given away
	Advertising in
	Newspaper
	Magazine

		Radio
		Other media
	Prizes and other expenses in holding contests or exhibitions	
	Contributions to various organizations for advertising purposes	
	Cost of displays, posters, etc. to attract customers	
	Publicity—generally speaking, all costs including entertainment, music, etc.	
	Christmas present to customers or prospects—de minimis rule	
Alterations to business property, if minor		
Amortization		
Attorney's fees and other legal expenses involving:		
	Tax strategy	
	Drafting of agreements, resolutions, minutes, etc.	
	Defense of claims against you	
	Collection actions taken against others	
	Any other business-related legal activity	
Auto expenses for business purposes, such as:		
	Damage to auto not covered by insurance	
	Gasoline	
	Oil	
	Repairs and maintenance	
	Washing and waxing	
	Garage rent	
	Interest portion of payments	
	Insurance premiums such as fire, theft, collision, liability, etc.	
	Lease payment	
	License plate	
	Driver's license fee	
	Depreciation	
	Wages of chauffeur	
	Section 179 deduction, for qualified vehicle	

B

	Bad debts—if previously taken into income
	Baseball/softball/soccer team equipment for business publicity
	Board and room to employee:
	All meals and lodging if for employer's benefit
	Temporary housing assignment
	Board meetings
	Bonuses as additional compensation to employees
	Bookkeeping services
	Building expenses, used for business, such as:
	Repairs to building
	Janitorial service
	Painting
	Interest on mortgage
	Taxes on property
	Water
	Rubbish removal
	Depreciation of building
	Heating
	Lighting
	Landscaping
	Burglary losses not covered by insurance
	Business, cost of operating office
	Business taxes—except federal income taxes

C

	Cafeteria plan—requires written plan
	Capital asset sale—losses
	Car and taxi fares

	Casualty damages, such as:
	Bombardment
	Fire
	Storm
	Hurricane
	Drought
	Forest fire
	Freezing of property
	Impairment or collapse of property
	Ice
	Heat
	Wind
	Rain
	Charitable contributions
	Checking account bank charges
	Child care—requires written plan
	Children's salaries
	Christmas presents to employees, customers, and prospects for advertising or publicity purposes, or goodwill, or if customary in the trade
	Collection expenses including attorney's charges
	Commissions on sales of securities by dealers in securities
	Commissions paid to agents
	Commissions paid to employees for business purposes
	Commissions paid to salesmen
	Condemnation expenses
	Contributions (deductible if made to organization founded for the following purposes, subject to some limitations):
	Religious
	Charitable
	Scientific
	Literary

	Educational
	Prevention of cruelty to children and animals
	Convention expenses, cost of attending conventions
	Cost of goods
	Credit report costs

D

	Day care facility
	Depletion
	Depreciation
	Discounts allowed to customers
	Dues paid to:
	Better Business Bureau
	Chamber of commerce
	Trade associations
	Professional societies
	Technical societies
	Protective services association

E

	Education assistance—requires written plan
	Embezzlement loss not covered by insurance
	Employee welfare expenses, such as:
	Dances
	Entertainment
	Outings
	Christmas parties
	Shows or plays
	Endorser's loss

	Entertainment expenses
	Equipment, minor replacements
	Equipment purchases—may require capitalization and depreciation
	Equipment repairs
	Exhibits and displays, to publicize your products
	Expenses of any kind directly chargeable to business income, such as:
	Renting of storage space
	Safe deposit boxes
	Upkeep of property
	Books to record income and expenses or investment income
	Experimental and research expenses

F

	Factoring
	Fan mail expenses
	Fees for passports necessary while traveling on business
	Fees to accountants
	Fees to agents
	Fees to brokers
	Fees to investment counsel
	Fees to professionals for services rendered
	Fees to technicians
	Fire loss
	Forfeited stock
	Freight charges

G

	Gifts to customers—limit $75
	Gifts to organized institutions, such as:

	Charitable
	Literary
	Educational
	Religious
	Scientific
	Group term insurance on employees' lives
	Guarantor's loss

H

	Health insurance
	Heating expense
	Hospitals, contributions to

I

	Improvements, provided they are minor
	Insurance premiums paid
	Interest on loans of all kinds for business purposes, such as:
	On loans
	On notes
	On mortgages
	On bonds
	On tax deficiencies
	On installment payments of auto, furniture, etc.
	On margin account with brokers
	Bank discount on note is deductible as interest
	Inventory loss due to damages
	Investment counsel fees

L

	Lawsuit expenses
	Legal costs
	In defense of your business
	In settlement of cases
	Payment of damages
	License fees
	Lighting
	Living quarter furnished employees for business's benefit
	Lobbying costs
	Losses, deductible if connected with your business or profession, such as:
	Abandoned property
	Accounts receivable
	Auto damage caused by fire, theft, heat, storm, etc.
	Bad debts
	Bank closed
	Bonds
	Buildings—damaged
	Burglary
	Business ventures
	Capital assets
	Casualties: fire, theft, heat, storm, etc.
	Damages to property or assets
	Deposit forfeiture, on purchase of property
	Drought
	Embezzlements
	Equipment abandoned
	Forced sale or exchange
	Foreclosures
	Forfeitures
	Freezing

	Goodwill
	Loans not collectible
	Theft
	Transactions entered into for profits

M

	Maintenance of business property
	Maintenance of office, store, warehouse, showroom, etc.
	Maintenance of rented premises
	Management costs
	Materials
	Meals, subject to limitation
	Membership dues
	Merchandise
	Messenger service
	Moving cost
	Musician expenses

N

	Net operating loss—may be carried back to previous years' income for refund and/or forward against future years' income
	Newspapers

O

	Office expenses, including:
	Wages
	Supplies
	Towel service
	Heating and lighting

	Telephone and telegraph
	Repairs
	Refurnishing, minor items
	Decorating
	Painting
Office rent	
Office rent—portion of home used for business	
Office stationery and supplies	

P

Passport fees
Pension plans—must be properly drawn
Periodicals
Physical fitness center
Plotting of land for sale
Postage
Professional society dues
Property depreciation
Property maintenance
Property repairs
Publicity expenses

R

	Real estate expenses of rental or investment property, including:
	Taxes of property
	Insurance
	Janitorial services
	Repairing
	Redecorating

	Painting
	Depreciation
	Supplies
	Tools
	Legal expenses involving leases, tenants, or property
	Bookkeeping
	Property management
	Utilities
	Commissions to secure tenants
	Maintenance—heating, lighting, etc.
	Advertising for tenants
	Cost of manager's unit, if on site and at employer's convenience
Rebates on sales	
Refunds on sales	
Rent settlement—cancel lease	
Rental property expense, such as:	
	Advertising of vacant premises
	Commissions to secure tenant
	Billboards and signs
Rent collection expense	
Rents paid, such as:	
	Business property
	Parking facilities
	Safe deposit boxes
	Taxes paid by tenant for landlord
	Warehouse and storage charges
Repairing of business property, such as:	
	Alterations, provided they are not capital additions
	Casualty damages, replaced, provided they are not capital additions
	Cleaning
	Minor improvements

	Painting
	Redecorating
	Repairing of furniture, fixtures, equipment, machinery, and buildings
	Roof repairs
	Royalties

S

	Safe deposit box rental
	Safe or storage rental
	Salaries (including bonuses, commissions, pensions, management fees)
	Sample room
	Selling expenses, such as:
	Commissions and bonuses as prizes
	Discounts
	Entertainment
	Prizes offered in contests
	Publicity and promotion costs
	Rebates
	Services, professional or other necessary for conduct of business
	Social Security taxes paid by employers
	Stationery and all other office supplies used
	Subscriptions to all trade, business, or professional periodicals
	Supplies, office or laboratory

T

	Taxes, all taxes paid except federal income taxes, such as:
	City gross receipts tax
	City sales tax
	State gross receipts tax

	State sales tax
	State unemployment insurance tax
	Federal Social Security tax
	State income tax
	State unincorporated business tax
	Real estate tax
	Tangible property tax
	Intangible property tax
	Custom, import, or tariff tax
	License tax
	Stamp taxes
	Any business tax, as a rule
	Auto registration tax
	Safe deposit tax
	Membership dues tax
	Gasoline tax
	Admission tax
Telephone and telegraphs	
Traveling expenses (includes: meals, taxi fare, rail fare, airfare, tips, telephone, telegrams, laundry and cleaning, entertainment for business purposes)	

U

	Unemployment compensation taxes paid by employer
	Uniforms furnished to employees

W

	Wages
	Workmen's compensation fund contributions

This list isn't comprehensive—there are unique deductions available to any business. Remember that the key is to follow the magic twenty-seven word guide to business deductions found in Internal Revenue Code Section 162(a):

> There shall be allowed as a deduction, all the ordinary and necessary expenses paid or incurred during the taxable year in carrying on any trade or business.

The IRS does not define "ordinary" or "necessary" for us in the tax code. Instead, figuring it out has been left to federal courts. Through many, many tax court cases they have determined:

> Ordinary expense: What is normal, common, and accepted under the circumstances by the business community.

> Necessary expense: What is appropriate and helpful.

Can the expense be shown to contribute to the business? The expenses must be ordinary and reasonable for the type of business that you have. Obviously, an auto wrecking company will have much different types of expenses necessary to do business than will an accounting office. It depends on your business.

Use the above list to spark your imagination. Check off items and add additional ones as you think of them. Then, go over the list with your tax advisor to discover how you can legitimately take the deductions.

Appendix C
Tax Strategy Examples for Multilevel Marketing Business Owners

Tax Strategies for Multilevel Marketing Business Owners

Following are three real-life examples of tax strategies developed and implemented for our CPA firm clients. Each strategy was customized for the client's personal issues and goals. You may find similarities to one or more of these clients, but keep in mind that each person is unique. We never recommend taking a boilerplate strategy and attempting to fit it to a unique situation. These are presented to demonstrate the possibilities each and every business owner has to greatly reduce their taxes and shield their personal assets. Always get competent and experienced tax advice from tax professionals before implementing any plan.

We suggest you use the Advisor Checklist in Chapter 3 for every advisor you intend to add to your team. Make conscious choices about what people you chose to listen to and consult with, as these are the critical relationships that will help you or harm you as you follow your own financial path.

EXAMPLE ONE: JOHN AND BETTY SMITH

John and Betty Smith were both employees of other companies. John was a middle manager at a large bank and Betty was a secretary for an insurance office. They had two small children who were in day care. They had busy lives, but saw that they weren't getting anywhere. They had "too much month at the end of their paycheck." John, as a banker, was aware of how dangerous living from paycheck to paycheck was. In his position, he had seen people suffer a small setback, or what should have been a small setback, and lose everything they owned. They simply had nothing to fall back on. Even though he knew the danger, he didn't know how to change their situation. Then they discovered a multilevel marketing opportunity. They worked diligently at it, spending evenings together cultivating leads and making many calls and presentations. After two years, they had reached a level of $30,000 per year coming from the MLM. The question they had was how much the MLM opportunity had helped them and how they could maximize the benefits.

EXAMPLE TWO: FRED JONES

Fred Jones was a great salesman in a floundering industry—travel bookings. He had spent a number of years cultivating client contacts and gaining expertise in the field. But the entire travel industry was in a sharp decline. The Internet had made travel bookings simple for the average consumer. They no longer had to rely on travel agents and had the ability to book whenever they wanted, often at reduced fares. He could see the writing on the wall for the travel industry.

He was single, and didn't have a lot of financial responsibilities, so he knew he could survive a financial hit. But he didn't relish the idea of going out and learning a new trade and then facing the risk of being outmoded again in ten years. The business world was rapidly changing and no one could foretell where it was going. He wanted to build his own business. He didn't have a lot of other skills and was not good at building systems.

He was drawn to a particular MLM opportunity that appealed to him. He especially liked the fact that he did not have to develop the systems to drive the business. Instead, he could concentrate on what he did best—sales, lead generation, and relationship building. In less than a year, he had built a business that brought in $30,000 per year in addition to his salary.

EXAMPLE THREE: MIKE AND MARIA GONZALES

Mike and Maria Gonzales were a highly successful multilevel marketing couple. They had worked at it for a number of years, devoting their full-time attention to their business. They also invested the proceeds in real estate, creating another stream of income. Mike and Maria and their ten-year-old daughter, Angela, had a good lifestyle with a lovely home in Southern California. Their main concern was protecting what they had built and finding a way to reduce their steadily increasing federal and state taxes.

Each of these examples are shown with the before and after snapshot of their taxes and how their tax structures and income streams worked.

The information presented here is for information purposes only and has been developed to help you see what benefits are possible. It has not been designed to make you a tax expert. Many crucial factors and critical steps have not been discussed in this abbreviated text. Additionally, this area of law is particularly dynamic. New tax codes, regulations, procedures, rulings, and precedential case law are constantly changing the practice of strategic tax planning. Make sure you consult with a qualified tax strategist before enacting any strategies discussed in this text.

JOHN AND BETTY SMITH DETAILS

After completion of their personalized strategy, we determined the following pertinent facts:

John's annual salary	$70,000
Betty's annual salary	30,000
2 children—child care	$4,000/child per year
Medical expenses	4,000
Travel	2,000
Computer	1,200
Annual home mortgage interest	10,000
Property tax	2,000

Before MLM opportunity: They paid $13,851 per year in federal taxes.

Tax Strategy:

John and Betty formed an S corporation for their MLM and Betty quit her job to devote her attention full-time to the business.

The S corporation filed a tax return, but the income or loss of the company was passed through to John and Betty's personal return. In this example, John and Betty had more legitimate business deductions than income, so they were able to create a corporate paper loss.

The S corporation showed:

Income	$30,000
Expenses:	
Automobile	(6,000)
Home office rent	(6,000)
Child care (corporate child care plan)	(8,000)
Meals (business purpose—50 percent)	(2,400)
Medical reimbursement plan	(4,000)
Travel (with business purpose)	(2,000)
Computer	(1,200)
Internet service	(200)
Salary paid to John and Betty	(12,000)
SIMPLE pension plans	(12,000)
Net (loss)	($23,800)

After the MLM, John and Betty now paid federal tax of $4,254—a decrease of $9,597 per year. But the benefits to them from the added business were actually much greater.

Benefits:

Reduced personal taxes by	$ 9,597

Plus:

SIMPLE pension fund per year	$12,000

What does this mean for John and Betty?

Each year they received a total benefit of $9,597 plus $12,000 into a pension fund.

In 10 years, at 15%, the tax and cash flow savings would equal	$ 194,855
In 10 years, at 15%, the pension account would equal	$ 243,645
In 20 years, at 15%, the tax and cash flow savings would equal	$ 983,151
In 20 years, at 15%, the pension account would equal	$1,229,323

FRED JONES DETAILS

After the completion of Fred's personalized strategy, we determined the following pertinent facts:

Fred's annual salary	$50,000
Medical expenses	1,000
Travel	4,000
Seminar and books	5,000

Before MLM opportunity: Fred paid $8,579 per year in federal taxes.

Tax Strategy:

Fred formed an S corporation for his MLM.

The S corporation filed a tax return, but the income or loss of the company was passed through to Fred's personal return. In this case, a corporate paper loss was created.

The S corporation showed:

Income	$30,000
Expenses:	
Automobile	(6,000)
Home office rent	(6,000)
Meals (Business purpose—50%)	(4,800)
Medical reimbursement plan	(1,000)
Travel (with business purpose)	(4,000)
Computer	(1,200)
Internet service	(240)
Seminars and books	(5,000)
Salary paid to Fred	(6,000)
SIMPLE pension plan	(6,000)
Net (loss)	($10,240)

After the MLM, Fred now paid federal tax of $5,709—a decrease of $3,870 per year. But the benefits to Fred, just like with John and Betty, were actually much greater.

Benefits:

Reduced personal taxes by	$ 3,870

Plus:

SIMPLE pension fund per year	$ 6,000

What does this mean for Fred?

Each year, he paid $3,870 less in tax plus invested $6,000 per year into a pension fund.

In 10 years, at 15%, the tax and cash flow savings would equal	$ 78,575
In 10 years, at 15%, the pension account would equal	$ 121,822
In 20 years, at 15%, the tax and cash flow savings would equal	$ 396,457
In 20 years, at 15%, the pension account would equal	$ 614,661

MIKE AND MARIA GONZALES DETAILS

After the completion of their strategy, we determined the following pertinent facts:

MLM	$360,000
Passive (real estate)	37,500

Currently operating MLM and real estate without any business structure
One child
Living expenses of $100,000 per year

Before tax strategy: They paid $147,700 in federal taxes and $15,400 in state taxes per year.

Tax Strategy:

Mike and Maria formed a C corporation in California (their home state) and a C corporation in Nevada. Considerations such as personal holding company status and controlled group status were addressed by ownership and the type of income received by the corporations.

A limited partnership was formed in California to hold their real estate investments, which were located outside California. The general partner of the LP was their Nevada C corporation. The Nevada C corporation also received a quarterly payment for marketing services for the California C corporation. The California C corporation received the MLM income.

The LP filed a tax return, but the income or loss of the LP interest was passed through to Mike and Maria's personal return. Both the California and the Nevada C corporations filed their own tax return and paid tax at their respective corporate rates.

For the LP, Mike and Maria showed basically the same amount of income they had shown before. This was put in place mainly for asset protection purposes. As always, get competent legal and tax advice for your own situation.

For the Nevada C corporation, the source of revenue is mainly for the marketing fees paid from the California C corporation. In Mike and Maria's case, a contract was drawn up calling for quarterly payments of $50,000 for marketing research and development. A clear trail of invoices, agreements, and work product was established. Following are the income and expenses for the Nevada C corporation:

Nevada C corporation:

Income	$200,000
Expenses:	
Salary	(100,000)
Defined benefit pension	(50,000)
Total expenses	(150,000)
Net income	$ 50,000

The California C corporation showed:

Income	$360,000
Expenses	
Automobile lease	(7,200)
Automobile lease	(7,200)
Gas, tires, etc.	(2,400)
Travel (for business development)	(10,000)
Meals	(6,000)
Nanny—on-premise day care	(18,000)
Salary	(50,000)
Physical fitness equipment	(2,000)
Medical reimbursement	(6,000)
Medical insurance	(3,000)
Gifts (promotion)	(3,000)
Home office rent	(12,000)
Marketing Nevada corporation	(200,000)
Total expenses	(326,800)
Net income	$ 33,200

The total tax that Mike and Maria paid, after the correct legal business structures were in place was only $53,500. This meant an annual savings of $110,000 in federal and state taxes.

What does this mean for Mike and Maria?

Each year, they received tax savings of $110,000 and a pension contribution of $50,000.

In 10 years, at 8%, the tax and cash flow savings would equal	$1,593,522
In 10 years, at 8%, the pension account would equal	$ 724,328
In 20 years, at 8%, the tax and cash flow savings would equal	$5,033,816
In 20 years, at 8%, the pension account would equal	$2,288,098

Appendix D
Sample Forms

Following are forms that are generic in nature. Seek good tax and legal advice before using any of the forms. They have been provided as examples for your use.

Worksheet
Brother-Sister Controlled Group Test

PART I:
80% CONTROL TEST

1. List those shareholders (individuals, estates, or trusts) who own voting stock in both corporations and the percentage of outstanding stock each owns.

Shareholders	Corporation X	Corporation Y	Corporation Z
_____	_____%	_____%	_____%
_____	_____%	_____%	_____%
_____	_____%	_____%	_____%
_____	_____%	_____%	_____%
Total	_____%	_____%	_____%

2. Does any combination of five or fewer of the above shareholders own 80% or more of the outstanding voting stock of both corporations?
   Yes _____ No _____

3. If the answer to question No. 2 is no, the corporations are not a brother-sister controlled group and no further testing is required.

4. If the answer to question No. 2 is yes, the 80% has been met. Proceed to Part II to determine the 50% test.

PART II:
50% IDENTICAL OWNERSHIP TEST

1. List the same shareholders whose combination of stock ownership in both corporations met the 80% test, the percentage of ownership in each corporation, and enter the lowest of the percentage ownership in Column 4.

	(1)	(2)	(3)	(4) Lowest Percentage
Shareholders	Corporation X	Corporation Y	Corporation Z	
_____	_____	_____	_____	_____
_____	_____	_____	_____	_____
_____	_____	_____	_____	_____
_____	_____	_____	_____	_____

2. Total of Column 4.

3. If the total on Line 2 is more than 50%, the 50% ownership test has been met and the corporations are a brother-sister group.

4. If the total on Line 2 is 50% or less, the test has not been met and the corporations are not a brother-sister controlled group.

Worksheet
Tax Calculation for Members of a Controlled Group

Each member of a controlled group (except a qualified personal service corporation) must compute the tax using the worksheet below.

1. Enter taxable income (Line 30, page 1, Form 1120)   1. $ _____

2. Enter Line 1 or the corporation's share of the $50,000 taxable income bracket, whichever is less   2. _____

3. Subtract Line 2 from Line 1   3. _____

4. Enter Line 3 or the corporation's share of the $25,000 taxable income bracket, whichever is less   4. _____

5. Subtract Line 4 from Line 3   5. _____

6. Enter Line 5 or the corporation's share of the $9,925,000 taxable income bracket, whichever is less   6. _____

7. Subtract Line 6 from Line 5   7. _____

8. Multiply Line 2 by 15%   8. _____

9. Multiply Line 4 by 25%   9. _____

10. Multiply Line 6 by 34%   10. _____

11. Multiply Line 7 by 35%   11. _____

12. If the taxable income of the controlled group exceeds $100,000, enter this member's share of the smaller of: 5% of the taxable income in excess of $100,000, or $11,750   12. _____

13. If the taxable income of the controlled group exceeds $15,000,000, enter this member's share of the smaller of: 3% of the taxable income in excess of $15 million, or $100,000   13. _____

14. Add Lines 8 through 13. Enter here and on Line 3, Schedule J, Form 1120   14. _____

Certified Copy of Resolutions to Liquidate the Corporation

I hereby certify that the following Resolutions were unanimously adopted at a Special Meeting of the Shareholders of _____ held on the _____ day of _____, 20____.

RESOLVED, that the Corporation be completely liquidated in accordance with the provisions of Section 336 of the Internal Revenue Code of 1986, as amended, and be it

FURTHER RESOLVED, that in accordance with such plan of complete liquidation, the officers, directors, and corporate counsel are hereby authorized and directed to see that the following steps are undertaken:

1. that within thirty (30) days of the date of this resolution adopting this plan of liquidation, counsel for the Corporation shall file Form 966 with the District Director of Internal Revenue, together with a certified copy of this resolution;
2. that the services of a disinterested qualified appraiser be obtained to determine the fair market value of the assets;
3. that the corporation shall proceed as far as possible to collect all outstanding accounts receivable and to settle any claims against it;
4. that thereafter, as soon as practicable, the Corporation, by its duly authorized officers and directors, shall distribute all assets, subject to any unpaid liabilities, to the shareholders in redemption and cancellation of all the outstanding capital stock of the Corporation, using their discretion as to how the assets and liabilities will be apportioned among the shareholders, but in no event shall they distribute to any shareholder net assets of a lesser value than is due him on a pro rata basis, using the appraisal values obtained in Item 2 of this resolution;
5. that the proper officers of the Corporation shall file a Certificate of Dissolution pursuant to state law;
6. that the proper officers and Corporation counsel shall file all other forms and documents required, including tax returns, as soon as possible after distribution of the corporate assets;
7. that specific authorization is given to _____, counsel for the Corporation, to prepare, sign and forward to the Commissioner of Internal Revenue, after the final tax return has been filed for the Corporation, a request for proper assessment of all federal taxes due from the Corporation; and
8. that the officers and directors of the Corporation are empowered, authorized, and directed to carry out the provisions of this resolution, and to adopt any further resolutions that may be necessary in liquidating and dissolving the Corporation in accordance with the expressed intent of the shareholders under the plan adopted.

_____
Secretary

Educational Assistance Program
[Sample Plan for Discussion Purposes Only]

1. **Purpose:** The Company Educational Assistance Program has been established for the exclusive benefit of the eligible employees of the Company. The Company desires to reimburse employees for all or a portion of the cost of attending educational courses related to the employees' success in the performance of their duties with the Company. It is intended that the Program meet the requirements for qualification under Code Section 127 of the Internal Revenue Code, and that benefits paid employees under the Program be excludable from gross income to the maximum extent allowed under Code Section 127.

2. **Plan Year:** The Plan Year is the 12-month period ending on December 31 of each year.

3. **Contributions:** Employees are not required or permitted to contribute to the Program.

4. **Eligibility Requirements:** Company employees meeting the following criteria are eligible:

   (a) Completion of a minimum of 6 months' service, before the start of the course of education for which reimbursement is to be provided under this plan,

   (b) Attainment of age 18,

   (c) Employed on a full-time basis, and

   (d) Continued employment for one year after satisfactory completion of a course. Any employees terminating within one year will receive a final paycheck adjusted for the amount of the educational benefit received.

5. **Qualifying Educational Programs:** Educational programs qualify under this plan if:

   (a) Participating employees limit their course load to a maximum of 2 courses or 6 credits per semester or school period.

   (b) Courses attended during regular working hours must receive prior supervisory approval, so no reduction in participant salary or status occurs.

   (c) The courses in degree programs are pertinent to the employee's functions or skill in performing his or her duties with the Company in a position of advancement to the participant's current position with the Company. An officer of the Company must decide whether an educational course meets this requirement before an employee's enrollment. If it is determined that an educational course does not meet this requirement, the plan will be administered in accordance with Article 11.

   (d) Courses are offered by an accredited school toward a recognized degree program or a definite plan of study. Tuition reimbursement will be at the state educational institution rate in effect at the time of enrollment. However, the employee must meet the requirements for reimbursement in Article 6.

   (e) If the Company specifically requires the employee to enroll in a course, the employee automatically meets plan requirements.

6. **Requirements for Reimbursement:** Upon completion of a prior-approved course, eligible employees must submit to the corporation a copy of the tuition statement and receipts for other items of qualified educational expenses (see Article 7), and a copy of the grade report. No reimbursement will be made without verified tuition and grade reports or if the employee receives educational assistance from other sources (i.e., financial aid or scholarships whether or not such financial aid or scholarships are offered by the company).

Reimbursement will be made according to the following schedule:

Undergraduate Courses		Other Courses	
Grade	Reimbursement	Grade	Reimbursement
A	100%	Pass	100%
B	85%	Fail	0%
C	60%		
Below C	0%		

7. **Educational Expenses Qualifying for Reimbursement:** The following items are reimbursable under this Program as qualified educational assistance: tuition, fees, books, supplies, and equipment related to an approved course of education. Tools or supplies (other than textbooks) that an employee may retain after the course completion are not eligible educational expenses under this Program. Also, meals, lodging, and transportation are not qualified educational expenses.

8. **Limitation on Benefits:** No more than 5% of the amounts paid or incurred by the Company under this Program for any Plan Year may be provided for the class of individuals who are shareholders (or owners) (or their spouses or dependents), each of whom own more than 5% of the stock (or capital or profits interest) in the Company. For purposes of determining stock ownership, the attribution rules of Code Section 1563(d) and (e) (without regard to purposes of determining stock ownership), and the attribution rules of Code Section 1563(e)(3)(C) apply. [For purposes of determining the capital or profits interest of an unincorporated trade or business, the rules under Code Section 414(c) apply.]

9. **Funding:** Qualifying educational expenses submitted for reimbursement by plan participants will be paid entirely from the general assets of the Company. The plan will be known as an unfunded plan.

10. **Plan Administrator:** The Plan Administrator shall be designated by the Board of Directors of the Company.

11. **Plan Administrator Authority:** The Plan Administrator is authorized to develop uniform rules and forms to be used in carrying out the purpose of the Program. The Plan Administrator shall determine all questions relating to eligibility. The Plan Administrator will interpret the terms and provisions of the plan. An interpretation shall be performed in a nondiscriminatory manner and shall be consistent with the purpose of the Program.

12. **Procedures for Reimbursement Denial:** The Board of Directors will review all educational reimbursement requests initially denied by the Plan Administrator. Any decision by the Board of Directors shall be binding on all parties.

13. **Amendment or Termination of Plan:** The Company reserves the right to change the plan provisions by amendment. All amendments, including the amendment to terminate the plan, shall be in writing and acknowledged by the Board of Directors through a resolution. No amendment shall affect the reimbursement of eligible educational expenses incurred by a participant enrolled in an educational course at the time the plan is amended or terminated. Instead, the participant shall be entitled to reimbursement under the terms of the plan at the time the course of study was initiated.

14. **Notification of Employees:** All employees eligible to participate in the program (see Article 4) will receive written notice of the terms and availability of the program. Each eligible employee shall receive a copy of the Summary Plan Description. Upon request, each eligible employee shall receive a copy of the Plan document.

Notice to Employees
Availability of Educational Assistance Plans
[Sample Plan for Discussion Purposes Only]

An educational assistance program has been established for the benefit of the employees of _____. The purpose of the program is to reimburse eligible employees for all or a portion of the cost of attending educational courses related to the employees' success in the performance of their duties.

Only courses offered by an accredited school toward a recognized degree program or a definite plan of study will be considered reimbursable under this plan. To participate in the educational assistance program, contact the Human Resources Department prior to enrolling in class.

Upon completion of an approved course, submit a reimbursement form with a copy of the tuition statement and a copy of your grade report. No reimbursement will be made without verified tuition and grade reports. Reimbursements are tax-free. Tuition reimbursements are made based on the grade attained as described in the plan document. Tuition reimbursements are limited to the rates charged at state universities.

Educational Assistance Plan
[Sample Plan for Discussion Purposes Only]

An educational assistance program (EAP) has been established for the benefit of the employees of _____. The purpose of the program is to reimburse eligible employees for all or a portion of the cost of attending educational courses related to the employees' success in the performance of their duties.

Am I eligible to participate? Employees who have worked a minimum of six months prior to the beginning of a course and who are employed on a full-time basis (30 hours per week).

How do I participate? If you have decided on a course of study, submit an Educational Assistance Reimbursement Form for approval before enrolling at the educational institution.

What happens if I terminate employment prior to completing the course? Employees who terminate service with _____ before completing the course will not be eligible for reimbursement under the plan. The plan is for the benefit of employees. Employees who terminate within one year of the satisfactory completion of a course must return any benefits received under this plan. An adjustment for the amount of the educational assistance received will be made to the final paycheck.

Is there a limit on the number of courses I may take? Yes. You are limited to a maximum of two courses or six credits per semester.

What other restrictions apply? The course must be related to your success in the performance of your duties at _____. Only courses offered by an accredited school will be considered reimbursable under this plan. You may attend a private university or college; however, your reimbursement will be at the state educational institution rate. If you are receiving educational assistance from other sources such as financial aid or scholarships, you are not eligible to participate in this program.

May I attend class during my normal working hours? You will need approval from your immediate supervisor before enrolling in a course that meets during your regular hours. However, once approval is received, you should not expect a reduction in pay or pay status (i.e., from full-time to part-time) if you attend classes during the workday.

How do I receive reimbursement? Upon completion of your course, resubmit the approved educational assistance form for payment and attach evidence of completion of the course, such as a grade report. You should also submit your tuition statement to show proof of expenses incurred.

What expenses qualify for reimbursement? Only tuition, fees, books, supplies, and equipment qualify as educational expenses. Any tools or supplies (other than textbooks) that you retain after the completion of the course are not reimbursable. In addition, meals, lodging, and transportation costs are not qualified as educational expenses.

Is there any restriction on the amount of reimbursement I may receive? Under the _____ EAP, you will not receive more than $5,250 during the plan year. The plan year is from January to December. In addition, you will be eligible for reimbursement based upon the grades received as shown in the following table:

Undergraduate Courses		_Other Courses_	
Grade	Reimbursement	Grade	Reimbursement
A	100%	Pass	100%
B	85%	Fail	0%
C	60%		
Below C	0%		

Are any benefits I receive taxable? It is intended that the Program meet the requirements for qualification under Code Section 127 of the Internal Revenue Code, and that benefits paid employees under the Program be excludable from gross income to the maximum of $5,250.

Is this plan permanent? _____ intends to continue this Program as a permanent plan. However, this Program shall be subject to termination at any time by a vote of the Company Board of Directors. Any employee enrolled in an approved course at the time of discontinuation shall be reimbursed in accordance with the terms of this Program.

Suggested Record Retention List

Type of Record	Suggested Retention Period	On File? Yes	No
I. CORRESPONDENCE			
General—All	3 Yrs.		
Tax & Legal Communications	*Indef.		
Production & Creative	8 Yrs.		
License & Traffic	6 Yrs.		
Sale & Purchase	6 Yrs.		
II. ACCOUNTING RECORDS			
Bank Statements & Deposit Slips	3 Yrs.		
Individual Payroll Records	8 Yrs.		
Payroll Time Card/Sheets	3 Yrs.		
Canceled Dividend Checks	6 Yrs.		
Expense Reports	6 Yrs.		
A/P & A/R Subsidiary Ledgers	6 Yrs.		
Other Subsidiary Ledgers	6 Yrs.		
Trial Balance (Monthly)	6 Yrs.		
Payment Vouchers—All	8 Yrs.		
All Canceled Checks	8 Yrs.		
Audit Reports	*Indef.		
General Ledgers & Journals	*Indef.		
III. CORPORATE RECORDS			
Expired Notes, Leases, & Mortgages	6 Yrs.		
All Cash Books	*Indef.		
Contracts & Agreements	*Indef.		
Property Deeds & Easements	*Indef.		
Registration of Copyrights & Trademarks	*Indef.		
Patents	*Indef.		
Corp. Charter, By-Laws, & Minute Books	*Indef.		
Capital Stock & Bond Records	*Indef.		
Stock Certificate & Transfer Lists	*Indef.		
Canceled Checks on Asset Purchases	*Indef.		
Canceled Checks for Taxes & Contracts	*Indef.		
Proxies	*Indef.		
Labor Contracts	*Indef.		
Retirement & Pension Records	*Indef.		
Tax Returns & All Work Papers	*Indef.		
IV. INSURANCE RECORDS			
All Expired Policies	4 Yrs.		
Accident Reports	6 Yrs.		
Safety Reports	8 Yrs.		
Settlement Claims	10 Yrs.		
Group Disability Records	8 Yrs.		
Fire Inspection Reports	6 Yrs.		
V. SALES & PURCHASE RECORDS			
Sales Contracts & Invoices	3 Yrs.		
Requisition Orders	3 Yrs.		
Purchase Orders	3 Yrs.		
VI. SHIPPING/RECEIVING RECORDS			
Export Declarations & Manifests	4 Yrs.		
Freights, Shipping, & Receiving Reports	4 Yrs.		
Bills of Lading Records	4 Yrs.		
Way Bills	4 Yrs.		
VII. PERSONNEL RECORDS			
Daily Time Reports	6 Yrs.		
Withholding Tax Statements	6 Yrs.		
Disability & Sick Benefits Records	6 Yrs.		
Expired Contracts	6 Yrs.		
Files of Terminated Personnel	6 Yrs.		

*Indef.—Records Must Be Kept Indefinitely

(1) The above Suggested Retention Periods for records were developed from IRS and federal regulations.

(2) It is suggested that because of the size and volume of business records that such records be inventoried periodically and those records that have expired, according to the Retention Period, be destroyed.

Medical Reimbursement Plan
[Sample Plan for Discussion Purposes Only]

Name: _____

1. **Benefits:** _____ will reimburse all eligible employees for expenses incurred on or after the effective date of the Plan for themselves, their spouses, and their dependents subject to the conditions and limitations established under this plan. It is the intention of _____ that the Benefits payable to these eligible employees be excluded from their gross pursuant to Section 105 of the Code.

2. **Employees Eligible to Participate:** Eligible employees means all of the employees of _____ except (a) employees who have not attained age 25 prior to the beginning of the plan year, (b) employees whose customary weekly employment is less than 25 hours, and (c) employees whose customary annual employment is less than seven months. Neither the age nor time requirements are mandatory if they are waived for all employees.

Note: The eligibility provision can have a three-year service requirement.

3. **Limitation:** Reimbursement or payment provided under this Plan will be made by _____ only in the event and to the extent that such reimbursement or payment is not provided under any insurance policy(ies), whether owned by _____ or the eligible employee, or under any other health and accident or wage continuation plan. _____ is relieved of any and all liability hereunder to the extent of the coverage under a policy or plan.

4. **Submission of Proof:** Any eligible employee applying for reimbursement under this Plan will submit to _____, at least once a year, validation for medical care for verification by _____ prior to payment. Failure to comply, at the discretion of _____, can terminate such eligible employee's right to reimbursement. The medical expense does not have to be paid by the eligible employee at the time reimbursement is requested, but the employee has an obligation to pay such medical bills.

5. **Payment:** _____ can, at its election, pay directly all or any part of the medical expenses in lieu of making reimbursement. When there is direct paying of medical expenses, _____ has no further responsibility.

6. **Amendment:** _____ has the right to amend the plan at any time as long as the amendments are not retroactive as to preclude reimbursement of medical expense prior to the later of the amendment's date or its adoption.

7. **Discontinuation:** _____ can terminate the plan at any time provided that medical expenses incurred prior to the termination will be reimbursed.

8. **Determination:** _____ will determine all questions arising from the administration and interpretation of the Plan. The decisions of are binding and conclusive on all eligible employees.

9. **Effective Date and Plan Year:** The effective date of the Plan is <u>January 1,</u> 20___. The Plan year is the same as the tax year of _____.

10. **Notification:** _____ will promptly notify all employees covered by this Plan and will furnish them with a copy. Acknowledgment is required from each eligible employee of his or her acceptance of the Plan by means of a signature.

_____   _____
Employee   Sole Proprietor

Cash-on-Cash Analysis

RECOMMENDED USE

We use the Cash-on-Cash Analysis form three different ways. First, we use the form to do an estimate of return before we make any offer for purchase of a property. Then, we use it after we have purchased a property to determine pricing. Finally, we perform another cash-on-cash analysis after we have rented or sold the property to see what the actual return was. We compare the actual return with the first estimate to help us better hone our estimating skills.

INSTRUCTIONS

Complete each line with estimate (if actual is not yet available) or the available number. There are two cases where the cash-on-cash return will look strange: 1) If you receive from your customer a deposit or option equal to the amount you have invested. This will give zero invested in the property; and 2) if you actually receive more back than you have invested. In these cases, your cash-on-cash return is higher than 100 percent, and is actually incalculable. Congratulations!

Property: _____

Invested:

Down payment   _____
(Actual, or estimated, based on information
  from your mortgage broker)
Closing costs   _____
(Actual, or estimated, based on information
  from your mortgage broker)
Fix-up costs   _____
(Actual, or estimated, based on information
  from contractor)
Holding costs   _____
(Actual or estimated—usually three months
  times monthly payment)

Total: This is the amount you have invested   _____ A

Cash flow in:

Down payment (lease deposit or option)   _____ B
(Depending on the type of deal you are doing this
  can be a down payment, a deposit, or option
  payment. It is the amount you receive from the
  new buyer/tenant.)

Monthly payment received: _____ C
(Rent or payment)

Monthly cash flow out:
If sold—mortgage payment   _____ D
     or——
(Buyer has responsibility for repairs, utilities, etc.)

If rented—mortgage payment   _____
Taxes and insurance   _____
Repairs   _____
(Generally 5 percent)
Property management   _____
Other   _____
Total cash flow out: _____ D

Formula for cash-on-cash ratio:

(C_____ — D_____) / (A_____ — B_____)
  (Monthly Payment Received) (Monthly Cash Flow Out)   (Amount Invested)   (Down Payment)

Answer will be the percentage return that your money is earning.

Formula for payback period

(A_____ — B_____) / (C_____ — D_____)
  (Amount Invested)   (Down Payment)   (Monthly Payment Received) (Monthly Cash Flow Out)

Answer will be, *in months,* the length of time it will take for you to get your
investment dollars back.

About the Author

Diane Kennedy, C.P.A., author of *Loopholes of the Rich: How the Rich Legally Make More Money and Pay Less Tax* in the Rich Dad's Advisor's series, the founder and owner of DKA (D Kennedy & Assoc) and a variety of investment companies, has been involved in every aspect of the accounting industry. Diane has built her reputation through empowering and educating others about the legal tax loopholes available to all individuals.

For over twenty years, Diane has assisted individuals and corporations in strategically structuring their businesses to take full advantage of the tax laws available. Her firm specializes in innovative tax planning that minimizes tax liability and maximizes legal protection.

Diane is highly respected within the accounting profession as the co-author of two college textbooks on accounting and computer topics and a book regarding corporate tax. She has authored numerous tax-related articles and has served as a past instructor at the University of Nevada, Reno. She was selected as a lecturer on U.S. tax laws to the People's Republic of China. Her notes are now part of the official documentation used in Beijing, China. She is a past recipient of the prestigious Blue Chip Enterprise award given to the business owner demonstrating the most entrepreneurial spirit in the State of Nevada. She is also a past recipient of the National Chamber of Commerce award for Excellence in Business. She has been featured on the internationally televised show *CNN's First Business*, as a successful and respected business owner and C.P.A.

Diane is an outspoken proponent of proactive tax planning allowing individuals and corporations to keep what they make. She is perhaps best known for her work with Robert Kiyosaki, as one of his selective Rich Dad's Advisor. She knows the secrets that the rich use to reduce their taxes and, with basic and simple understanding, discloses those secrets to everyone.
Diane Kennedy can be reached through her website at www.legaltaxloopholes.com.

CASHFLOW® TECHNOLOGIES, INC.

CASHFLOW® Technologies, Inc., and richdad.com, the collaborative efforts of Robert and Kim Kiyosaki and Sharon Lechter, produce innovative financial education products.

The Company's mission Statement is
"To elevate the financial well-being of humanity."

CASHFLOW® Technologies, Inc., presents Robert's teaching through books: *Rich Dad Poor Dad™, Rich Dad's CASHFLOW® Quadrant™, Rich Dad's Guide to Investing™,* and *Rich Kid Smart Kid™*; board games *CASHFLOW® 101, CASHFLOW® 202,* and *CASHFLOW for Kids®*; and tape sets. Additional products are available and under development for people searching for financial education to guide them on their path to financial freedom. For updated information, see richdad.com or contact info@richdad.com.

Rich Dad's
ADVISORS™

Rich Dad's Advisors is a collection of books and educational products reflecting the expertise of the professional advisors that *CASHFLOW®* Technologies, Inc., and its principals, Robert and Kim Kiyosaki and Sharon Lechter, use to build their financial freedom. Each advisor is a specialist in their respective areas of the B-I Triangle, the business foundation taught by *CASHFLOW®* Technologies, Inc.

Robert Kiyosaki's Edumercial
An Educational Commercial

The Three Incomes

In the world of accounting, there are three different types of income: earned, passive, and portfolio. When my real dad said to me, "Go to school, get good grades, and find a safe secure job," he was recommending I work for earned income. When my rich dad said, "The rich don't work for money, they have their money work for them," he was talking about passive income and portfolio income. Passive income, in most cases, is derived from real estate investments. Portfolio income is income derived from paper assets such as stocks, bonds, and mutual funds.

Rich dad used to say, "The key to becoming wealthy is the ability to convert earned income into passive income and/or portfolio income as quickly as possible." He would say, "The taxes are highest on earned income. The least taxed income is passive income. That is another reason why you want your money working hard for you. The government taxes the income you work hard for more than the income your money works hard for."

The Key to Financial Freedom

The key to financial freedom and great wealth is a person's ability or skill to convert earned income into passive income and/or portfolio income. That is the skill that my rich dad spent a lot of time teaching Mike and me. Having that skill is the reason my wife, Kim, and I are financially free, never needing to work again. We continue to work because we choose to. Today we own a real estate investment company for passive income and participate in private placements and initial public offerings of stock for portfolio income.

Investing to become rich requires a different set of personal skills, skills essential for financial success as well as low-risk and high-investment returns. In other words, the knowledge to create assets that buy other assets. The problem is that gaining the basic education and experience required is often time consuming, frightening, and expensive, especially when you make mistakes with your own money. That is why I created my patented educational board games, trademarked as CASHFLOW.

Three Different Games

CASHFLOW, Investing 101®:

CASHFLOW® *101* teaches you the basics of fundamental investing, but it also does much more. *CASHFLOW*® *101* teaches you how to take control of your personal finances, build a business through proper cash flow management, and learn how to invest with greater confidence in real estate and other businesses.

This educational product is for you if you want to improve your business and investing skills by learning how to take your ideas and turn them into assets such as your own business. Many small businesses fail because the owner lacks capital, real-life experience, and basic accounting skills. Many people think investing is risky simply because they cannot read financial statements. *CASHFLOW*® *101* teaches the fundamental skills of financial literacy and investing. This educational product includes the board game, a video, and audiotapes. It takes approximately two complete times playing the game to understand it. Then we recommend that you play the game at least six times to begin to master the fundamentals of cash flow management and investing.

Price $195 U.S.

CASHFLOW, Investing 202®:

CASHFLOW® 202 teaches you the advanced skills of technical investing. After you are comfortable with the fundamentals of *CASHFLOW® 101*, the next educational challenge is learning how to manage the ups and down of the market, often called volatility. *CASHFLOW® 202* uses the same board game as *101*, but it comes with a completely different set of cards and score sheets and more advanced audiotapes. *CASHFLOW® 202* teaches you to use the investment techniques of qualified investors—techniques such as short selling, call options, put options, and straddles—that can be very expensive to learn in the real market. Most investors are afraid of a market crash. A qualified investor uses the tools taught in *CASHFLOW® 202* to make money when the markets go up and when the markets come down.

After you have mastered *101*, *CASHFLOW® 202* becomes very exciting because you learn to react to the highs and lows of the market, and you make a lot of paper money. Again, it is a lot less expensive to learn these advanced trading techniques on a board game using paper money than trading in the market with real money. While these games cannot guarantee your investment success, they will improve your financial vocabulary and knowledge of these advanced investing techniques.
Price $95 U.S.

CASHFLOW, Investing for Kids®:

Could your child be the next Bill Gates, Anita Roddick of the Body Shop, Warren Buffet, or Donald Trump? If so, then *CASHFLOW for Kids®* could be the family's educational and fun game that gives your child the same educational head start my rich dad gave me. Few people know that Warren Buffet's father was a stockbroker and Donald Trump's father was a real estate developer. A parent's influence at an early age can have long-term financial results. *CASHFLOW for Kids®* includes the board game, book, and audiotape.
Price $59.95 U.S.

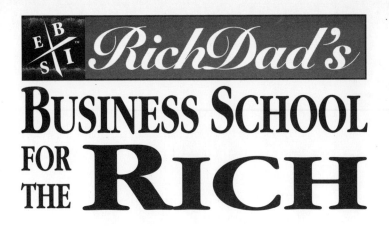
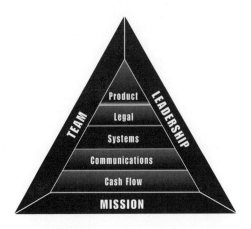

Please visit our Web site,
www.richdad.com
to review:

- Additional Information About Our Financial Education Products
- Frequently Asked Questions (FAQs) About Our Products
- Seminars, Events, and Appearances with Robert Kiyosaki

Thank You,

To Order Books, Visit: www.twbookmark.com

North America/South America/Europe/Africa:
CASHFLOW™ Technologies, Inc.
4330 N. Civic Center Plaza, Suite 101
Scottsdale, Arizona 85251
USA
(800) 308-3585 or (480) 998-6971
Fax: (480) 348-1349
e-mail: info@richdad.com

Australia/New Zealand:
CASHFLOW™ Education Australia
Reply Paid AAA401 *(no stamp required)*
PO Box 122
Rosebery NSW 1445, Australia
Tel: 1 300 660 020 or (61) 2 9662 8511
Fax: 1 300 301 998 or (61) 2 9662 8611
e-mail: info@cashfloweducation.com.au

RichDad.com